Application Servers
for
E-Business

Application Servers for E-Business

LISA M. LINDGREN

CRC Press
Taylor & Francis Group
Boca Raton London New York

CRC Press is an imprint of the
Taylor & Francis Group, an **informa** business

AN AUERBACH BOOK

First published 2001 by CRC Press

Published 2019 by CRC Press
Taylor & Francis Group
6000 Broken Sound Parkway NW, Suite 300
Boca Raton, FL 33487-2742

© 2001 by Taylor & Francis Group, LLC
CRC Press is an imprint of the Taylor & Francis Group, an informa business

No claim to original U.S. Government works

ISBN 13: 978-0-8493-0827-7 (pbk)
ISBN 13: 978-1-138-46856-6 (hbk)

Visit the Taylor & Francis Web site at
http://www.taylorandfrancis.com

and the CRC Press Web site at
http://www.crcpress.com

Library of Congress Cataloging-in-Publication Data

Lindgren, Lisa.
    Application servers for e-business / Lisa M. Lindgren.
        p. cm.
    Includes bibliographical references and index.
    ISBN 0-8493-0827-5 (alk. paper)
    1. Electronic commerce. 2. Application software—Development. I. Title.

HF5548.32 .L557 2001
658′.0553—dc21   00-050245

Library of Congress Card Number 00-050245

Dedication

To Anu

Contents

Preface

This book was written to provide a useful and comprehensive overview of the technologies related to application servers. The modern application server is a complex platform that is the linchpin of an enterprise environment that includes a very wide range of technologies — Web document formatting, Web protocols, server-side scripts, servlets, applets, programming languages, distributed object technologies, security capabilities, directory and naming services, load balancing, system management, and others. As such, it can be a daunting task to try to learn and comprehend these systems, because they touch on so many different technologies.

Therefore, this book was written explicitly for an audience that has a need to understand application servers, the role they play in the modern enterprise IT infrastructure, and the environment in which they operate. It is intended to be a single, authoritative reference source and tutorial for all issues pertaining to application servers. It provides a technical explanation and description of the technologies utilized in modern application servers to facilitate electronic business (e-business), including CORBA, Java, Enterprise JavaBeans, Java 2, Web servers, and legacy systems. It also includes implementation considerations for application servers, including security, scalability, load balancing, fault tolerance, and management.

This book is targeted at IT management and staff responsible for specifying, designing, evaluating, and implementing e-business solutions. It does not include the programming details or detailed specifications that may be of interest to programmers, Web authors, or other technology implementers. Sorry, but there are numerous books out there that go into the gory details on programming EJBs and CORBA objects and other related topics. The intent of this book is to describe the technologies, providing a comprehensive understanding of what they do and where they fit in the overall picture.

Chapter 1 provides an overview of application servers, the evolution of computing that took us from hierarchical, mainframe-centric environments to the Web model of computing, and the rationale for e-commerce and e-business.

Chapters 2 through 5 cover specific technologies. More specifically, Chapter 2 covers the Web technologies — from Web browsers and servers to applets and servlets. Chapter 3 provides an overview of Java technologies, and Chapter 4 covers CORBA. Chapter 5 discusses application servers in detail.

Because application servers increasingly support the key, mission-critical processes of an enterprise, it is critical that organizations deploying them build in "enterprise-class" facilities for security, scalability, load balancing, fault tolerance, and management. These enterprise deployment design issues are discussed in Chapter 6. The book concludes with Chapter 7, which provides several detailed examples of the advantages of application servers in large enterprises, two case studies illustrating the decision process, and an overview of 17 application servers.

The book is intended to be read sequentially. However, readers can easily skip sections or chapters that are not relevant to them or that cover topics they already understand. The chapters are organized in a straightforward manner, with sections and subsections clearly indicated so that they can easily be skimmed.

The technologies covered by this book are changing and evolving. For example, both the Java 2 Enterprise Edition (J2EE) platform and CORBA are undergoing major enhancements that are very pertinent to the subject of application servers. Readers who are interested in pursuing a particular subject in more detail are encouraged to check out some of the Web sites provided as references and also those provided in the "For More Information" section.

IT professionals who are reading this book because they are about to embark on a new e-business project utilizing application servers may find the whole topic daunting and complex. Application servers really do force us to stretch, learn, and grow because they touch on so many different, important, and complex technologies. However, I hope you enjoy the voyage, as I have done trying to capture all of this in a single, and hopefully, comprehensive source.

Lisa M. Lindgren
Lake Winnipesaukee, New Hampshire

Acknowledgments

This book never would have been written without the support and encouragement of my partner, Anura Gurugé. The idea was his, and his confidence in me was unwavering. His assistance and advice kept me on track and focused, and his understanding and support made the task easier. Thank you, Anu.

I appreciate the involvement of André Taube of BuildPoint Corporation and Krishnan Subramanian of FoliQuest International N.V. and for providing insight into their decision making processes and their implementation of application servers. Having real-world examples of implementations can help bring technology discussions alive, and these two gentlemen very generously provided us all with a glimpse into their projects. Thank you.

I also owe a debt of gratitude to a number of people working for some of the application server companies for the contacts, assistance, insight, and technical clarification they provided: Jeff Reser, Jason R. McGee, and Mike Wu at IBM; John Kiger, Maria Mariotti, Christina Grenier, and Liz Youngs at BEA Systems; Erik O'Neill and Jonathan Weedon at Inprise Corporation.

My thanks also go to Theron Shreve, my editor, for his patience and support and to Claire Miller for her assistance in making the project happen.

Thanks to Danielle and Matthew for helping out and for the fun when you are here. Winston and Maggie provided a welcome break at the end of the day. My friends and e-mail buddies — Brenda Weiler, Randie Johnson, Donna Kidder, Susan ("Schultzie") Swenson, Janet Hoffmann, Kristen Eldridge, and all my other friends — have given me lots of laughs and often brightened my day. Thanks to all. Finally, my thanks to my parents, Gene and Alice Lindgren, and my brother, Tom Lindgren, for their love and support.

Chapter 1

Introduction

To say that the World Wide Web has changed the face of computing is a vast understatement. In the first year or so of its existence, the Web was simply an interesting enhancement to the user interface of the Internet. Prior to the Web, the Internet was a network used heavily by government and educational institutions. The user interface of the Internet was character-based and cryptic, and therefore most users of the Internet were relatively sophisticated computer and network users. The Web offered a simple user interface and an easy way of interconnecting documents of related information. The Web technologies eventually evolved to support sophisticated interaction with users, which laid the groundwork for a new paradigm for transacting business. The Web has spawned entire new industries and has rendered the term "dot-com" a common adjective to describe the new companies and industries. The letter "e" (E) is being used to preface nouns, adjectives, and verbs and signifies the new electronic economy. The Web has created thousands of millionaires and billionaires from Internet initial public offerings (IPOs) and has leveled the playing field between new startups and established "brick-and-mortar" companies.

Economists regularly use the terms "new economy" to describe stocks and companies that enable an Internet model of doing business, and "old economy" to describe stocks and companies that sell goods and services in the traditional manner. The new-economy companies offer products or services for conducting business-to-consumer (B2C) and business-to-business (B2B) transactions. Yahoo!, America OnLine, eBay, and Amazon.com are premier examples of new-economy companies. While the new-economy companies have received a lot of press and have been the darlings of the NASDAQ stock market, the old-economy companies are not standing still. Almost without exception, they all have some form of Web presence and many are making dramatic movements in embracing the Web model of doing business. Economists and stock analysts are now saying that the old-economy companies, with their vast resources, brand recognition, and distribution channels, are poised to overtake

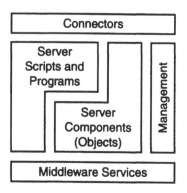

Exhibit 1.1   General Architecture of an Application Server

many of their new-economy competitors. In fact, some analysts predict that some new-economy companies will cease to exist once their more traditional competitors ramp up the Web parts of their businesses.

Computing architectures have been changing rapidly to accommodate the new Web model of doing business. An application server is a relatively new breed of product that allows enterprises to augment their Web servers with new applications that are comprised of new business logic. Many application servers also integrate transactions and data from mission-critical, legacy hierarchical and client/server systems. Application servers represent the marriage of architectures. They allow organizations to build, deploy, and manage new applications that are based on the Web model but that integrate a wide variety of existing systems. Exhibit 1.1 depicts the very general architecture of an application server.

Before the Web, computing architectures evolved over years or even decades. The mainframe dominated computing from the 1960s until the 1980s. The mainframe model dictated a hierarchical architecture in which the mainframe controlled all communication, and end-user devices (terminals) had no local computing power.

With the advent of the personal computer and the intelligent workstation in the 1980s, the client/server era of computing began. Early advocates of client/server computing giddily pronounced the end of the mainframe era and the hierarchical model. In reality, there were several issues (cost, complexity, platform compatibility, and proprietary interfaces) that prevented the client/server architecture from completely replacing existing hierarchical systems. By the early 1990s, object-oriented architectures were being developed and deployed to overcome some of the problems with traditional client/server programming.

Then came the Web. With its ubiquitous user interface (the Web browser) and low cost of entry, the Web model quickly dominated. Enterprises of all sizes began to deploy Web servers for public access over the Internet, employee access over corporate intranets, and business partner access over corporate extranets. Throughout this book, the term "i*net" will be used to refer collectively to the Internet, intranets, and extranets. I•nets are, by definition, based on Web and Internet technologies. This means that they utilize TCP/IP as the networking architecture, Web browsers as the means of accessing information and applications, Web servers as the entry point (or "portal") to the enterprise, and Internet standard technologies for security, name resolution, and application deployment.

The application server is a special breed of product that spans the decades, seamlessly integrating the variety of different systems and architectures that a typical enterprise has deployed, and providing enterprise access to all i•net users. The application server is based on object technologies and has interfaces to visual development tools, allowing brand new applications to be built much more quickly than in the past. The object orientation promotes the ability to reuse code and potentially to integrate off-the-shelf, commercially available components, enhancing time-to-market and code quality. Application servers represent the pinnacle of server-based computing that integrates the high availability and advanced security capabilities demanded by today's enterprises. Application servers, in summary, facilitate the implementation of enterprisewide E-commerce and E-business systems.

The Evolution of Computing Architectures

Most enterprises have built their IT systems, applications, and infrastructure over a period of many years. The mission-critical systems have been created and fine-tuned to run the key business processes of the enterprise with 99.999% availability. In many cases, the mission-critical applications run on legacy systems and there is no compelling justification to move the applications to Web servers. The vast investment in building and maintaining these systems, estimated at trillions of dollars, must be protected because the scalability and reliability of the mission-critical systems have been proven over time.

However, enterprises that wish to harness the power of the Web to their advantage must find ways to integrate the new with the old. Because of the massive installed base of legacy equipment, systems, and applications, a brief overview of the evolution of computing architectures as implemented in enterprises is provided here. This is not an idle diversion into ancient history. The Web architects of today may need to accommodate a variety of legacy systems, architectures, and technologies if they hope to achieve full integration of the Web with their key business processes.

Legacy Systems

The early business computer systems were mainframe computers. Early mainframes were extremely expensive and somewhat rare. Programs and data were encoded on punched cards or tape and read into the system. The common programming languages were assembly, a low-level machine language, and

COBOL, a higher level language geared to business applications. The mainframes were cared for by an elite legion of systems programmers that wielded ultimate power in apportioning system resources to various jobs and applications. Mainframes are physically large machines that reside in secure data centers that have sophisticated environmental controls.

IBM was an early entrant into the business computer market, and its mainframe systems dominated the computer market for many years. By the mid-1980s, virtually all medium and large enterprises worldwide had at least one IBM or IBM-compatible mainframe in their IT infrastructure. Many of the largest enterprises, such as General Motors, Sears, and AT&T, had hundreds or thousands of IBM (and compatible) mainframes running their key business applications.

A handful of vendors competed against IBM in the mainframe market by making a compatible computer that would run the same applications and offer the customer a lower price or greater functionality. Others competed against IBM by defining their own business computers that were not compatible with IBM mainframes. Programs written for one type of system would not necessarily run on other systems. The most successful of the IBM competitors were known as the BUNCH, which is an acronym of the five top firms — Burroughs, Univac, NCR, Cray, and Honeywell. Although these firms enjoyed a good deal of success in certain markets and certain vertical applications, their installed base is small compared to that of IBM. The IBM mainframe continues to have a substantial market share and installed base. And, as students of Wall Street know, the IBM mainframe continues to sell in fairly large numbers today and has helped IBM to maintain its position as a key worldwide supplier of technology.

Mainframe computers were highly popular for large public and private organizations that required the power and capacity of a mainframe computer to crunch vast amounts of data and manage huge customer databases. However, not all applications required the power and capacity of a mainframe. The minicomputer was the answer to the need for computing at a lower cost point and lower capacity. Minicomputers were used for both scientific and business applications. Perhaps the most popular minicomputer ever was the Digital Equipment Corporation (DEC) VAX system, although other companies like Wang, Data General, and Prime Computer achieved a good deal of success in the minicomputer market. Early minicomputers, like mainframes, each had a proprietary operating system but eventually some minicomputers supported one or more UNIX variants. The minicomputer boomed from the late 1970s until the late 1980s, when it was eventually edged out of existence by powerful PC and UNIX servers.

IBM participated in the minicomputer market as well, marketing a line of products that it called a midrange system. These systems were popular for business applications and sold as departmental systems as well as complete systems for small and medium businesses. IBM dominated the business midrange market, initially with its highly successful System/38 and System/36 product families. In the late 1980s, at the same time that the rest of the minicomputer market was waning, IBM introduced the AS/400 product line. Thousands of business applications written for the AS/400 are available from IBM and third-party suppliers, and it is estimated that more than 450,000 AS/400 systems have been sold since its introduction. The AS/400 is still being sold today and comes equipped with Web server software and Web-enabled applications.

The majority of legacy systems were designed to interact with end users who were stationed at fixed-function terminal displays. These terminals were the precursor to PC screens. The initial terminals offered a very basic interface of alphanumeric characters. The user interface is often described as "green-on-black" because the typical screen had a black background and green characters. Later, terminals offered a choice of color combinations (e.g., amber-on-black) and eventually even multiple colors and graphical symbol support. Most early terminals support 24 or 25 rows and 80 columns of characters, although various other sizes were available as well. Terminals were dedicated to a particular system or application. Therefore, if a particular office worker needed to access a mainframe system, a minicomputer, and a System/38 midrange system, he or she would need to have three different terminals on his or her desk.

Once PCs began to proliferate in the enterprise, a new breed of software — the terminal emulator — was created. As the name implies, terminal emulator software mimics or emulates the functions of a traditional fixed-function terminal device. A PC user with this software can access the legacy application and eliminate the terminal device from his or her desktop. By opening multiple emulators or multiple copies of a single emulator, the end user can communicate with multiple legacy host systems. However, in most cases, the user continues to interact with the legacy host using the rather cryptic and dated character-based interface typical in legacy applications. Even if the PC running the emulator offers the latest version of Windows, a 21-inch screen, and millions of colors, the user still sees a traditional 24 × 80 screen with a black background and alphanumeric characters within the emulator's window.

The architecture of these legacy systems is hierarchical. The mainframe supports all of the business logic and controls all network resources. The terminal devices cannot operate independently of the legacy host system. IBM's Systems Network Architecture (SNA) is by far the most widely deployed example of this architecture. SNA was IBM's strategic networking architecture, implemented within its mainframes, midrange systems, and networking hardware and software products. Most mainframe and minicomputer vendors that competed against IBM implemented a portion of the SNA architecture so as to be able to interoperate at some level with IBM systems. The native protocols employed by these IBM competitors, however, were typically their own proprietary variants of asynchronous or synchronous protocols. Exhibit 1.2 depicts a typical large enterprise with a variety of legacy systems. Chapter 2 describes how some legacy systems are being integrated with Web environments.

The legacy systems were the early pioneers of the computing industry. However, there were a number of issues that later computing architectures strove to overcome, including:

- *Proprietary operating systems and environments.* Each system required applications that were written specifically for that environment. The networking architectures varied, making it difficult to create a single, integrated network. Customers became dependent on one vendor and one product line for continued operation. The cost of owning multiple different systems could be astronomical.
- *Centralized control.* Especially with large mainframe systems, a central IT group controlled the resources and the priorities of competing projects. Business units and departments did not have the resources under their control to initiate their own new applications. The backlog for new applications was often measured in years — not months.
- *Underutilized resources.* PCs and workstations were not fully leveraged to offload processing from centralized systems.
- *Static and hierarchical architecture.* In most environments, all resources were predefined. Network adds, moves, and changes imposed a huge administrative overhead. The hierarchical nature imposed a large overhead on the centralized systems and did not allow for the flexibility that users were demanding.
- *Cryptic user interface.* The character-based interface often required weeks or months of training before an end user was considered proficient.

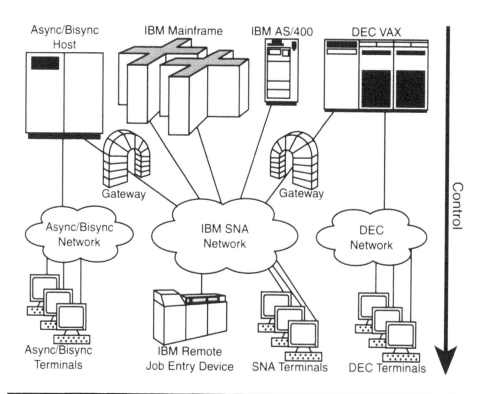

Exhibit 1.2   Legacy Hierarchical Systems

Beginning in the 1980s, many of the proprietary systems and environments began to be replaced by more open solutions. UNIX servers supplanted many of the proprietary minicomputer systems. Customers demanded that mainframe and midrange systems add support for open networking protocols (i.e., TCP/IP) so that interoperability with other platforms was possible. SNA, the dominant enterprise network architecture of the 1980s, evolved to support intelligent devices and a level of dynamic definition and flexibility not previously available. Application programming interfaces (APIs) were added to the mainframe and midrange systems so that new client/server applications could be built.

Today, most large educational, governmental, and commercial organizations have a variety of legacy systems. Some of the legacy systems have been isolated from updates and upgrades in the rest of the IT infrastructure. In some cases, organizations are afraid to make changes to the legacy systems for fear that something may break that they will not be able to fix. Other legacy systems have evolved and now support new applications and Web technologies. For example, today IBM's mainframe operating system comes bundled with a TCP/IP stack and a Web server. Nonetheless, even new mainframes running a TCP/IP stack will often still support some of the legacy, mission-critical applications that are based on the old hierarchical model. I*net users can gain access to these legacy applications through a new breed of Web-to-host gateway products. These are described in Chapter 2.

Client/Server

In the early days of client/server, the new architecture was seen by some to represent a revolution in computing rather than an evolution. Client/server, which enables the deployment of servers and applications at the departmental level, promised to break the hold that a central IT department had upon the end-user community. The proletarian masses would be free to implement applications at will. The central hierarchy and its mainframe computers would slowly wither and die. In fact, a respected weekly computing magazine actually sponsored a contest, inviting contestants to guess the date on which the last mainframe computer would be unplugged. This contest was a little optimistic, to say the least.

The name "client/server" pretty accurately captures the essence of this architecture. It is a two-tier architecture in which clients, intelligent end-user devices like PCs and workstations, communicate with servers to carry out transactions, move data, and process business logic. The application is somehow split between the client and the server. For example, the client device usually has all of the user interface logic and other local processing responsibilities. The server may contain the customer database and the logic for manipulating that database. The client and server must agree on a protocol or an API through which they will communicate. The servers may be distributed to the departmental level or they may be centralized in a data center.

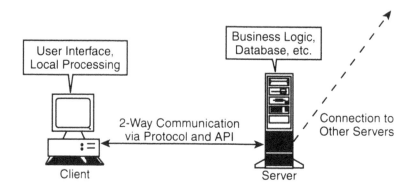

Exhibit 1.3   Client/Server Environment

There may be a hierarchy of servers as well. The client may communicate with a primary server, which in turn communicates with other servers (e.g., a mainframe) to access database records or process transactions. Exhibit 1.3 illustrates a client/server environment.

Conceptually, client/server is a relatively easy concept and architecture. Once standard APIs are agreed upon and implemented in various products, new client/server applications can interface to a variety of different systems (including legacy systems). Thus, for example, a new customer service application that resides on a UNIX server can gather customer billing information in the form of database records from a mainframe system. It can invoke a credit checking application on a different UNIX system utilizing remote procedure calls.

Client/server can, however, be extremely complex to implement. For each application or type of application, a standard protocol or API must be devised and implemented on both the client and the server. During the 1980s and 1990s, standards bodies were kept very busy defining standards for file transfer, database access, mail, network and system management, transaction interfaces, etc. Many vendors, out of frustration with the standards bodies or for competitive reasons, implemented proprietary interfaces within their products.

Another difficulty in implementing client/server is the variety of clients and servers within an enterprise. For each unique desktop operating system, for example, a different version of the client software has to be designed, written, tested, deployed, and maintained. At the desktop, Microsoft's DOS gained an early foothold, and since then the Windows family has dominated. However, there are several other desktop platforms that have gained support in the enterprise. Apple's Macintosh platform and operating system has always been favored by those involved in desktop publishing. IBM pushed for many years to get its OS/2 operating system accepted as the corporate desktop standard. While IBM eventually abandoned this attempt in the face of the dominance of Windows, OS/2 still exists in some large enterprises, particularly in financial organizations in the United States and throughout European and Asian markets. Finally, UNIX workstations have been common in technical and engineering environments.

There are similar platform issues at the server. While Microsoft's Windows NT and Windows 2000 have gained widespread enterprise deployment in the last several years, that has not always been the case. UNIX was the overwhelming choice for servers, and remains very popular. Sun Microsystems, Hewlett-Packard, and IBM have all sold numerous UNIX-based servers. Unfortunately, there is not one single standard for UNIX. There were early initiatives to come up with a UNIX standard, but the competing vendors could not agree completely on the standards. As a result, several different UNIX variants exist in the marketplace. Linux, a recent addition on the scene, offers an open approach with its freely available source code, but in the end adds one more variation to the set of UNIX server options.

In addition to the application-level protocol or API, client/server requires that the client and the server agree on and utilize a common networking architecture. The protocols common in the mainframe/legacy environment would not suffice due to their hierarchical nature and dependence on a centralized definition, administration, and session management. There were two options available: either the existing, mainframe-oriented protocols could be adapted to support client/server systems, or new standards could be defined that would be adopted by all client and server systems. Both options were pursued, resulting in three different competing protocols:

1. *Advanced Peer-to-Peer Networking (APPN)*. Architected and implemented by IBM, this was a follow-on to Systems Network Architecture (SNA), IBM's dominant hierarchical networking environment. Unlike SNA, APPN was licensed to any vendor wishing to implement it. Critics claimed it was not dynamic enough to support new networking requirements, and not open enough because the architecture was controlled and defined by IBM. APPN was implemented by many large IBM enterprise customers, and still exists in many networks.
2. *Open Systems Interconnect (OSI)*. This was a complete set of standards for networking, designed from the ground up by standards bodies. OSI defined a reference model of seven layers of networking, which is still a model used today to describe various networking approaches and protocols (see Exhibit 1.4). Although it had widespread backing from the user and vendor communities, it ultimately failed to gain critical mass. TCP/IP, which had been around for many years, was implemented by many instead of waiting for the promise of OSI.
3. *Transport Control Protocol/Internet Protocol (TCP/IP)*. TCP/IP was defined in the 1960s and 1970s to support U.S. governmental defense initiatives and research. It formed the basis of ARPANET, which was the precursor to the modern Internet. As such, it was widely deployed by governmental organizations, defense contractors, and higher education. It eventually evolved and was adopted by many commercial enterprises as a standard networking architecture.

Despite the complexity and cross-platform issues, client/server has been widely deployed in large and small enterprises. Packaged client/server products

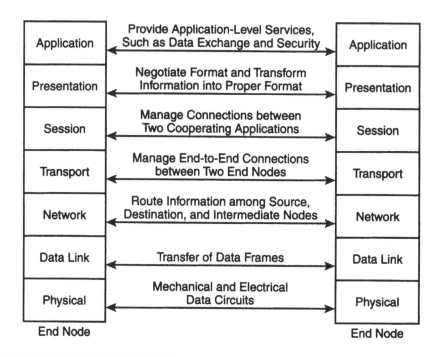

Exhibit 1.4   Seven-Layer OSI Reference Model

from PeopleSoft, SAP, and Baan have been implemented by large and small enterprises around the world. Sybase and Oracle have enjoyed enormous success selling and deploying distributed database management systems to support client/server environments. Lotus Notes pioneered the market for groupware and has gained support in many organizations. Microsoft's Back-Office suite of products has an enormous installed base and offers a complete set of server solutions targeted at the branch office, departmental environment, or mid-sized business.

Distributed Object Model

Object-oriented programming got its start in academia and has been a staple in Computer Science curricula since the early 1980s. The goal and the premise of object-oriented programming is that one can build reusable pieces of code that are written such that the implementation details are not seen or even relevant to the user of that code. Programmers can utilize existing "objects" that have defined operations that they perform ("methods"). This eliminates the writing and rewriting countless times of similar code that performs similar operations on a particular type of object.

Objects are structured into *classes* that are organized hierarchically. A particular object is defined as being an *instance* of a particular class. Its class has ancestor classes (*superclasses*) from which it inherits attributes and methods. Each class may also have "children," which are its own offspring and inherit attributes from it (*subclasses*).

A simplistic example from real life is my dog, Maggie. She is an instance of the class "Golden Retriever." This class is a child of the class "dog." The "dog" class defines attributes and methods that are common to all dogs (e.g., the methods: bark, eat socks, protect territory). The "Golden Retriever" class refines and adds to the "dog" class those methods and attributes that are specific to Golden Retrievers (e.g., the attributes: good with kids, sweet but slightly dumb, good worker). Maggie can perform all methods that are allowed by the definition of the class "dog" and its child class "Golden Retriever," but not methods that are defined to the class "human." Note that "dog" class and "human" class could be related somewhere in the ancestor tree and share certain methods and attributes. Also, "Golden Retriever" could have subclasses that more specifically define the attributes of major blood lines within the breed, for example.

If a programmer wanted to create a program about Maggie, the task would be greatly simplified if he or she could find the "dog" class definition and the "Golden Retriever" class definition in the marketplace. The programmer would not have to create these from scratch, and could instead focus his or her efforts and talents in creating the unique instance, Maggie.

A distributed object model utilizes object-oriented concepts and defines how objects can be distributed throughout an enterprise infrastructure. The distributed object model details how the objects communicate with one another and how an object is defined. A distributed object model builds upon rather than replaces the client/server architecture. Objects can be implemented on and accessible through client systems and server systems. While a client/server environment is often termed a two-tier environment, a distributed object environment is often referred to as a three-tier or an N-tier environment because it has a middleware component that brokers communication between objects. Exhibit 1.5 depicts a distributed object model.

The distributed object model requires a common approach to defining the attributes and methods of classes and the relationships between classes. This rather important and monumental task was undertaken by the Object Management Group (OMG), a consortium of more than 800 companies representing many different areas and disciplines within the computer industry. The result is the Common Object Request Broker Architecture (CORBA). There is one notable company abstaining from the OMG — Microsoft. It has defined a competing object architecture, previously called Distributed Component Object Model (DCOM) but now called COM+. Java also has a defined server-side distributed object model, Enterprise JavaBeans (EJB).

The deployment of object models is in various stages in enterprise environments. Some enterprises were early advocates and have a rich installed base of object technologies; other enterprises have avoided the object models until recently. The proliferation of Web-based systems has not derailed the implementation of object-based systems. Indeed, the two complement one another. Java, a set of technologies tied to the Web, and CORBA are being married to create object-oriented Web environments. In fact, many application servers support both Java technologies and CORBA technologies. These technologies are explored fully in Chapters 3 and 4, respectively.

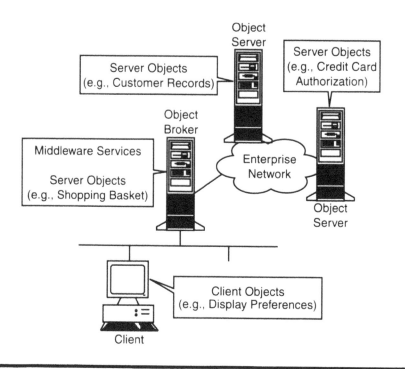

Exhibit 1.5   Distributed Object Model

Web Model

Sir Isaac Newton said: "If I have seen further it is by standing on the shoulders of giants." Likewise, the World Wide Web did not spring fully formed from the ether in the early 1990s. The World Wide Web is built on top of a network that had been proven and deployed for many years.

Beginning in the mid-1970s, the Defense Advanced Research Projects Agency (DARPA) funded research into establishing a network of networks (an internetwork) that would join various governmental agencies, research labs, and other interested organizations, such as defense contractors, to communicate and share information easily. The result was called ARPANET. Based on TCP/IP, the network linked the university and governmental organizations as early as the late 1970s. Eventually, ARPANET evolved and extended to more organizations and became known as the Internet.

The early users of the Internet were primarily governmental labs, universities, and defense contractors. The interface was character-based and somewhat cryptic. It allowed knowledgeable users to "Telnet" to other sites (i.e., log on to and access), share files via the File Transfer Protocol (FTP), and perform other permitted operations. Internet Protocol (IP) was and is the underlying transport protocol of the Internet. Many applications use the higher-level Transport Control Protocol (TCP) on top of IP to provide reliable, end-to-end transmission of the data.

The World Wide Web came about in 1994 as an extension to the existing Internet, pioneered by Tim Berners-Lee and associates. The Web adds a unique, location-independent, graphical navigational ability on top of the Internet. Users with Web browsers can navigate an interconnected space of information. The Web is controlled and managed by no single person or entity. Documents and information are hyperlinked together, creating a virtual Web or fabric of information.

The early Web model of computing focused on the easy dissemination of information. HyperText Markup Language (HTML), the basic document description language of the Web, allows individuals and organizations to easily publish information on Web servers. The basic architecture of the Web model is described as a "thin-client" architecture because the client machine only needs to support a browser, which was, at one time, a pretty basic piece of software.

Over time, however, the Web model has grown to include more complex client capabilities (i.e., a fatter thin client). Extensible Markup Language (XML) and Wireless Markup Language (WML) have been added to HTML and its extensions as common content description languages. Programs (applets) are executed within the browser environment at the client side to enhance the client's local processing beyond the capabilities of a Web browser. Server scripts, servlets, and distributed objects enhance the sophistication of the Web server. Finally, new types of products add host access, distributed computing, and middle-tier application services to the whole Web environment. Chapter 2 provides an overview of the various Web technologies, including HTML, XML, WML, Java, ActiveX, applets, servlets, and Web-to-host technologies.

Electronic Commerce and Electronic Business

The Web has truly revolutionized our collective vision of what is possible with computers and with networks. The Information Superhighway that was loftily projected by governmental policy wonks and the educated elite in the early 1990s has in fact become a reality with the Internet and the Web. The impact that it has wrought on everyday life and the speed with which it has become pervasive in everyday society is completely unprecedented. It has become an accepted maxim that commercial entities without a Web strategy will cease to exist within a few years. Governmental organizations are beginning to worry out loud about the "digital divide" that appears to be ready to leave an entire segment of the population in the dust as the Internet economy booms.

Merely having a presence on the Web is not sufficient. Organizations typically begin their Web presence by simply publishing information to Web visitors. Once that level of presence is established, end users demand a more interactive, dynamic environment that is able to support a wide range of interactions with the organization. Organizations that master the Web eventually integrate all key business processes with their i*net.

Three Stages of Web Presence

Enterprises typically evolve their presence on the Web in three stages. In the first stage, an enterprise creates a Web site that provides Web visitors with static information about the enterprise, its products, and its services. This type of Web site is often called brochureware because it provides the same type of noncustomized, marketing-oriented information that is often published by organizations in brochures. This is also the reason the term "publishing" has been prevalent in describing the use of the Web for dissemination of information.

In the second stage of Web presence, the Web site is made dynamic through the introduction of forms, drop-down lists, and other ways to allow the end user to interact with the Web site. A simple example of this type of dynamic interaction is the request of a valid userID and password before a particular operation is undertaken. A more sophisticated example is the shopping cart and credit card authorization functions on a retail Web site. This second stage of Web presence is made possible by writing scripts, which are programs executed by the Web server. Chapter 2 discusses Web server scripts in more detail.

In the third stage of Web presence, the Web site becomes the portal through which employees, customers, and business partners carry out a rich and complex set of transactions with an enterprise. In this stage, the Web site is seamlessly integrated with existing systems and all systems are reachable through a single piece of software — the Web browser. The Web site in the third stage of evolution presents a different face to three different types of users — employees, business partners, and consumers. Each constituency is offered a unique set of choices and applications based on what is relevant to them and what they are allowed to do. For example, employees can access company holiday schedules, fill out time cards and expense reports, and access each of the internal applications relevant to doing their job. Business partners can enter orders, track shipment status, and resolve billing issues. It offers customers the ability to confirm availability of items, check on the status of back-ordered items, gain approval of credit terms, and access detailed shipping information. This is all possible because the Web server is integrated with all of the key-back office systems of the enterprise. It has access to customer databases, MRP systems, and all other systems that run the business. Application servers enable the third stage of Web presence.

Electronic Commerce

Electronic commerce can take place beginning in the second stage and in the third stage of Web presence. For the purposes of this book, *electronic commerce (E-commerce)* will be defined as the sale of goods and services and the transfer of funds or authorization of payment through a Web site. The customer of an E-commerce transaction may be a consumer or it may be another business entity.

To many, business-to-consumer (B2C) E-commerce is the most visible aspect of the Web. Consumers can surf the Web, purchasing just about any kind of good or service from retail Web sites. A new breed of company has materialized, the E-tailer, that only offers goods and services via its Web site and has no physical store presence on Main Street or in the shopping malls. Amazon.com and eBay are two early examples, but the segment has grown with the addition of a newer set of entrants such as pets.com. Traditional retailers, eager to capitalize on their brand loyalty to keep Web shoppers, have joined the E-tailers. Just about every major brick-and-mortar retailer is offering a Web-based shopping alternative to visiting its stores. The savvy ones are marketing the benefits of shopping over the Web from a company with local presence for customer service such as processing the return of merchandise.

Another major form of B2C E-commerce is in the area of financial services. Consumers have eagerly and rapidly moved to the Web model for trading stocks and performing basic banking tasks. Charles Schwab, the established national discount broker, was an early participant and is now the top online trading site. E-Trade and other new online brokerage houses without traditional brokerage offices have taken customers and accounts from some of the traditional brokerage firms. Finally, even the most conservative brokers are offering Web-based trading to augment their more traditional broker-based services.

The rationale for B2C E-commerce is relatively straightforward and simple to understand. From the consumer's perspective, they now have access to virtually any good or service and can easily shop for the best prices and terms. From the perspective of new E-tailing firms, they are able to tap a potentially huge market without requiring the time and huge costs of building a physical presence throughout the nation. Established retailers are reacting to the threat of the new E-tailers and attempting to grow their market share at the same time. Experts estimate that 17 million U.S. households shopped online in 1999, for a total sales volume of $20.2 billion. Furthermore, 56 percent of U.S. firms are expected to sell their products online in the year 2000, which is up from only 24 percent of firms in 1998 (http://www.internetindicators.com/facts.html).

Although the B2C examples of E-commerce are the most visible, business-to-business (B2B) E-commerce is a vibrant and growing area. Companies like Cisco Systems, Dell Computer, and Sun Microsystems are offering Web-based purchasing to their existing customers. These systems are somewhat different than B2C E-commerce sites because they must accommodate the purchasing authority, approvals, and paperwork commonly used by corporations and other organizations to procure goods and services. They also typically require that a proper sales agreement and prior approval are in place before they will process orders. The B2B E-commerce initiative is growing rapidly as companies realize the cost benefits of submitting routine purchase transactions across the Web. According to Cisco Systems, the company now receives 85 percent of its orders via its Web site (http://www.cisco.com), representing more than $32 million in sales every day.

The business justification for pursuing B2B E-commerce is both cost reduction and improved efficiencies. Consider the case of a Cisco Systems customer that needs to add a few Ethernet switches to its network. Prior to the Web, the network manager would phone the Cisco sales representative. The sales representative may not be immediately available, necessitating the network manager to leave a voice mail asking for a return call. Several rounds of voice-mail messages may occur before the two are able to speak. The order itself, if it's covered under an existing purchase agreement, could take only minutes to produce but it may take many valuable minutes from both the network manager and the sales representative to get to this point to conclude the business. Multiply this inefficiency by tens of thousands and one gets a sense of how much time can be wasted in nonproductive activities for Cisco sales representatives and their customers. By making routine equipment purchases through the Web, the network manager is able to devote more time to solving real network problems and the sales representative is able to devote more time to supporting customers in ways that are more valuable.

E-commerce for B2C and B2B is quickly becoming a way of life for many and is changing our relationship with our retail and business providers. As more and more companies sell their goods and services via the Web, the remaining firms with no E-commerce Web presence will surely suffer and will eventually lose customers to competitors that offer the convenience and time savings of shopping via the Web.

Electronic Business

E-commerce is an important evolution for many organizations. However, the ultimate goal for organizations wishing to maximize the potential of the Web is electronic business. IBM, the first major computer vendor to coin the term, defines electronic business (E-business) as "the transformation of key business processes through the use of Internet technologies." (http://www.ibm.com/e-business/info/). Using this definition, it is clear that E-commerce is a subset of E-business, because the sales function is just one of the key business processes a commercial enterprise supports. Stated another way, E-commerce is a necessary but not sufficient criteria for achieving E-business.

The term "key business processes" in the definition has another strong implication for E-business. Unless an enterprise is very young to the extent that all IT infrastructure is based on Web and Internet technologies (e.g., Amazon.com), the key business processes of an enterprise may rely on a variety of mission-critical legacy systems. Therefore, the achievement of E-business implies that an enterprise may have to integrate its Web systems with its legacy hierarchical and client/server systems. By definition, the enterprise that has achieved E-business is in the third stage of Web presence.

A primary example of a B2C E-business site is the Charles Schwab site. It was previously cited as the leading online brokerage firm. It seems there are new surveys and rankings every day of online brokerages, and Charles Schwab consistently ranks at or near the top. One of the reasons for the consistent ranking is the richness of the Web site. Customers can perform a wide range of functions and services through the single, secure customer portal. The services currently offered to customers via its Web site include:

- open new accounts
- receive delayed and real-time securities quotes
- view detailed account information, including overview, balances, positions, and history
- compare holdings against market indices
- move money into or out of one's account, or between various Schwab accounts
- place orders for stocks, mutual funds, options, corporate bonds, U.S. treasuries, futures, and after-hour trades
- view status of orders
- access company news, information, and charts
- access a rich set of research material
- receive customized alerts
- analyze current asset allocation and compare it to a model allocation
- gain access to independent financial advisers
- access various online planners to assist in setting goals and plans for retirement, college funding, etc.
- modify account password, e-mail address, mailing address, and phone number
- request checks, deposit slips, deposit envelopes, W-8 form, and W-9 form
- fill out forms to transfer accounts to Schwab, set up electronic or wired funds transfer, receive IRA distribution, apply for options trading, and many other customer service functions

This incredibly diverse list of services differentiates the Charles Schwab Web site from many of its competitors. It is clear by examining the list that Charles Schwab has crossed the line from E-commerce to E-business. Its core commerce function, securities trading, is available on the Web, but it augments that E-commerce offering with a rich set of customer service and account management features, external news feeds, external research services, and proactive alert services. Essentially, virtually every transaction or request that a customer would require to interact with Charles Schwab can be satisfied via its Web site. Of course, the company continues to offer a 1-800 service for customers who need additional assistance. And it continues to operate and even expand its network of branch offices to assist its customers in person.

The Charles Schwab E-business Web site has not replaced the company's traditional customer service mechanisms, but the Web site has allowed Charles Schwab to grow its asset and customer base faster than it would have been able to do so using traditional means. The traditional way of servicing more customers would have meant the expansion of its network of branch offices and also the expansion of its telephone call center for handling customer service inquiries. The addition of each new customer would have required a certain investment in new staff and infrastructure to support that customer. In the E-business model, each additional customer requires only a modest incremental investment in new infrastructure and systems and some fractional new investment in call centers and branch offices. The required investment for the traditional model versus the E-business model is likely on the order of 100:1 or 1000:1. These cost efficiencies and the ability to scale the operation are the driving forces behind the deployment of B2C E-business solutions.

A premier B2B E-business site is Cisco Systems' Web site, Cisco Connection Online. This site is certainly geared to providing E-commerce. As already stated, Cisco receives more than 85 percent of its orders, valued at more than $32 million per day, through its E-commerce Web site, the Cisco Marketplace. This site offers Cisco customers and resellers a rich set of capabilities, including online product configuration, access to up-to-date pricing, and 24-hour access to order status.

But the site goes beyond providing E-commerce. In particular, its Technical Assistance Center (TAC) is considered a model in the industry for providing online customer service and support. Developed over a period of years, the TAC site offers customers around the world immediate access to Cisco information, resources, and systems. In fact, customers can gain online access to many of the same systems and tools that are utilized by Cisco's TAC engineers in providing service and support. In that way, customers can often diagnose and troubleshoot their own network problems without incurring the turn-around delay of contacting a TAC specialist. However, when a TAC specialist is required, the TAC site serves as the primary initial interface into the Cisco support organization. The benefit to customers is a more responsive support environment. Cisco has benefited enormously from an early investment in the TAC site and online tools. Just as the Charles Schwab site has enabled that company to scale its business faster than if it did not have the Web, the Cisco TAC site has enabled Cisco Systems to grow its business faster. More TAC engineers can take care of more customers when some of the problems are handled via the Web. In the tight high-tech labor market, the TAC Web site has allowed Cisco to maintain high standards of customer service during a period of exponential growth of its customer base.

Another area that Cisco is just beginning to explore with its site is E-learning. Cisco Systems executives regularly talk about the Internet as a force that will change education in the future. Cisco is beginning to offer a set of training modules available on its Web site for its customers, partners, and consultants. E-learning will enable more people to become proficient on Cisco products and technologies than would have been possible with more traditional, class-room-based approaches.

Although some examples of B2C and B2B E-business have been examined, there is a third constituency in the i*net world — employees. Organizations that are conducting E-business with their customers and business partners usually offer their employees a customized, secure portal through which they can carry out all of their day-to-day essential functions. One could call this type of portal a B2E site because it links a business to its employees. Exhibit 1.6

Exhibit 1.6   Example of Employee Portal Page (© Anura Gurugé, 2001)

illustrates an example of the employee portal page of a fictitious company. This page is like a company-specific version of a personalized Excite! start page. It allows the company to efficiently broadcast successes and other important news to all of its employees. The portal can give access to all of the applications that are relevant to that particular employee as well as employee-specific messages such as the number of new e-mails waiting. Finally, the portal can provide online employee access to benefits, vacation information, and all other human resources functions. The employee portal can greatly increase the efficiency and the satisfaction of all workers with its appealing and easy-to-use graphical interface. The employee portal can also ease the regular and day-to-day dissemination of key enterprise information to the workforce.

Chapter 7 details two case studies of organizations that have utilized application servers to achieve B2C, B2B, and B2E E-business.

E-commerce has fueled the growth of the Web. In just a few short years, the Web has become a pervasive force in the worldwide economy. Consumers and businesses around the world are discovering the efficiencies and the convenience of buying goods and services over the Web. E-commerce, while a necessary step in the Web presence of for-profit organizations, is not the final goal. The final goal is E-business, in which *all* key business processes, *including* the sales process, are fully integrated with the Web. Once E-business is achieved, organizations can realize vast efficiencies in their business processes. They will be able to serve more customers and partners more efficiently. Their employees will be more productive and will require less training.

What is an Application Server?

An application server is a component-based, server-centric product that allows organizations to build, deploy, and manage new applications for i*net users.

It is a middle-tier solution that augments the traditional Web server. The application server provides middleware services for applications such as security and the maintenance of state and persistence for transactions.

An application server usually also offers a variety of back-ends that communicate with a variety of legacy applications, allowing organizations to integrate the data and logic of these legacy applications with the new, Web-oriented applications. Thus, application servers enable organizations to achieve E-business. Refer to Exhibit 1.1 for a view of the general architecture of an application server. Exhibit 1.7 illustrates where an application server fits in the overall enterprise i*net infrastructure.

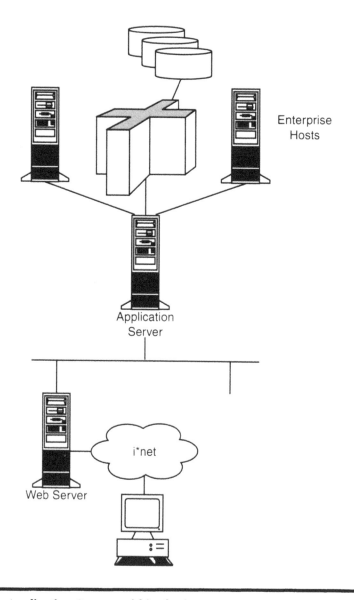

Exhibit 1.7   Application Servers within the i*net

There are a variety of vendors offering application servers today, including IBM, Inprise, BEA Systems, iPlanet, Microsoft, and many others. Each of the implementations is different, and each product has a different technology emphasis. For example, Inprise's product is built upon the company's CORBA Object Request Broker (ORB) and thus has a CORBA-based architecture, although the product supports the Java objects and the EJB architecture as well. The iPlanet Application Server, on the other hand, is a Java-based solution but it interoperates with CORBA platforms and applications. Microsoft sells a solution that is solely based on the company's COM/DCOM architecture and technologies.

The clients of an application server may be a variety of devices, but the commonality is that they support Web-oriented protocols and technologies. The devices may be PCs, laptops, personal digital assistants (PDAs), digital mobile telephones, or a variety of handheld devices. The devices usually do not communicate directly with the application server; instead, they communicate with a Web server, which in turn communicates with the application server. In these cases, the end-user device supports one or more of the protocols supported by Web servers and Web browsers: HyperText Markup Language (HTML), eXtensible Markup Language (XML), or the new Wireless Markup Language (WML). However, in some cases, the devices communicate directly with the application server without first going through a Web server. Depending on which technologies are supported by the application server, these devices could be running Java applets or applications, ActiveX controls, programs that communicate using a CORBA-based protocol, or programs utilizing a proprietary protocol over TCP/IP.

The application server software is installed on a server somewhere in the enterprise infrastructure. It may run on the same server that is also running Web server software, but this is not a requirement. In fact, there are compelling reasons (e.g., scalability) to run the application server and Web server separately. Application servers are available that run under a wide variety of operating systems, including Windows NT, a variety of UNIX systems, Linux, OS/390, OS/400, Novell NetWare, and others. The application server is often referred to as a middle-tier solution because it logically (and maybe physically) resides in the "middle" of the infrastructure, upstream from clients and Web servers and downstream from enterprise data.

The application server engine that runs the new programs is usually based on Java or CORBA technologies. The engine supports interactions between objects, applets, servlets, and legacy hierarchical or client/server programs. Chapter 5 explores the architecture and elements of an application server in much more detail. Chapters 2 through 4 provide an overview of all of the technologies relevant to application servers to provide a foundation for the discussion in Chapter 5.

The application server usually supports a variety of back-ends to communicate with other servers and hosts. The set of back-ends supported varies from product to product, but some of the possible systems and programs supported by specific back-ends include:

- database management systems using standard APIs and/or protocols
- transaction processing systems using terminal datastreams
- transaction processing systems using published APIs
- client/server applications using published APIs
- CORBA applications
- Java applications
- Microsoft DCOM/COM applications

The application server model relies on the creation of new applications. These new applications rely heavily on standard interfaces and components to leverage the existing IT infrastructure and investment in applications. Nonetheless, a programmer who understands a variety of different, sophisticated technologies must create the new applications. To assist in the building of these new applications, most application servers support one or more integrated development environments (IDEs). These are toolkits that simplify the development process by providing a visual interface to the programmer. Using a visual drag-and-drop interface, the programmer can concentrate on the unique business logic of the new application rather than the mechanics of writing code from scratch. IDEs are available from a number of different vendors, including IBM, Microsoft, Borland (Inprise), and Symantec, among others. Some application server vendors provide support for a set of common IDEs, while other vendors offer their own proprietary IDE product as an adjunct to the application server.

System Design Considerations

The goal of deploying new applications based on application servers is to achieve E-business. Again, according to IBM, E-business is "the transformation of key business processes through the use of Internet technologies." This is a very aggressive goal. After all, most IT infrastructures have been very carefully built and tested over a period of years. Overall system availability is often measured in terms of the number of "nines" that are beyond the decimal point (i.e., 99.9999 percent). Many system and network professionals are compensated based upon the continued high availability of systems. Consider, for example, the case of Cisco Systems. Just the E-commerce portion of its site is worth approximately $22,000 in revenue every minute, or $370 every second. Even a minor outage is unacceptable.

All mission-critical systems must ensure that the confidential data and systems of the enterprise are safe from outside observation and attack. They must demonstrate appropriate scalability to handle the anticipated load of requests. They must demonstrate the ability to continue to operate despite the failure of one or more components. Finally, they must provide sufficient tools to allow system and network managers to manage the environment. Because application servers will be an important component in many E-business initiatives, it is critical that the application servers seamlessly support the ability to build secure systems that offer appropriate scalability, load balancing, fault tolerance, and management.

Security

Any enterprise involved in E-commerce and E-business will likely rank security as the top concern. Almost everyone has read the news stories about the bright teenagers with a moderate level of technical knowledge hacking into the Central Intelligence Agency and DARE sites, or launching denial-of-service attacks that crippled CNN, eBay, Yahoo!, Amazon.com, and ETrade for a period of hours. Security must be of paramount concern, particularly when all key business systems are integrated into the i*net and therefore potentially accessible by anyone with an Internet connection. It is a very serious and potentially crippling occurrence to have a Web site attacked. However, the threat is of a different magnitude when the attack could potentially extend to an enterprise's entire base of mission-critical applications and data.

The good news is that there are a wide variety of security mechanisms available that can safeguard E-commerce and E-business systems. Of course, the bad news is that there are a wide variety of mechanisms available. An IT organization needs to implement multiple levels of security to safeguard its systems. It is not sufficient to say, for example, that one has implemented Secure Sockets Layer (SSL), one of the many Web standards for security. SSL is an important element of an overall security architecture, but SSL alone does not suffice.

An overall security architecture for E-commerce and E-business includes the following elements:

1. *Encryption:* the encoding of data so that it is illegible to anyone trying to decipher it, except for the intended recipient
2. *Authentication:* the verification of the identity of a user (e.g., the use of passwords and digital certificates)
3. *Authorization:* the granting or denial of access to a particular application, resource, or data based upon the identity of the user and some security policy

In an E-commerce and E-business infrastructure that includes access to the public Internet, a corporate intranet, and business partner extranets, the overall security architecture can become quite complex. A variety of systems and security products may be involved, including firewalls, policy servers, routers configured with filtering and other security mechanisms, etc. Adding complexity is the multi-tier nature of an architecture that includes Web servers, application servers, client/server systems, and legacy host systems. For example, should one employ encryption at each stage of the process, or is it sufficient to only encrypt the data once it leaves the corporate intranet and travels across a public wide area network or the Internet? Should users be able to access multiple systems with a single logon, or should they be forced to log in separately to each system? These are just two of the many questions that need to be answered before a comprehensive security plan can be devised. Chapter 6 explores some of the key security technologies in more detail.

Scalability

Scalability means that a computer system or network is able to grow to accommodate new users and new traffic in an approximately linear fashion. A scalable system has no design thresholds that, once reached, become a bottleneck for continued growth. A scalable system recognizes that there are finite resources (e.g., network bandwidth, CPU power) and it makes parsimonious use of those resources.

Scalability is a critical design consideration for E-commerce and E-business systems. As organizations that have already achieved E-business know, a successful system quickly becomes very popular. The demand for the system and the number of users and amount of traffic can escalate quickly. But what happens if the system becomes overwhelmed and the response time increases dramatically or the system fails altogether? Users will quickly become disillusioned with the system, and customers may even desert to the competition.

There are several important aspects that must be considered in an overall scalable design for E-commerce and E-business:

1. *Network*. An enterprise has no control over the access speed that an Internet user has or the overall capacity of the Internet. However, the internal network must be designed with sufficient bandwidth available to handle planned peak loads with some growth in those loads factored in. The typical scalable campus network infrastructure today is based on high-speed LAN switching. The enterprise wide area network must also be considered if i*net traffic will traverse a private WAN.
2. *Server*. The individual servers upon which the overall E-business system is based should gracefully scale to support increasing user and transaction loads. Obviously, any system will have a limit but some systems scale better than others. For example, UNIX servers are generally recognized to scale better than Windows NT systems. Scalable servers will be equipped with sufficient memory, disk, and network interfaces so that these are not a bottleneck. The software systems that run on the servers should be designed to scale easily. For example, systems that support multiple end users should employ multithreading so that multiple transactions can be processed simultaneously.
3. *Server complex and multiprocessing*. Any individual processor will eventually become a bottleneck, given enough end users or transactions. The E-business environment should be designed to support a complex of multiple servers or utilize symmetrical or asymmetrical multiprocessing approaches. This allows the overall system to grow and continue to support an ever-increasing number of users by adding servers or

processors to the complex. Some of the well-known Web sites require hundreds of different Web server machines to handle the load.

4. *Intermediate processing.* Very often, i*net traffic must traverse multiple systems and networks to complete a transaction. Each system and network in the path from the end user to the application server(s) has the potential of introducing a bottleneck. For example, any single router in a network can become temporarily busy, resulting in data that waits in a queue to be forwarded to the next node. Each layer of security adds its own processing overhead. For example, encryption imposes a large processing load at both ends of the encrypted link. If a single transaction is encrypted twice on its way to its destination, there are four different encryption/de-encryption steps in each direction.

Designing scalable systems is an ever-changing task because each new addition to or modification of the existing systems results in a change in the amount, type, or timing of traffic and transactions. Organizations need to devise an overall strategy to achieve a scalable E-business system. They also need to continually monitor the environment on a day-to-day basis so that future bottlenecks can be detected before they become a problem.

Load Balancing

Load balancing is something that is employed once a particular application is deployed across two or more servers. As described in the previous section, this is used to build scalable systems. Load balancing is a mechanism to balance the users or the transactions across the available pool of servers. The goal of load balancing is to ensure that the available servers are all handling more or less the same amount of work at any given time so that no single server becomes overloaded. Load balancing should be deployed in such a way that the end user is not aware of the fact that there are multiple servers. The end user should only be concerned with defining or specifying a single location, and the pool of servers should appear logically to the user as a single device. Exhibit 1.8 illustrates the concept of a pool of servers.

The importance of load balancing increases as the scale of the system increases. Early Web sites, for example, sometimes tried to solve the scalability problem by having the end user select a particular Web server to contact based upon some criteria. Microsoft, for example, requires that users select a particular server from which to download software based on the server that is in closest proximity. This scheme can work for awhile, as long as there are no more than a few choices and the probability of successfully completing a transaction on the first try is pretty high. If, on the other hand, there are hundreds of server choices and some high percentage of them are already working at capacity, users will quickly become frustrated and give up.

Load balancing algorithms are varied. Some are simple round-robin schemes, in which servers are allocated new sessions or transactions in sequence. This works reasonably well if the sessions or transactions are similar

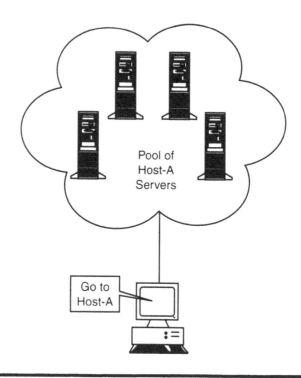

Exhibit 1.8   Pool of Servers

in nature and the servers are roughly equivalent in capacity. More sophisticated mechanisms take into account various metrics of each server, including perhaps CPU utilization, number of active sessions, queue depth, and other measures.

Load balancing is related to scalability because the entire concept of load balancing is based on the premise that there are multiple servers performing the same tasks. Load balancing systems can also help to maintain high overall system availability and fault tolerance.

Fault Tolerance

A fault-tolerant system is able to tolerate the loss of a component and continue to operate around the failed component. Note that fault tolerance does not mean the absence of faults or failures. Computer components and systems are often rated based on the mean time between failure (MTBF), measured in hours. MTBF is a measure of the frequency with which a particular component or system will fail. Fault tolerance, on the other hand, is a measure of how well or poorly the system tolerates the failure of components.

The fault tolerance of a single component such as a PC, server, or network component can be enhanced using primarily hardware capabilities. Power supplies, which are often the component with the lowest MTBF of all components, can be dual and hot-swappable. This means that the system has two power supplies, with one as the primary supply. If it fails, the secondary supply will take over with no disruption to the operation of the system. The hot-swappable part means that the failed supply can be replaced while the system is up and running. Thus, the system is available 100 percent of the time during the failure of a key hardware component and its replacement. Many PCs, servers, and network equipment such as switches and routers support redundant and hot-swappable power supplies, disk subsystems, and network interface adapters.

In a scalable environment in which multiple applications or Web servers are pooled together to form a virtual unit, fault tolerance principles imply that the failure of a single server will allow the continued operation of the remaining available servers. If one Web server of a pool of five Web servers fails, the i*net users should still be able to access the Web site. There may be a slight degradation in overall performance, but the users will still be able to perform all of the functions they are permitted to perform.

There is often a single product that is implemented in the virtual server pool environment that provides both load balancing and fault tolerance. This is because they are related ideas. Sessions or transactions should be load balanced across all available servers. It would not make sense for a load balancer to allocate sessions or transactions to a server that has failed. For that reason, most load balancing products have a mechanism to periodically query the health of the servers in the pool. They remove from the list of potential servers any server that is not responding or is otherwise deemed "not healthy."

Load balancing and fault tolerance are often implemented in a device within the network. However, they can also be implemented in the destination server that runs the application. For example, IBM offers its mainframe customers a capability called Parallel Sysplex. With Parallel Sysplex, customers can implement a virtual pool of mainframe processors. All active sessions are logged to a central facility. If any single application processor fails, all active sessions are seamlessly transferred to a remaining, active system. There are pros and cons to this approach. If there are a variety of different hosts, then each must have its own capability similar to Parallel Sysplex. The optimum approach combines the benefits of network-based fault tolerance devices in addition to host-based fault tolerance capabilities. Parallel Sysplex and other load-balancing and fault-tolerance capabilities are discussed in more detail in Chapter 6.

Management

One cannot focus on the management of an application server without examining the environment as a whole. As illustrated in Exhibit 1.5, the environment in which an application server exists is complex and includes a variety of different server types (e.g., Web servers, legacy hosts, application servers). The application server environment may also include a complex network infrastructure that includes switches, routers, and firewalls. Finally, the environment may include network application servers such as domain name servers, directory servers, and security policy servers.

Each platform and device in the environment has a built-in default management capability. The goal of a management strategy should be to have a unified set of system and network management tools that allows a network operations staff to proactively and reactively manage all systems and components. A comprehensive management strategy includes each of the following elements: fault management, configuration management, accounting/billing, performance management, and security management. The emphasis in many organizations is on fault and configuration management. The importance of accounting/billing may vary from organization to organization. However, with the rapidly growing demands of i*net users on the infrastructure, performance and security management are becoming critical elements.

A detailed overview of the various standards and common tools for system and network management is provided in Chapter 6.

Final Thoughts

IT organizations around the world are being challenged to implement E-commerce and E-business infrastructures to allow their enterprises to take advantage of the explosive growth of the Web. Senior management views the goal of mastering the Web as both a carrot and a stick. The carrot is the promise of greater revenues, increased customer satisfaction and loyalty, streamlined business processes, and the elimination of an outdated set of interfaces to customers and business partners. The stick is the threat that organizations that do not master the Web will cease to exist.

But achieving E-business involves the transformation of the organization's key business processes. The application server is a new breed of product that will allow organizations to deploy new, Web-oriented applications for their i*net users while maximizing the power of and the investment in their wide variety of legacy systems. It is, admittedly, a complex undertaking that involves the integration of many diverse technologies under a single, cohesive architecture. And because the answer to the question, "When does this all need to be complete?" is almost always "Yesterday," IT organizations often feel that they are trying to change the tires on a bus that is barreling down the highway at 65 miles per hour while ensuring the safety of all its passengers.

Nonetheless, many organizations have already successfully demonstrated the advantages of implementing applications servers to achieve the goal of E-business. This new breed of product will allow countless organizations to integrate new Web-oriented applications for i*net users with the mission-critical systems that are powering the enterprise today.

Chapter 2

A Survey of Web Technologies

Application servers are inextricably connected to the Web and Web-related technologies. This chapter provides an overview of how Web browsers and servers operate and details many of the technologies that are prevalent in today's i*net environments. The chapter is intended to provide a concise description of important Web technologies for the reader who does not have an extensive Web programming background.

Overview of Web Browser and Server Operation

There are two necessary software components required to complete a Web transaction: the Web browser and the Web server. The Web browser is software that resides on a client machine, which could be a PC, laptop, personal digital assistant, Web phone, or a specialized appliance. The Web server is a program that runs on a server machine, which is usually equipped with lots of power, memory, and disk capacity to support many concurrent users. The Web server software is often referred to as a HyperText Transfer Protocol (HTTP) server because HTTP is the protocol used to transmit information to browsers. Web servers are available that run on a wide variety of operating systems, including many UNIX variants, Linux, Microsoft Windows NT, Novell NetWare, IBM OS/390, and IBM OS/400.

The Web browser and server are examples of a client/server pair of programs. The Web browser is the client program and the Web server is the server program. The client sends requests to the server and the server responds to those requests. The usual browser request is for the server to retrieve and transmit files. It is the client that decides what to do with the information (e.g., display the text or image, play the audio clip). A set of standard formats and protocols work together to ensure that Web browsers can properly access Web servers and receive data from them.

The first set of standards for this two-way communication is at the networking level. As explained in Chapter 1, Transmission Control Protocol/Internet Protocol (TCP/IP) became the *de facto* standard of networking in client/server environments and the underlying networking protocol of the Internet and the Web. More precisely, IP is the protocol that manages the transmission of data across a network or set of networks. TCP is a higher-level protocol that makes sure the data arrives complete and intact.

Every computer that wishes to communicate using IP has a unique address assigned to it that is in the form 123.456.789.123. These addresses represent a hierarchy of network-subnetwork-individual computer (host). Because these numeric addresses are difficult for humans to deal with, IP allows each address to be associated with a unique name. A specialized type of server called a Domain Name System (DNS) performs the translation from name to numeric address. Each host on a TCP/IP network may support multiple applications, such as file transfer, mail, and Web requests/responses. IP deals with this by allowing each host to have multiple ports, one for each application it may utilize. The standard port used by Web browsers and Web servers is port 80, although any other port number could be specified as long as the two agree.

The second standard for Web browser and server communication defines the protocol for the request and the response. This protocol, HTTP, can be logically viewed as being "on top" of TCP/IP. Exhibit 2.1 illustrates the relationship between IP, TCP, and HTTP.

HTTP is a standard that specifies the format that the Web browser will use to phrase its request and that the Web server will use to format its response. Version 1.0 of the HTTP standard is the original version that was implemented by all Web browsers and Web servers. Although documented in an informational Request For Comment (RFC) — the mechanism used by the Internet Engineering Task Force (IETF) to document practices and protocols for potential adoption as a standard — Version 1.0 never became an IETF standard. A new, standards-track RFC (RFC 2616) enhances the original HTTP and is known as HTTP/1.1.

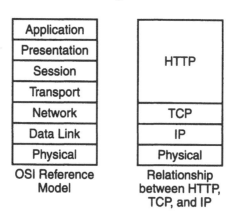

Exhibit 2.1   **Relationship between HTTP, TCP, and IP**

An HTTP request from the browser to the server includes:

- action requested (called the *method*)
- Universal Resource Identifier (URI), which is the name of the information requested
- HTTP version
- (optional) message body

The list of methods permitted depends on the version of HTTP being utilized (see Exhibit 2.2 for a list of HTTP/1.1 methods). The most common method is "Get," which is used when the Web browser wishes the Web server to send it a document or program. The URI specifies the name of the file that should be retrieved; HTTP/1.1 demands that all URIs are absolute references, not relative references. The protocol version indicates which version of the HTTP standard is being utilized. The message body, if included, contains information that modifies or supplements the request.

The Web server responds to the request from the browser with the following information:

- HTTP protocol version
- status code
- reason phrase
- (optional) message body

The protocol version, as in the request, indicates which version of HTTP is being utilized. The status code is a three-digit numeric code that indicates whether the request was successful or not; if it failed, the status code describes the type of failure. The reason phrase is a textual phrase that corresponds to the status code, intended to allow a human user or programmer to understand the status code without needing to look up the code in a reference. The

Exhibit 2.2   Methods Supported by HTTP/1.1

Method Name	Action
OPTIONS	Request for information about the communication options available for a request/response chain
GET	Retrieve whatever information is specified by the Request-URI
HEAD	Retrieve the meta-information stored in the HTTP headers of a GET method but do not retrieve any data
POST	Request that the server accept the body as a new subordinate of the resource identified by the Request-URI
PUT	Requests that the enclosed entity be stored at the Request-URI
DELETE	Requests the server to delete the entity identified by the Request-URI
TRACE	Invoke a remote, application-layer loopback of the request method

Exhibit 2.3   Some Common MIME Types

MIME Type	Description
text/plain	ASCII text
text/html	A document formatted using HTML
image/gif	An image encoded in the GIF format
image/jpeg	An image encoded in the JPEG format
application/postscript	A document formatted using Adobe's PostScript format
video/mpeg	A video clip encoded in the MPEG format
audio/basic	An audio clip

message body, if included, contains the results of the request (e.g., the HTML document).

The third type of standard used by Web browsers and Web servers defines the type of data contained in the message body response. The Web has borrowed a standard from the e-mail world called Multipurpose Internet Mail Extensions (MIME) to describe the type of information (or "document") that is contained in a particular file or response. Utilizing conventions, the Web browser knows how to display or otherwise respond to the data it is receiving. For example, the Web browser understands how to properly format and display a Web page that utilizes the HyperText Markup Language (HTML) as its page description language or how to play an audio file. The type of data is called the media-type. The Internet Assigned Number Authority (IANA) registers valid media-types. Exhibit 2.3 lists some common MIME media-types used in Web documents.

Take a look at a simple example to illustrate this process. Assume that the browser and the server are communicating using HTTP version 1.0. In this example, the user has a PC with a browser. The user, who wants to take a look at today's weather maps, has bookmarked the Universal Resource Locator (URL) associated with weather map page on CNN's Web site. The user selects the bookmark. Exhibit 2.4 lists the sequence of events.

The user's browser sends a request looking for the IP address that corresponds with the name in the URL. A DNS node at the user's Internet service provider (ISP) responds with the appropriate IP address. The browser then sends a request to the appropriate IP address specifying a port number of 80. The server, which is "listening" on port 80 for requests, receives the Get request from the browser that requests that the headline page be sent. The server parses the request and determines that the page /WEATHER/images.html should be located and returned to the client. The client also sends additional information in the message body indicating, for example, which browser it is running and what types of files it can accept. Assuming that the client can receive a file of type HTML and the server has the file named /WEATHER/images.html stored locally, the server fulfills the client's request. The appropriate version, status code, and reason text are returned in the header response and the message body includes information

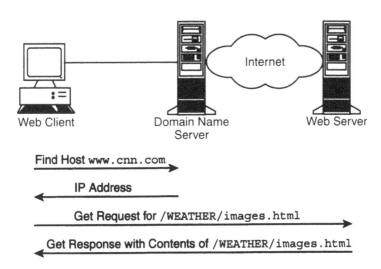

Exhibit 2.4 Example of Browser Request for a Page

about the server, the current data and time, the content type and length, the last modified date, and finally the contents of /WEATHER/images.html.

It is the responsibility of the browser to understand how to decode and display the HTML file. Note that all the server did was locate the file and send it along with certain information about the file (size, last modified date) to the browser. For example, if the /WEATHER/images.html file contains an anchor that represents a link, the browser will utilize its preconfigured or default variables to display the active link with the appropriate color and underlined text. If the file contains an anchor for a graphic image such as a gif image, that image is not a part of the HTML file downloaded because it is a different MIME file type and it resides in its own file (with a filename suffix of .gif) on the server. The browser will automatically build and send a new Get request to the server when it parses the anchor for the image, requesting the transmission of that gif file.

The cause of this serial request-response sequence is that the browser — not the server — is responsible for examining the content of the requested file and displaying or playing it. Obviously, Web pages that have many different images, sounds, etc. will generate a lot of overhead in terms of sequential Get requests. To make matters worse, each individual Get request is a separate TCP connection to the network. Therefore, each Get request results in the establishment of a TCP connection before the request can be sent, followed by the disconnection of it after the result is sent. If there are proxies or gateways between the browser and the server, then even more TCP connections (one per hop) are set up and torn down each time. If the file contains five different gif images, then the browser will serially build and send five different Get requests to the server and result in the setting up and disconnecting of at least five different TCP connections. To the end user, it appears as if the network is slow because it takes a long time for the browser to completely display a single complex Web page.

Fortunately, the new, standards-track version of HTTP, HTTP/1.1, addresses the inefficiencies just described. HTTP/1.1 allows a single TCP connection to be set up and then maintained over multiple request-response sequences. The browser decides when to terminate the connection, such as when a user selects a new Web site to visit. HTTP/1.1 also allows the browser to pipeline multiple requests to the server without needing to wait serially for each response. This allows a browser to request multiple files at once and can speed the display of a complex Web page. It also results in lower overhead on endpoints and less congestion within the Internet as a whole. HTTP/1.1 also makes more stringent requirements than HTTP/1.0 in order to ensure reliable implementation of its features.

Document Formatting

The basic way that a user interacts with Web servers is via Web pages. A Web page can be static or dynamic. A static Web page is the same for each user and each time it is viewed. An example of a static page is the home page of the FedEx Web site, www.fedex.com. This page contains graphics, fill-in forms, drop-down lists, and clickable navigational menus to direct the user somewhere within the site. The page is the same every time it is viewed until the FedEx Webmaster posts another version of the page to the Web site.

A dynamic Web page, by contrast, is created on-the-fly by the Web server or another program. A dynamic page contains the result of an operation. An example of a dynamic page is the result page of a FedEx tracking request. When a user types an airbill number into the appropriate form on the FedEx site, the next page the user sees contains the tracking information for the particular package represented by the unique airbill number.

Whether a page is static or dynamically created, the page must adhere to certain standards so that Web browsers can properly display the page as intended by the Web author. The original standard for document formatting for the Web is HyperText Markup Language (HTML). New standards are being developed for a follow-on language, eXtensible Markup Language (XML), and one that is specific to wireless devices, Wireless Markup Language (WML). These are the major specifications for controlling the user interface of the browser, although they are not the only specifications being discussed within the Web community or the standards bodies. For more complete and detailed information, visit the Web sites of the World Wide Web Consortium (www.w3c.org) and the IETF (www.ietf.org).

HTML

HTML has been the document description language of the Web since its inception in the early 1990s. HTML is based on Standard Generalized Markup

Language (SGML), an earlier and more generic standard, and has evolved over time. Anyone who used the Web in 1994 or 1995 will remember the very basic formatting used by most Web sites (i.e., left-justified text, few fonts, etc.). The IETF created a working group to address HTML and document the current practices, with the result the HTML 2.0 standard (RFC 1866). The HTML working group was then disbanded, and the World Wide Web Consortium (W3C) continued to work on evolving HTML. HTML 3.2, documented in 1996, added commonly used features such as tables, applets, text flow around images, and other features. HTML 4.0, first documented in late 1997, contained the next major revision. It was eventually superseded by HTML 4.01, which was finalized in late 1999. The W3C is now working on a new recommendation, called XHTML 1.0, which reformulates HTML in XML.

HTML uses tags to structure text into headings, paragraphs, lists, links, etc. Each tag comes in a pair delimiting the begin and the end of the text to which the tag should apply. For example, the beginning of a paragraph is delimited with <p> placed before the first word in the paragraph and with </p> after the last word in the paragraph. The Web author must adhere to the conventions of HTML and can only use the tags allowed by the particular version of HTML that he intends to support.

Some Web authors and programming tools attempt to utilize HTML for page layout (i.e., controlling the exact placement of text and images) but HTML was intended for the purpose of defining structural elements within text. Cascading Style Sheets (CSS) is a capability that is being promoted by the W3C, among others, to be used by Web authors to control document styles and layout. Although related, HTML and CSS are independent sets of specifications.

Dynamic HTML (DHTML) is a term that describes HTML with dynamic content. DHTML is not a separate standard or a new version of the HTML standard. Instead, DHTML encompasses three different technologies and standards: HTML, CSS, and JavaScript.

XML

HTML is fine for publishing pages of information to end users with browsers. However, with the growing dominance of E-commerce and E-business, the Web is becoming a vehicle for application-to-application communication. For example, a retail Web site will have the user fill in a form with the address to which the merchandise should be sent. When rendered in HTML, it is not easy to programmatically pick out this information and create an invoice. The program creating the invoice may need to know that address information is in the fifth paragraph of the HTML page. However, if the page changes in the future and now the address information is in the sixth paragraph rather than the fifth paragraph, the invoicing application will need to change as well. This creates real problems for maintaining and updating programs that extract and exchange information via the Web.

Exhibit 2.5   Sample XML Code

```
<name>
   <title>Ms.</title>
   <first-name>Lisa</first-name>
   <last-name>Lindgren</last-name>
</name>
<address>
   <street-addr>123 Main Street</street-addr>
   <apt></apt>
   <city>Anytown</city>
   <state>AB</state>
   <zip>01010</zip>
</address>
```

The eXtensible Markup Language (XML) was created to overcome this and other limitations of HTML. Like HTML, XML is based on SGML, a standard that has been around since the 1980s. Like HTML, XML utilizes a pair of tags to delineate data. Unlike HTML, however, XML allows the creator of the tags to define what the tags mean and how they should be acted upon. For example, the tag <p> in an XML file may delimit a paragraph, but depending on the context it may mean something totally different (e.g., person, place). XML also permits attributes in the form name=value, similar to the attributes used in HTML. A simple example of XML is illustrated in Exhibit 2.5. With this example, it is a trivial matter for the invoicing application to locate all of the individual elements of the customer's name and address. And, although the intent of XML is to simplify the programmatic access of data, XML is simple for a human user or programmer to understand as well.

The work on XML began in 1996. The first specification that resulted, XML 1.0, was issued by the W3C in February of 1998. However, XML is not a single standard; rather, it is a family of related standards. The W3C has had multiple working groups working in parallel to refine and define certain aspects of XML. 1999 saw the publication of recommendations for namespaces in XML and linking style sheets in XML (XML uses CSS). As of this writing, W3C working groups are actively working to specify the following XML-related technologies:

- XML Query
- XML Packaging
- XML Schema
- XML Linking Language
- XML Pointer Language
- XML Inclusions
- XML Base
- continued refinement of XML Syntax, XML Fragment, and XML Information Set

WML

The population of wireless subscribers is growing rapidly throughout the world. According to some experts, the number of wireless subscribers will be 520 million by the year 2001 and 1 billion users by the year 2004. Mobile telephones and other handheld wireless devices are being equipped with Web browsers to allow users to get e-mail and push and pull information over the Internet from these mobile devices.

The Wireless Application Protocol (WAP) is a family of protocols and standards designed to support data applications on wireless telephones and other handheld wireless devices. The WAP Forum is a new forum that has been formed to develop and promote these standards. Founded in June 1997 by Ericsson, Motorola, Nokia, and Phone.com, the WAP Forum now has members from a wide range of vendors, including wireless service providers, software developers, handset manufacturers, and infrastructure providers. The WAP Forum works with other organizations and with standards bodies (such as the W3C and the IETF) to coordinate related activities.

According to the WAP Forum, Web access using wireless devices is distinctly different than PC-based Web access. Wireless devices have much lower CPU and memory capabilities than a PC. A wireless device has less power available to it and a much smaller display area than a PC. Wireless networks are characterized as having less bandwidth, higher latency, and less connection stability than wired networks. Finally, wireless users want a much simpler user interface than a PC and they want access to a limited set of capabilities from their wireless devices than they would from a general purpose PC (e.g., e-mail retrieval, stock ticker lookup).

As one of the WAP-related protocols, the WAP Forum is working on a specification for the Wireless Markup Language (WML). WML is based on XML but is designed for the lower bandwidth of wireless networks, smaller display areas of the wireless device, and user input devices that are specific to wireless devices (e.g., pointer). WML supports a slimmed-down set of tags that is appropriate to the lower memory and CPU capabilities of a handheld device. Unlike the flat, page-oriented structure of HTML, WML allows a WML page to be broken up into discrete user interactions, called cards. Wireless users can navigate back and forth between cards from one or multiple WML pages.

The WAP Forum released version 1.1 of the WAP specification in June of 1999 and is currently working on version 1.2. As of this writing, products supporting WAP are just being released to the market.

Client-side Programs

The original Web model was pretty simple. Web servers downloaded pages requested by browsers. The browsers displayed the textual and graphical information and played the audio or video clip. This was called a "thin-client" model, and it had enormous appeal for many because it avoided one of the major problems with the traditional client/server model — the distribution and maintenance of individual software programs to each and every client PC or workstation.

Consider the case of a large multinational auto manufacturer. The IT staff of this firm had 40,000 desktop PCs to maintain. Each time a new version of client software was released, the IT staff had to configure and install the software on each of the 40,000 desktops — a job that typically took two years to accomplish. Of course, by the time the new version was fully installed on all desktops, it had already been superceded by one or two new versions. This distribution and maintenance problem is exacerbated if the IT staff cannot directly control the desktop. As an example, the same multinational auto manufacturer had a large network of dealers. The IT staff supported client/server programs that allowed the dealers to interact with the manufacturer to enter orders, check delivery, etc. The dealers, which are independent companies not under the direct control of the manufacturer's IT staff, were supposed to install and configure new versions of client software as they were released. However, the IT staff could not ensure that each dealer would install and configure the new software correctly or in a timely manner. The dealers also had a variety of different operating systems. The IT staff was stuck supporting multiple revisions of client software and had enormous help-desk costs as a result.

The thin-client model offers organizations the promise of eliminating the headache of distributing, configuring, and maintaining client software. The client PCs only have to have a browser installed, and new content is added only to the Web server. Users have the benefit of accessing the latest and greatest information each and every time they access the Web server.

However, this benefit is only achieved if the browser itself does not become a bloated piece of software that is continually changing. For example, say a new multimedia file type is devised. In the absence of some other mechanism, the new multimedia file type could not be distributed and played until a sufficient number of Web browsers had been updated to recognize and play the new file type. Because a Web browser, like any other client software in a client/server environment, is installed on each system, the large automobile manufacturer's IT staff has the same problem it had before in distributing and maintaining new revisions of Web browser software. It is important to keep the frequency of new revisions of browser software to a minimum.

There is a second problem in that not all client/server computing needs can be satisfied with the traditional Web browser and server model. For example, Web browsers in the past did not recognize the light pen as an input device. Because the browser would not recognize the light pen, there was no way for Web server applications to act upon light pen input. Organizations that relied on the light pen as the source of input to the application were effectively barred from using the Web model. Some applications require a greater level of control over the client system than is possible through a Web browser.

The answer to these problems was to extend the Web model to allow programs to be executed at the client side. The trick was to devise ways to leverage the Web browser and Web server without incurring the client software distribution and maintenance problems. There are three major approaches utilized for client-side applications in the Web environment: plug-ins, Java applets, and ActiveX controls.

Before examining each of the three types of client-side applications, there is an important concern about readily available and easily distributed client-side applications — security. Applications that can be downloaded with the click of a mouse pose a potential threat to end systems and the networks to which they are connected. Viruses, worms, and other hazards can hide within what appears to be a legitimate application. Each of the client-side application approaches varies with respect to how it deals with this security concern.

Plug-ins

Netscape originally devised the concept of a plug-in. Quite simply, plug-ins are programs that behave as if they are a part of the browser itself but they are separate programs written to a browser API. Typically, plug-ins are written by third-party developers that wish to propagate support for a new MIME type. The browsers of both Netscape and Microsoft support plug-ins. Common examples of plug-ins include:

■ Macromedia's Shockwave for interactive multimedia, graphics, and streaming audio
■ RealNetwork's RealPlayer for real-time audio, video, and animations
■ Adobe's Acrobat plug-in for displaying Portable Document Format (PDF) documents within a browser window

End users usually obtain plug-ins by downloading the code from a Web site, and plug-ins are usually free. The code is automatically installed on the client system's hard drive in a special plug-in directory. When a user opens a document that contains a MIME type not defined to the browser itself, the browser searches the appropriate directory for a plug-in that is defined to support the given MIME type. The plug-in is loaded into memory, initialized, and activated. A plug-in can be visible or hidden to the user and it can be within the browser frame or in an independent frame, depending on how the designer has specified it. A plug-in to display movies, for example, will probably define its own frame and play the video for the movie within that frame. An audio plug-in, by contrast, will usually be hidden.

A plug-in is a dynamic code module rather than a self-standing application. The browser must activate it and it runs within the browser's environment. A plug-in is also platform specific and distributed as compiled code. Therefore, a plug-in provider must write a version of the plug-in for each and every operating system platform it intends to support. Because it is compiled before distribution rather than interpreted, a plug-in can be written in any language.

A plug-in, once invoked, has all system resources available to it allowed through the plug-in API. Therefore, a plug-in can potentially damage systems and other resources accessible to it via the network. Most plug-in vendors rely on digital signatures to verify the identity of the vendor as proof that the plug-in is safe. Before the plug-in is installed on the client system, the identity of the creator is revealed to the end user. If the user decides to trust plug-ins from that particular vendor, then the installation proceeds. This is made possible through the use of digital certificates, which are described in detail in Chapter 6.

Java Applets

Java, a language and a set of technologies defined by Sun Microsystems, has seen incredibly rapid adoption given its backing by Sun, Netscape, IBM, Oracle, and other powerhouses in the computing industry. In fact, the list of vendors committing significant development resources to Java technology is huge and growing. The coalition of Java backers is often called ABM — Anyone But Microsoft. To be fair, Microsoft's products support Java, albeit less enthusiastically than its own ActiveX and related technologies.

Java has evolved into a very comprehensive set of technologies that includes server-side and object-based computing and is explained more fully in Chapter 3. Initially, however, Java was a new programming language based on the strengths of C++. Its primary goal was to be a platform-independent, object-oriented, network-aware language. To achieve platform independence and portability to the degree that Sun calls "Write Once, Run Anywhere" (WORA), Java is rendered into byte-code and interpreted by the destination platform rather than being compiled into a platform-specific code module. An overriding design goal for Java was for robustness; therefore, the language eliminated some of the more error-prone and "dangerous" aspects of C++, such as the use of pointers.

To interpret the Java native byte-code and thus run Java programs, a platform must support the Java runtime environment, called the Java Virtual Machine (JVM). The JVM is written to be specific to the operating system on which it runs because it needs to directly access system resources. Therefore, a JVM written for Windows is different from a JVM written for the Mac. However, to the Java programmer, the two JVMs are identical because the Java libraries available for use by the Java program are the same. This allows the Java byte-code to be identical for all JVMs, and thus fulfills Sun Microsystem's goal of WORA. Web browsers are packaged with an embedded JVM. Java programs invoked by the browser run on the browser's JVM.

A Java applet is a client-side Java program that is downloaded along with an HTML page that has an `applet` tag encoded. The browser displays the HTML page and then downloads the applet from the Web server and executes it using the embedded JVM. It continues to execute the applet until it terminates itself or until the user stops viewing the page containing the applet. A Java application is different from an applet. A Java application can be distributed through the use of a Web server, but it is then installed on the client system and runs independently of the browser and the browser's JVM.

One of the early criticisms of the Java applet model was that a large applet could degrade a network and require users to wait a long time for an applet to download. Although the name "applet" may imply that these are small applications, that is not necessarily the case. Applets can be very small or they can be as large as regular, stand-alone applications. Consider the case of a large enterprise with 20,000 desktops. If all of these users require a particular Java applet that is 3 megabytes in size, then each time the applet is downloaded to the user base, the operation requires 60 gigabytes of network bandwidth. Initially, applets were downloaded every time the user accessed the HTML page containing the applet tag. This has been changed so that applets can be cached on the hard drive. When the page containing the applet tag is downloaded, the Web browser compares the version of the cached applet with the version stored on the Web server. If there is a match, the cached applet is executed. It is only if the cached applet is out of date that the download is initiated. When there is a new version of an applet available, the IT organization only needs to propagate the new applet to its Web servers. The update of the user base will occur automatically, and network bandwidth is only consumed when necessitated by an update of the applet.

To address the concern about security, Java applets originally could only perform certain tasks and could not access any system resources such as the hard drive. This is referred to as a "sandbox" model of security because the Java applets operated within the strict confines of a sandbox and could not reach out of the sandbox to harm the underlying system. While secure, this model of security limited the capabilities of Java applets and was eventually relaxed. Most applets implement digital certificates to address the security concern.

Many vendors and IT organizations provide Java applets to extend the capability of the browser and utilize the software distribution capabilities inherent in the Web model. Sun maintains a Web site devoted to Java applets at http://java.sun.com/applets/index.html.

ActiveX Controls

ActiveX controls are similar to Java applets in that they are downloaded with Web pages and executed by the browser. ActiveX is a set of technologies defined by Microsoft and based on a long history of Microsoft technologies. ActiveX is language independent and platform specific, which directly contrasts with the language dependence and platform independence of Java applets. Although Microsoft claims that ActiveX is supported on a variety of platforms, in reality it is closely tied with the Windows 95/98/2000 desktop operating system. Senior Microsoft executives have clearly stated that the Windows platform will always have priority and will always gain new functionality first when it comes to ActiveX.

ActiveX technologies have evolved over time from the initial object technologies within Windows. Object Linking and Embedding (OLE) was introduced in 1990 to provide cut-copy-paste capabilities to Windows applications.

It is OLE that allows one to embed an Excel spreadsheet within a Word document. OLE evolved over time to be more generalized for building component-based software applications, at which point OLE became known as Component Object Model (COM). COM evolved to allow components in different networked systems to communicate with one another, at which point it became known as Distributed Component Object Model (DCOM). When the Web came along and Microsoft embraced it as a strategic direction, ActiveX was created. ActiveX is essentially DCOM specifically geared to delivery of applications over the Internet and intranets. An ActiveX control is a client-side component that can communicate in a local or networked environment. Recently, DCOM has been enhanced once again. It is now called COM+ and includes the ability to integrate component-based transactions that span multiple servers.

Caching of ActiveX controls has always been allowed, so that ActiveX controls are only downloaded the first time a user visits a page with an ActiveX control and again when the control is updated. Because ActiveX controls are based on OLE, they can access any of the system resources available to any client application. This includes the ability to write to the hard drive or any other system resource, and even includes the ability to power down the system. This fact was dramatized early on by the Java camp, and many articles have been published about the inherent security problems of ActiveX. The positive side of this is that ActiveX controls are more tightly integrated with the system and can offer things such as better printing control. In reality, both Java applets and ActiveX controls today utilize similar digital certificate and entrusted source techniques to address the security concern.

Early on, vendors offering downloadable client-side applets/controls usually selected one or the other. The market was bifurcated, and vendors chose either the Java camp or the Microsoft camp. Since then, the furor has died down somewhat and many vendors have gone beyond the religion of Java versus Microsoft. Many now offer versions of their client-side code in both Java applet and ActiveX control versions.

Server-side Programs

An alternative to client-side programs is to extend the Web model through the introduction of programs on the Web server. Server-side programs are invoked by the Web server, and allow the introduction of dynamic Web pages. Scripts and other server-side programs are common for implementing user authentication, shopping carts, credit card purchases, and other E-commerce and E-business functions that are best performed in a centralized and secure location such as on a server. Proponents of the server-side approach claim the following benefits over client-side programs:

1. *Minimal bandwidth requirements*. Because the programs are installed and run on the Web server, they do not need to be downloaded to

each individual client. This can dramatically diminish overall network bandwidth requirements, and users connected to slow links are not hampered by extremely long download times.

2. *Security*. Tampering with a Web server is more difficult than planting a malicious applet or control somewhere that will be downloaded to anyone accessing the page containing the applet/control. Web servers, and other host servers, are protected by physical and logical security mechanisms, making it relatively difficult for a hacker to plant a malicious application on a server and go undetected.

3. *Protection of intellectual property and business logic*. Code and data downloaded to the client is potentially vulnerable to decoding or reverse-engineering.

4. *Manageability*. Server-side applications can be easier to monitor, control, and update than client-side applications.

5. *Performance*. Operations that require extensive communication with other hosts (e.g., frequent database queries) will be more efficient if they are implemented in close proximity to the other hosts. Client-side applications in these scenarios will consume excessive bandwidth and incur higher latency.

6. *Minimal client computational requirements*. Some clients, such as handheld appliances, have limited CPU capabilities and memory. By implementing the computationally intensive operations on a server, the client can be very thin. This is particularly important for Web phones and other handheld appliances that utilize Web access.

7. *Virtual elimination of client software distribution and maintenance*. Server-side programs allow advanced and new capabilities to be added to the server. The client can remain very "thin" and will probably not require extensive updates, even to the Web browser software. Because all new logic is introduced on the server, the task of distributing and maintaining client software is virtually eliminated (with the single exception being the browser).

One potential downside to server-side programs is scalability. Depending on the programming approach used, server-side programs can consume a lot of resources (i.e., CPU, memory) on the server. This can lead to a dramatic curtailment of the number of concurrent users that a server can support.

The Web server can be enhanced through a variety of approaches. The oldest approach is for the Web server to support one or more application program interfaces (APIs) that call server-side scripts, which are programs written in a variety of languages and either interpreted or compiled. Three newer approaches are Java servlets, Java server pages, and Active server pages.

Scripts, Forms, and APIs

Scripts are programs that are accessible and initiated by the Web server in response to invocation by the user. Although the name "script" may imply to some that these programs can only be written in an interpreted language such as Perl or UNIX shell, most scripts can be written in any language. Programs written in languages such as BASIC, C/C++, and Fortran must be compiled before they can be used as a script.

The Web server and the script communicate through an application programming interface (API). The first API used by Web servers is the Common Gateway Interface (CGI). This is a simple interface and is in widespread use. However, both Netscape and Microsoft have developed various proprietary APIs that their servers support in addition to the standard CGI. Scripts and forms are described in terms of CGI, followed by a brief description of the major proprietary Netscape and Microsoft APIs.

A CGI script is invoked through a URL reference, whether typed in by the user or selected via an anchor in an HTML document. The Web server can determine that a particular URL reference is referring to a CGI script by one of two ways:

1. The file extension in the URL reference is a type defined to the server as a CGI script file (e.g., `.cgi` or `.exe`).
2. The file in the URL reference is located in a directory on the server reserved for CGI scripts (e.g., `/cgi-bin`).

Once the Web server determines that a particular URL refers to a script, the server invokes the script and passes it any variables that are contained in the URL. Once invoked, the script can access information from other servers, such as database servers, and it can interact with the user using forms. The script must build the Web page that responds to the user's request and pass that page back to the server to conclude the transaction. With CGI, the script can be written in any language (interpreted or compiled). There is a new instance of the CGI script created each time it is invoked, which can cause high system overhead if there are many users invoking the same script simultaneously.

A common way to provide input to a script is through the use of HTML forms. Web pages that utilize input boxes, check boxes, radio buttons, and drop-down lists may be using forms. Forms have defined anchors within HTML so that the browser knows how to display the special fields and what to do with the input that the user provides.

The use of forms with CGI scripts implies a two-step process requiring two separate connections and two separate and distinct transactions between the user and the server. In the first step, the user selects a URL that indicates that he would like to initiate a CGI script. As an example, a university student has accessed the school's library system and has clicked on a link indicating he would like to search for a particular book in the system. This link contains a URL reference indicating a CGI script on the university's Web site. The script is invoked and it downloads the empty form to be filled in by the user. At this point, the connection is terminated because the transaction is complete and one cannot maintain session state between different invocations of the Web server and CGI script.

The user fills in the form, then selects the Submit button, and the browser sends a new request to the server. This request again indicates the URL of the CGI script but this time it also includes the search data that the user has included in the form. In this example, suppose the user has typed `appli-cation servers` in the fill-in box for subject. The script is invoked a second time and the variables and values (e.g., `subject=application+servers`) filled in by the user are passed to the script. For this, the script executes on the unique data provided by the user. For this example, the search for books on application servers is performed and the search results are formatted into an HTML page and returned to the user. The connection is terminated and the second step is complete.

The Netscape Server API (NSAPI) is an API that extends the functioning of the Web server itself, and is therefore not positioned as an alternative or replacement for CGI, which is used to write applications. NSAPI is a set of C functions that allows programmers to extend the basic functionality of the Netscape server. These extensions to the basic operation of the server are called server application functions (SAFs). The Netscape server comes with a set of predefined SAFs and then programmers can define additional SAFs. These new SAFs are known as server plug-ins, which is an appropriate name because they extend the function of the Web server much as a browser plug-in extends the function of the Web browser. An example of a server plug-in is a program that modifies how the server responds to each `Get` request from a browser by appending special information to each response.

Netscape supports a second API that allows new programs to process HTTP requests that are sent to the Netscape Web server and therefore extend the functionality of the Web server. Web application interface (WAI) applications can be written in C, C++, or Java. WAI applications run in their own process separate from the Web server. A unique aspect of WAI is that it is a CORBA-based interface and its use requires that Inprise's Visibroker be installed on the same server. The WAI application and the Web server communicate using CORBA protocols. *Note:* WAI is supported in current versions of the Netscape server but the server documentation clearly states that the interface may not be supported in future versions.

Microsoft has defined its own proprietary server interfaces. The current strategic thrust is Active Server Pages (ASP), which is described in a later section. Predating ASP, however, and still supported on Microsoft Internet Information Services (IIS) server is the Internet Server API (ISAPI). ISAPI, unlike the two Netscape APIs discussed, is intended to support Web applications and therefore is positioned as an alternative to CGI. Microsoft, while fully supporting the CGI standard, encourages developers to write applications to ASP or ISAPI rather than CGI. ISAPI is positioned as offering much better performance and lower utilization of the server compared to CGI. ISAPI applications are written in C++; they can run in the same process and memory space of the Web server, providing optimum use of system resources. ISAPI applications are also activated only once and then can be called by multiple users concurrently, minimizing the impact on the server when server traffic increases. Finally, ISAPI communicates with the Web server using more effi-cient system calls than used for CGI.

The use of scripts and script APIs is extremely prevalent. Most early Web sites relied on Web scripts to interact with the user and provide dynamic content. Today, CGI and the vendor-specific APIs can still be gainfully used to enhance a Web site. However, as Web technology has evolved, the choices for server-side programs have grown.

Java Servlets and Java Server Pages

Netscape was always a public and visible supporter of Sun's Java initiatives, and its Web server was usually one of the first products to implement new Java technologies. The relationship between the two organizations has become more formalized. After America OnLine purchased Netscape, the iPlanet alli-ance was formed. iPlanet is the result of a formalized collaboration between Sun and AOL, and the Netscape Server has evolved into the iPlanet Web Server. As a result of the history and the new collaboration, the iPlanet Web Server offers support for a complete array of Java technologies, including Java servlets and Java Server Pages.

Java servlets have been around since about 1997. Quite simply, Java servlets are like Java applets, except that they run on the server rather than the browser. Servlets are Java objects that are loaded by the Web server's Java Runtime Environment (JRE) when the servlet is needed. (By definition, of course, the Web server must support Java objects and have a JRE in order to run Java servlets.) The servlet is invoked using a lightweight thread, which contrasts to CGI scripts that require an entirely new process to be spawned. Servlets communicate with the Web server via the servlet API and, like CGI scripts, are invoked through URL invocation.

A servlet, unlike a CGI script, does not need to terminate once it has returned a response to the user. This means that a servlet can maintain persistence. Servlets can use persistence to carry out multiple request/response pairs with a particular user. Alternatively, servlets can use persistence to maintain a single connection to a particular back-end process such as a database server. Persistence can dramatically reduce the overhead compared to CGI scripts, thereby increas-ing the scalability of the Web server and potentially improving user response time.

The servlet approach to server-side programs requires the servlet program-mer to include HTML tags and presentation information within the Java object that is on the server. This can be a problem because in many organizations the people who design the presentation of a Web site and the programmers who extend the functionality of the server are different people with different skill sets. By embedding the presentation logic in with the application logic, the programmer of the servlet must be involved each time the presentation of the page or site needs to change. For this reason, the servlet API was enhanced and the concept of a Java Server Page (JSP) was introduced.

A JSP is essentially a Web page (like an HTML page) that has application logic embedded within it. The application logic can involve several different types of Java technologies (JavaBeans, JDBC objects, Remote Method Invocation; see Chapter 3). The presentation logic is defined using standard HTML or XML, and the dynamic content is generated by the application logic. The presentation logic can be changed without requiring any changes to the application called by the page, and vice versa. The JSP code is identified through the use of JSP tags, which are coded just like HTML/XML tags with angled brackets. Unlike HTML or XML pages, however, it is the server — not the browser —that interprets and acts upon the JSP tags. The server uses the information within the tags to initiate the appropriate program to create the dynamic content. JSP pages are dynamically compiled into servlets when they are requested; thus, from that point on, they act as servlets to the server and have the same benefits as servlets (e.g., persistence).

Active Server Pages

Active Server Pages (ASP) technology is very similar in concept to JSP. Like JSP, ASP involves the creation of Web pages using standard HTML/XML and embedding code within the page to handle the dynamic content. Like JSP, the dynamic content is created through the execution of a program on the Web server. Like JSP, ASP allows the programmer to define application and session variables that are maintained across multiple pages so that session state can be maintained. Unlike JSP, ASP is not based on Java component architecture or on Java APIs. Instead, ASP is an extension of Microsoft's ActiveX technologies to the server. Thus, ASP is supported only on Microsoft platforms. ASP is a feature of Microsoft's Internet Information Server (IIS) 3.0 and above.

ASP supports server-side scripts and components. The scripts are embedded within the HTML/XML file defining the page. Microsoft's server natively supports VBScript and JScript scripting languages, although plug-ins are available from third-party suppliers to support REXX, Perl, and Python scripting languages as well. Compiled programs can be created using Java, C/C++, Microsoft Visual Basic, and other languages. These programs are then defined as ActiveX server components and accessed via a script.

ASP and ASP components can be defined as running within the same process as IIS or in separate processes. Running all three (IIS, ASP, components) in a single process provides the best performance because new processes do not have to be created when the ASP or component is invoked. However, this option offers the least protection because a faulty component or ASP can crash the Web server. Running all three in separate processes, by contrast, consumes more system resources but offers the best isolation and protection.

Server-side Programs versus Application Servers

The various types of server-side programs that have been discussed allow Web programmers to create dynamic content, communicate with database servers and other hosts, and in some cases maintain persistence and session state. Why, then, would one require an application server? Is it not possible to perform any E-commerce or E-business application using standard CGI scripts or one of the other server-side programming models discussed above?

The answer to the second question is yes. The server-side programming models provide the necessary capabilities to allow a Web programmer to create a wide variety of E-commerce and E-business applications and incorporate multiple back-end systems. What an application server offers is a framework and a set of common tools, interfaces, and object models that provide a set of services for the new applications. The application programmer can utilize these common services and focus on creating new business logic rather than creating these services from scratch for each and every application.

Web-to-Host Solutions

Chapter 1 introduced the notion that E-business, by IBM's definition, occurs when an organization has transformed its key business operations to include access via corporate intranets, extranets, and the Internet (i.e., i*nets). Because many IT infrastructures have been built over a period of many years, these infrastructures include a variety of legacy applications on a variety of different host systems. To transform the key business operations, it is necessary to either rewrite the legacy applications specifically for the i*net model or provide access to the legacy data and business logic through some sort of "gateway" technology. In this context, the term "gateway" applies to any technology that allows Web-based users to access the legacy data and business logic without changing the legacy applications in any way.

Rewriting legacy applications to support Web-oriented technologies is not usually feasible. Many IT organizations have already reengineered some of their legacy applications in the client/server model. These applications often have well-defined public interfaces (e.g., ODBC for database access) that can be easily leveraged and utilized in today's client-based or server-based Web applications. However, a huge base of older legacy applications that continue to rely on a character-based interface still exists. These applications are often the lifeblood of an organization, and there is a myriad of reasons that the applications cannot and will not be rewritten to support the Web model of computing. Some of the reasons include:

1. The applications are working, and the risk of changing them is too immense.
2. The source code is unavailable or poorly documented, making it very difficult to reverse-engineer.
3. A business case justification cannot be made to rewrite the application.
4. The mainframe or other legacy system on which the application resides provides security and scalability unavailable on other platforms.
5. The sheer size of the undertaking to rewrite the applications is simply too immense.

6. The scarce programming resources available to an organization can be put to better use building new business logic.
7. Off-the-shelf solutions exist to enable Web-based users to access the legacy applications without changing those applications.

Perhaps the most important rationale for not rewriting applications is the last one listed — that is, solutions exist from a variety of vendors that allow Web-based users to access the legacy host applications. In addition to simple access, solutions exist that allow the legacy data and business logic to be seamlessly integrated with new applications that are based on the Web model. IT organizations can unlock the vast potential of the legacy data and applications to Web-based users while preserving the integrity of the legacy system.

One issue that is of paramount concern when providing Web access to legacy host systems is the issue of session persistence and session integrity. This is because legacy applications were written to communicate with a known set of users, and sessions were expected to persist over a series of individual transactions. Without session persistence and integrity measures, the Web environment, which includes a potentially large pool of unknown users that may require only a single transaction with the host system (e.g., account lookup), can seriously compromise the security of the legacy systems. Because these systems often house the "crown jewels" of the organization, it is critical that IT organizations implement solutions that will not allow an unauthorized user to piggyback on the session of an authorized user, for example.

There are both client-based and server-based solutions for Web-to-host access. Each of the major approaches is described in the following sections. Before the Web-to-host solutions are addressed, a brief overview of traditional host access is provided.

Traditional Host Access

Chapter 1 provided an overview of some of the different types of legacy systems utilized in the 1970s and 1980s. By far the most prevalent legacy systems still used by enterprise organizations today are the IBM-compatible mainframe, the IBM AS/400 minicomputer, and UNIX systems and other minicomputer systems that use DEC VAX-compatible terminals and protocols.

These systems all evolved over time and support client/server APIs and protocols. However, the original applications implemented on these legacy systems were designed to interact with end users who were stationed at fixed-function terminal displays. These terminals were the precursor to PC screens. The initial terminals offered a very basic interface of alphanumeric characters. The user interface is often described as "green-on-black" because the typical screen had a black background and green characters. The host application is responsible for the user interface. Therefore, the host application formats the screen and defines the attributes and characteristics of each field on the screen (e.g., highlight, input field, protected). The host application builds a "datastream" that is a string of codes and text that describes a screen to the terminal. When the user responds by filling in data fields and pressing the Enter key or a PF key, a new datastream is built and returned to the host application. (Note: This describes block-mode operation rather than character-mode operation, in which individual characters are sent to the host.)

The definition of the datastream, its codes, and the protocols used to communicate between the host and the terminal differ from host system to host system. Invariably, the name of the protocol was taken from the model type of the terminal. Therefore, the IBM mainframe protocol for host-to-terminal communication is called 3270 because this is the model number designation of the IBM mainframe family of terminals. Similarly, 5250 describes the protocol and datastream for the AS/400 because its terminal family model designation is 5250. In the DEC world, there were multiple, related terminal families called VTxxx, where VT stands for Virtual Terminal and xxx is a two- or three-digit model number, usually 52, 100, 200, or 400. The datastream traverses the network using a networking protocol. SNA was used for 3270 and 5250, while TCP/IP was used in the UNIX and DEC VAX environments.

When PCs began to replace terminals on many workers' desktops, terminal emulator software, which mimics or emulates the functions of the traditional terminal devices, became common. Most corporate users accessing legacy host systems today gain that access using terminal emulation software. This software initially provided basic access and connectivity to legacy hosts. Today, these are complex applications that contain a wide variety of features. Typical feature sets include:

- choice of network connectivity options (direct, LAN, WAN, gateway)
- customizable user interface (screen colors, keyboard mapping)
- user productivity features (cut/copy/paste, scripting, hot spots, record/playback)
- support for multiple sessions and multiple host types
- host printing and file transfer
- data integration capabilities
- support for client/server APIs for new applications

The network connectivity options of terminal emulation are an important facet to understand in order to understand Web-to-host solutions. In the UNIX and DEC VAX environments, the network is assumed to be TCP/IP and the upper-layer protocol Telnet is used to transmit the terminal data. In the IBM mainframe/midrange environment, SNA was the protocol employed. With the prevalence of TCP/IP in enterprise networks, however, many large organizations would prefer to use TCP/IP rather than SNA to transport the mainframe/midrange data. In the mid-1980s, the Telnet protocol was extended to carry 3270 and 5250 data. The resulting standards are known as TN3270 and TN5250, respectively. These standards are still in the process of evolving with continual enhancements, and the newer versions of the standard are commonly called TN3270E and TN5250E ("E" for enhanced or extended). These protocols allow the 3270 and 5250 datastreams to be carried within a TCP/IP packet rather than an SNA packet. Additionally, Telnet protocols are used at the beginning of the session to indicate the capabilities of each end.

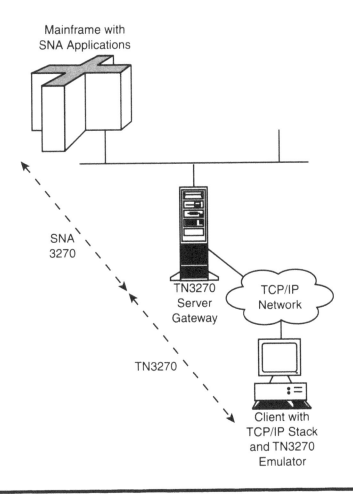

Exhibit 2.6   Example of TN3270 Client and Server

Telnet is a client/server protocol. In the terminal emulation environment, the client is implemented within the terminal emulation software and is therefore on the desktop wishing to access the host. The server end of the protocol is implemented either on the host system itself or on an external gateway server. No matter where it is implemented, the server is responsible for translating the protocol from Telnet to the native protocol. In the case of UNIX and DEC VAX environments, there is no server because the host's native protocol is Telnet. In the case of IBM mainframe and midrange systems, the server converts from TN3270 to SNA 3270, or from TN5250 to SNA 5250. Exhibit 2.6 illustrates an example in which an external gateway server is translating from TN3270 to SNA 3270. Web-to-host solutions build on this Telnet client/server model to provide access to legacy host systems from Web-based devices.

Applet-based Approaches

One approach to provide host access to Web-based users is to download the appropriate logic to the client. The common way this is done is by packaging terminal emulation software as a Java applet or an ActiveX control. Users either type in a URL or click on a link that indicates they wish to access a particular host or host-based application. The URL is associated with an applet or control, which is downloaded unless the current version is already cached or installed on the client system.

The browser invokes the applet or control. The screen representing the host session may run within the browser's window or it may run in a separate window, depending on the implementation and possibly the configuration. The benefit of having the host session display in a separate window is that users can continue to use the browser window independently while the host session is active. Nonetheless, at this time, users will probably see a traditional emulator screen and can gain access to any host they are authorized to access and to which they have a valid login and password. Exhibit 2.7 illustrates an example of a user accessing an IBM mainframe using a terminal emulator Java applet.

The applet or control is usually a subset of a full, traditional emulator. The product usually only supports the Telnet options for host access (i.e., TN3270, TN5250, VTxxx) because the Web-based client, by definition, is using TCP/IP. It may or may not support the full list of user customization and user productivity features. The reason an applet or control may not support all of

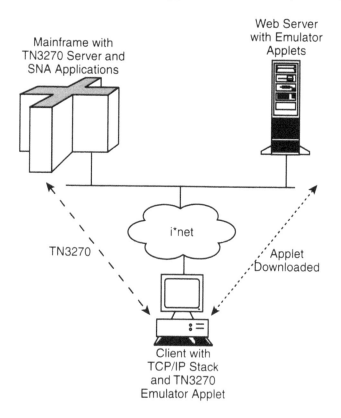

Exhibit 2.7   Mainframe Access Using Java Emulator Applet

the features of its traditional, "fat-client" counterpart is to minimize the time and bandwidth required to download the software. Even if the applet or control is cached, it must still be downloaded when it is updated. If the applet or control is very large, this can wreak havoc with an enterprise network. Therefore, some vendors offer a minimum of features in their applet or control products. Others offer a variety of applets or controls in different sizes so users can select the feature set they require.

Because the applet or control is based on terminal emulation software, the user interface is usually the dated, cryptic, green-on-black, alphanumeric display that dates back to the days of fixed-function terminals. This display is usually adequate for users who are familiar with the interface, such as data entry personnel. This interface is not sufficient for new or casual users, such as the general consumer population. Some products support tools and technology that allow the character-based interface or terminal emulation applets or controls to be rejuvenated with a new Web-style interface. Menus are converted to drop-down lists or buttons. Input fields are converted to the input trenches common on Web pages. These solutions usually implement some sort of pattern-matching scheme or knowledge base to identify the different types of host fields and convert them to Web equivalents.

A traditional terminal client program does not usually offer any explicit security features. This is because the host performs all of the security mechanisms, such as user authentication and authorization. One of the first screens a legacy host user is presented with is a login screen in which the user enters a userID and password. If the host authorizes the user for a particular application, the user can access that application. This model for security works well when all users are within the corporate firewall. However, as soon as the user is outside the firewall (as in the case of extranet and Internet users), there is a major hole in security — namely, the userID and password logins can be read by prying eyes. For this reason, all major applet and control vendors offer encryption to protect the integrity of the data. Initially, most client applet/control vendors have supported encryption negotiated using Secure Sockets Layer (SSL), and some gateways support SSL as well. However, the IETF group responsible for defining TN3270 and TN5250 is moving to adopt Transport Layer Security (TLS) as the standard method of negotiating encryption. Both the applet/control and its appropriate TN3270 or TN5250 gateway must support the same security method. Fortunately, TLS is backward-compatible with SSL.

Another way that some vendors implement security for applets and controls is to introduce a middle-tier server. This server is implemented on Windows NT or UNIX servers and provides centralized administration, usage metering, and other administrative capabilities in addition to security. Except in the case of one vendor's implementation, the server does not actually contain any of the client functionality. Exhibit 2.8 illustrates a middle-tier server environment.

The applet/control method of Web-to-host access is most appropriate as a replacement for traditional fat-client emulators. For this reason, the typical user of an applet/control product will be a user within the corporate firewall who has been using a traditional emulator. These users tend to login to one

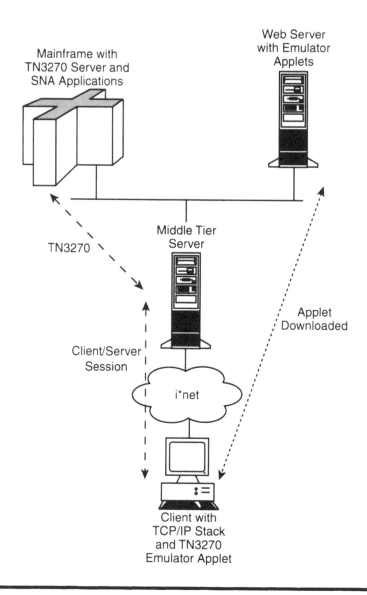

Exhibit 2.8   Mainframe Access Using Java Emulator Applet and Middle Tier Server

or a few applications in the morning and maintain sessions throughout the day. These users are also usually proficient in the use of the character-based interface. In other words, these users are characteristic of a traditional legacy host user. The applet/control approach is attractive for this segment because it provides most or all of the functionality these users have had in the past while eliminating the cost and effort of manually installing and configuring fat-client emulation software on each and every desktop. These users are usually connected to a relatively fast, LAN-based infrastructure and thus the applet/control download time is relatively insignificant.

The applet/control approach is not optimal, however, for new users such as business partners and consumers. These users are not familiar with the operation of the cryptic alphanumeric user interface, and would require training to become proficient. These users also have a completely different session profile than internal users. Typically, these external users only require occasional access to the host for short-duration sessions. Finally, these users are usually connected via slow-speed dial-in links. For these reasons, the applet/control approach, with its default character-based interface and applet download, is not optimal for these external users. Server-based approaches such as HTML conversion and host integration servers better meet their needs.

HTML Conversion Approaches

The alternative to downloading applets or controls to the client is to perform all Web-to-host functionality on the server. There are two major types of server-based Web-to-host products on the market: HTML conversion servers and host integration servers. The HTML conversion server offers a subset of the functionality offered on most host integration servers.

The HTML conversion server is a server-side program that converts legacy host datastreams into HTML pages. In the simplest case, this is a one-to-one conversion. For each host screen that a terminal or emulator user would see, there is a single Web page that is its equivalent. However, instead of seeing a black background with green characters, users would perhaps see a tiled image in the background and text of any font or color supported by the browser. Instead of seeing cryptic strings at the bottom indicating program function key assignments and actions (e.g., PF3=END), users would see a button that they would click to initiate the action. Standard host menus and input fields are converted to radio buttons, drop-down lists, and input field trenches.

The conversion from the host datastream to HTML is typically done on-the-fly, in real time, as the user navigates through the host application. HTML conversion servers usually support 3270 and 5250 datastreams, and some support VTxxx hosts as well. The HTML conversion products are usually implemented as CGI scripts or Active Server Pages, and they interface with a Web server to download the pages to the user. Exhibit 2.9 depicts an HTML conversion server.

Some HTML conversion servers offer advanced user interface rejuvenation capabilities. For example, a product may support the default transformations performed on-the-fly in addition to more advanced scripting that allows programmers to rearchitect the user interface completely. Instead of seeing a one-to-one relationship between host screen and Web page, users may see a many-to-one or even one-to-many relationship. Advanced scripts can be created that change the way in which users interact with the application, and scripts can even combine the data from multiple hosts and multiple applications into a single Web page.

HTML conversion servers do not directly communicate with the end user; they utilize the Web server to send pages and forms to the user and to receive input back from the user. This approach has benefits and drawbacks. One of

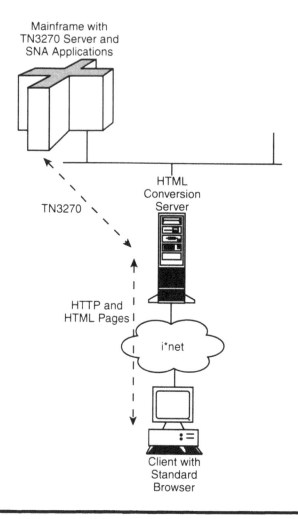

Mainframe with
TN3270 Server and
SNA Applications

HTML
Conversion
Server

TN3270

HTTP and
HTML Pages

i*net

Client with
Standard
Browser

Exhibit 2.9   HTML Conversion Server

the benefits is that the HTML conversion server can leverage any security that is already being used between the client and the server. Therefore, if they both support SSL for security, then the HTML conversion server gets security "for free" and does not have to implement it. Another big benefit of this approach is that the only software required at the client is a standard browser. There is no download or applet or control code, and the browser does not have to be at the latest and greatest level.

One of the drawbacks of the HTML conversion approach is the lack of persistence. As described earlier in this chapter, a CGI script cannot maintain persistence across different interactions with a user. This is potentially disastrous to legacy hosts, because one unauthorized user could potentially gain access to an open session of an authorized user and thus compromise the entire host-based authentication and authorization scheme. All vendors of HTML conversion servers have implemented some mechanism to ensure session persistence so as to avoid this problem.

Another drawback of the HTML conversion approach is that the browser does not provide the same information to the server as that of a traditional terminal device. For example, the browser does not recognize light-pen input and therefore cannot respond to input to a light pen and convey that input to the server. Program function key support is also missing from browsers. Because a large installed base of legacy applications relies on light pens or program function keys, most HTML conversion vendors have devised schemes to circumvent this limitation.

An additional major drawback of the HTML conversion approach is the potential for server overload and therefore a lack of scalability. With each transaction from the host to the user, the server must parse the datastream, convert it based on some rules to a Web page equivalent, and send the page to the Web server. The HTML conversion server must also maintain all session state information and obey all of the rules of TN3270, TN5250, and/or VTxxx. Early HTML conversion servers were limited to very few sessions, often only about 100 concurrent sessions. For large organizations, with potentially thousands or tens of thousands of concurrent users, this was a major drawback. Scalability of some of the solutions has improved, but HTML conversion on-the-fly is still a resource-hungry operation.

HTML conversion servers offer IT organizations the ability to immediately offer at least some rejuvenation to the legacy applications and therefore open up access to these applications to a whole new breed of user. This approach is best suited to Internet-based users because the relatively slow-speed link does not get consumed downloading new code to the client. In addition, these users typically demand a relatively light transaction load because their host access is usually casual and sporadic. A single server can serve a large number of this type of user before it is overwhelmed.

Host Integration Servers

One of the issues with client-based applets/controls and with HTML conversion servers is that both approaches focus on only a subset of legacy host applications, namely those that are accessed via a character-based datastream. Granted, these applications have the largest installed base. However, there are a number of other legacy applications around that organizations need to integrate with their Web-based environments.

A host integration server is a server-centric Web-to-host integration solution that provides more generalized access to a variety of different legacy host systems. An HTML conversion server is a subset of a full-fledged host integration server, which has the following characteristics:

- It runs on either a middle-tier server or the destination host server and may support one or more different server operating systems, including perhaps NT, UNIX, NetWare, OS/390, OS/400, or Linux.
- It supports zero-footprint clients, sending standard HTML (and perhaps XML) to the clients.

- It communicates upstream with a variety of legacy host applications through a variety of transaction, batch, and programmatic interfaces (e.g., 3270 datastream, 5250 datastream, VT, ODBC/JDBC, MQSeries, CICS API(s)).
- It includes the means to utilize a visual development tool to easily integrate the host data and applications into new Web pages. It may or may not provide on-the-fly conversion for host datastreams.
- It may include security, scalability, and fault tolerance features such as SSL, load balancing, and hot server standby.
- It interoperates with Web servers and possibly with new application servers.

Modern host integration servers offer much more capability than basic HTML conversion servers. One obvious and apparent difference is in the support for different types of host applications and different data sources. With a host integration server, one can build Web pages that integrate data from a variety of different legacy host applications. For example, a home banking Web page may include the customer's name and address from a mainframe CICS application, current account activity from a Sybase database located on a Tandem system, and special promotions that the customer may take advantage of from an AS/400 back-office system. By contrast, an HTML conversion server can only communicate with mainframe and minicomputer applications that use the same datastreams supported by the conversion server.

Another difference between the early HTML conversion products and true host integration servers is in the assumed amount of scripting and customization. Modern host integration servers presume that the new user interface will not simply be a one-to-one correlation between host screen and HTML-based Web page. Therefore, host integration servers are focused on providing customization studios (or interfaces to standard customization studios) that allow programmers to easily design brand new Web-style interfaces that incorporate host data. On the other hand, HTML conversion products are geared toward providing quick and easy access to host applications with some level of rejuvenation. The on-the-fly conversion capability is usually relied upon to do the majority of the user interface rejuvenation. Most HTML conversion servers, as stated in the previous section, also support some level of scripting or programming to allow more sophisticated rejuvenation, but the simplicity of the on-the-fly conversion is the real selling point of these products.

Thus, with its sophisticated user interface redesign capabilities, how does a host integration server compare with an application server? Application servers have many of the characteristics listed above for host integration servers. The major differences between the two is that the application server:

- is targeted to the development of new business logic rather than the access of existing legacy business logic

- is built upon an object model, supporting some combination of CORBA, Enterprise JavaBeans, and Microsoft's COM
- contains connectors to legacy data and applications, but the list may not be as complete as those provided with host integration servers

In reality, host integration servers and application servers can be synergistic products. The application server can focus on providing the object framework and other application services, and it can rely on a host integration server to provide back-end hooks to legacy systems. Some application server vendors are beginning to package host integration servers with their products or to recommend one or more host integration servers.

Final Thoughts

The technologies underpinning the Web have been evolving since its inception. The original Web model was elegant in its simplicity — browsers request documents, which include text, graphics, audio, and video content, from a server and then display or play the document content. Each request is viewed as a distinct request or transaction, and users are free to surf through a vast maze of interconnected documents without needing to know how they arrived at their current location.

The unprecedented success of the Web model for delivering content ultimately necessitated the evolution of that model to accommodate the delivery of new applications. These new applications needed to support the creation of dynamic Web content and the secure and persistent interaction with the user. Both client-centric and server-centric approaches were devised and have been successfully utilized in a variety of different types of applications.

The client-centric approach of downloading Java applets or ActiveX controls to the user device is appropriate primarily for intranet environments in which users regularly perform the same tasks. These users typically perform the same type of transaction time and time again and, therefore, having the client system execute the logic rather than a centralized server is the most scalable way of supporting these users. Because these users tend to use a small set of applications and they are usually attached to high-speed internal networks, the download of applet/control code is manageable. Finally, because these users are downloading applets or controls that were intentionally placed there by the IT staff, the security risks of downloadable client code are mitigated.

The server-centric approach, over the long run, will be the approach that better meets the needs of external users and also internal users who only use a particular application on occasion. The server-based approach offers IT organizations a variety of different technologies that can be selected based on the particular needs of the application or user base. The server-based approach supports the widest range of browser-based access devices, including handheld wireless devices, PDAs, and traditional PCs and laptops. This approach offers other benefits over the client-based approach:

1. minimal bandwidth requirements
2. more tamper-resistant
3. protects intellectual property and business logic
4. easier to monitor and control
5. can provide superior performance
6. virtual elimination of client software distribution and maintenance
7. the server is the fundamental piece to support a distributed object model

Large organizations with a complex variety of business applications will likely build, over time, a hybrid infrastructure that includes the "standard" Web model (i.e., HTTP, HTML, CGI), client-based applets and controls, and server-based scripts and programs. As they begin to integrate more and more legacy data and applications with the Web model, organizations should begin to implement an infrastructure based on one or more distributed object models based on Java, CORBA, or Microsoft's COM+. These distributed object models, and the application servers that are built using them, provide advanced application services and reusability and will allow IT staffs to be more nimble and to more quickly deploy new business logic.

Chapter 3

Java

Most application servers are built on a framework of Java, CORBA, or a combination of the two. This chapter provides a detailed look at many of the components and technologies of Java, particularly those related to distributed objects and server-side technologies, in order to provide a foundation for the chapters that follow.

History and Overview of Java

The term "Java" does not really apply to any single thing or technology. If one asked a room full of people what Java is, one would likely hear all of these responses, and more:

- computer language
- means of distributing programs over the Internet
- set of application programming interfaces (APIs)
- runtime environment
- distributed object framework
- development kit
- platform for computing
- compliance program
- the coolest logo that the computer industry has seen in a long time
- an attempt by Sun and many other vendors to diminish the dominance of Microsoft

The reality is that Java is all of the things listed. Java has been evolving since it first was introduced by Sun in 1995. Initially, Java was only a new language, albeit an exciting new language that garnered a lot of attention. It was designed for the Web, designed to be platform independent, and based on C++. Over the last few years, Java has grown and evolved into a complex set of related technologies based on a core of the Java language. Although Sun once considered handing the responsibility for Java to standards committees, Java remains managed and controlled by Sun today, although it provides a mechanism for the vendor community to provide input and direction. Nonetheless, Java has gained the support of many key players, including IBM, Oracle, and many others. Once more hype than reality, Java has matured and become an established cornerstone of many development tools and production products.

During the first year of Java's existence, Sun made great progress in attracting and keeping widespread attention focused on Java. Netscape added Java support in version 2.x of its browser and Sun's own HotJava browser was released. Sun formed JavaSoft as a separate division and tasked it with proliferating Java throughout the industry. Major licensees, including Microsoft, IBM, Apple, and SCO, signed up to support Java. The first version of the Java Development Kit (JDK) was released and included a compiler, an interpreter, class libraries, and a debugger. A database interface was created (Java Database Connectivity, JDBC) and a means of invoking Java methods remotely was introduced (Remote Method Invocation, RMI). The major tool vendors, including Borland and Symantec, announced that they would create tools for Java application development. An avalanche of technical books began to appear, and downloads of early Java specs and the JDK exceeded 40,000 per month. The JavaOne Conference, an annual user conference centered around Java and held in the San Francisco area of California, was launched.

By 1997, downloads of the Java JDK had increased to 300,000 per month. Java was evolving into a distributed component model with the 1996 introduction of JavaBeans and the 1997 introduction of Enterprise JavaBeans. Java was also gaining a growing number of APIs, including those for naming and directory services, richer security, multimedia content, and transaction services. The Java Foundation Classes (JFC) framework was enabling easier creation of GUI-based Java applications. Sun introduced the 100% Pure Java certification program to allow independent software vendors to certify their implementation of Java in their application. The third major release of the JDK, 1.2, was released in late 1997 and Java implementations were moving from the PC client to the server and small handheld devices such as smart cards.

During 1998 and 1999, Java continued to gain momentum both in terms of the number of active Java programmers and the number of commercially available Java products. In 1999, the Java 2 platform was announced, which marked a true point of technical maturity for Java technologies. With Java 2, developers have a complete computing platform upon which they can build. The Java 2 platform is available in a few different packages (micro, standard, and enterprise), allowing the developer to select the packaging of technologies appropriate for that particular application environment. The Java 2 platform, beyond packaging of various Java technologies, provides advances in the areas of security, deployment, performance, and interoperability.

The Java Language(s)

Java is a single computer language that was developed at Sun Microsystems. As already noted, the Java language is based on C/C++. It is compiled into byte-codes that are either interpreted at runtime or just-in-time compiled and then run. Java is a full-fledged computer language that offers strong type checking and other powerful features typical in compiled computer languages.

JavaScript is a scripting language that is, at least from a positioning standpoint, a cousin of Java. However, JavaScript was developed independently from Java at Netscape and was originally called LiveScript. JavaScript is often embedded within an HTML page and executed on-the-fly by the browser. Like many scripting languages, JavaScript is positioned as a simple language for non-programmers to use, in this case to easily enhance Web pages by adding dynamic elements.

Java

According to Sun, Java is "[a] simple, object-oriented, network-savvy, interpreted, robust, secure, architecture-neutral, portable, high-performance, multithreaded, dynamic language."[1] Whew! That is quite a mouthful. Each of the adjectives is examined in turn.

Simple

Java is similar in syntax to C++, a computer language used by thousands of computer programmers and students worldwide. However, Java is missing some capabilities of C++ that its creators believed were esoteric, confusing, and error-prone. Java's advocates thus claim that Java is a simpler language to learn and to use. The absence of certain C++ capabilities, such as the use of pointers, also makes Java a "safer" language in that it does not allow a programmer to accidentally (or intentionally) corrupt memory.

One capability built into Java and lacking in many other languages is the automatic allocation and deallocation of memory. Programmers do not have to explicitly allocate memory for use in their programs and then worry about freeing up the memory; the system occasionally performs what is known as garbage collection to retrieve unused chunks of memory. This makes the programs easier to code but also less prone to bugs because memory reference errors are a common source of bugs in other languages such as C++.

One capability that is intentionally lacking in Java and present in other languages is the use of pointers. In languages such as C and C++, a pointer to a variable can be passed between subroutines and programs rather than the variable itself. Arithmetic operations can also be performed on the pointer. Pointers offer flexibility but are a very common source of bugs that are often very difficult to find and fix. Java eliminated pointers, thus simplifying the language and eliminating a common problem in other languages.

Java also eliminates the concept of a header file. The header file, in C and C++, is the place that the programmer places definitions of classes and data structures. The executable source files then reference the header files used in that particular program, method, or subroutine. However, if a header file changes, then all source files that refer to that header file must be recompiled, relinked, and retested. This can sap programmer productivity and makes the entire development process more unwieldy.

Also missing from Java, and present in C++, is the concept of multiple inheritance. In C++, one class can inherit characteristics from two different classes. There has long been a debate over the utility of multiple inheritance. Its relative usefulness must be balanced by the fact that multiple inheritance adds considerably to the complexity of the program and of the compiler. Java allows a class to inherit from only a single other class.

Having made all of these points about the simplicity of Java, it should be noted that Java remains a complex, high-level computer programming language. One should not expect a non-programmer, such as a Web author, to be able to pick up a book and learn to program in Java over a weekend (despite the claims that the books make). Its simplicity is relative to other high-level programming languages such as C, C++, and Smalltalk.

Object Oriented

Java was designed from the start to be an object-oriented language. The concept of object orientation was described in Chapter 1. Quite simply, in object-oriented programming, one defines *objects* and *methods*. The objects are the nouns and the methods are the verbs. Therefore, one programmer can create an object called a customer with certain allowable methods that can be applied to the customer object: change address, add transaction, credit payment, etc. The actual details of how the customer is implemented are hidden from other programmers and programs, but others can utilize the object class. This enhances reuse of code and adds greatly to overall productivity.

Java supports two characteristics of strongly object-oriented programming languages: inheritance and polymorphism. Inheritance, as described in Chapter 1, allows one class to inherit the characteristics of another class, creating a tree-like structure of inheritance. Thus, the class *book* can inherit all of the characteristics of the class *product*. The creator of the class *book* then only needs to design the unique characteristics of that class and inherit the common characteristics of all products (e.g., price, size, weight, order lead-time). Polymorphism refers to the ability to process things differently, depending on the particular class. For example, the class *product* can have a method *salestax* that calculates the state sales tax on an item. However, the sales tax might depend on the type of product. Clothing and food items may have no tax; most other products may have 6 percent tax, and luxury items may have 10 percent tax. Polymorphism allows the derived classes (book, clothing, food, etc.) to redefine the *salestax* method so that it is always correctly calculated for all products.

The promise of a vast marketplace of Java objects is becoming fulfilled. Third-party developers are offering Java components for sale that will vastly simplify and speed the deployment of new applications. For example, classes and components are available in the marketplace for an online shopping cart, an online catalog, credit card processing, etc. Organizations that wish to deploy a new E-commerce application can purchase the various components and focus on adding the unique characteristics of the application.

Network Savvy

Java was created with the Internet in mind. As such, it has native support for TCP/IP and higher-level related protocols such as File Transfer Protocol (FTP) and HTTP. Java allows programmers to open URLs and access objects across the network as easily as they can access files on the local file system. Java includes Remote Method Invocation (RMI), which allows remote, network-connected objects to be easily invoked. RMI handles the details of setting up the communication link between the two systems and passing data back and forth.

Interpreted

Java is an interpreted language. When a programmer creates a Java program, it is (usually) compiled into a byte-code stream. In a traditional compile-and-link process such as used with C++, the output of the compile-and-link stage is object code that is specific to the particular platform for which it was compiled. With Java, on the other hand, the byte-code that results from the compilation stage is machine independent. It is when the Java program is run that the byte-code is interpreted into machine-specific instructions. For example, a Java applet is downloaded from a Web server in Java byte-code format. When the applet is executed on the client's machine, the virtual machine on the client system interprets the byte-code into machine-specific instructions that are executed on-the-fly.

The downside of an interpreted program compared to a compiled program is in execution speed. The processor must read the byte-code and transform it into machine-dependent code before it can actually execute the code and do the work. This is done for each byte-code instruction, so the processor ends up doing much more work than if the code were all ready to execute in native machine language. Early critics of Java (such as some at Microsoft) often cited this performance problem as a reason why Java would not replace traditional, compiled programming approaches. Since then, however, the emergence of just-in-time (JIT) compilers has virtually eliminated the Java performance hit. With a JIT compiler, the entire byte-code stream is compiled into native machine code before the application is initiated. With this approach, the only performance hit is taken at the very beginning, when the application is first initiated. JIT compilers have brought the performance of Java applications almost to parity with applications written in C++. Some JIT compilers can even take in Java source code and directly create machine code without the explicit intervening step of byte-code, thus even eliminating the up-front hit.

Robust

A robust language is one that prevents problems from occurring and detects problems before they are able to corrupt or crash the system. In other words, a robust language avoids and detects bugs before they become a problem.

As already detailed in the discussion on Java's simplicity, there are several error-prone and bug-inducing features of C++ and other languages that are omitted in Java in order to enhance Java's robustness. Java provides automatic allocation of memory when required and periodically performs garbage collection to return memory that is no longer being referenced to the pool of available memory. This prevents memory depletion problems, in which a system's memory is depleted because memory is allocated but never freed, and memory corruption problems, in which memory is freed but a reference to it remains and is used in the future. The other important omission from C++ to enhance robustness is the lack of pointers. Because pointers in C++ can be arithmetically manipulated, it is a simple task for a programmer to inadvertently modify a pointer to legitimate data. By manipulating the pointer, it now points to a completely unintended and arbitrary place in memory. If the application begins to write to that memory, the results can be catastrophic. Worse, pointer reference errors are very difficult to troubleshoot and fix. By eliminating these two common causes of errors, Java can claim to be a more robust language.

Java is a strongly typed language. This means that the compiler enforces explicit data type declarations so errors can be detected at compile time rather than at runtime. Although C and C++ are also strongly typed, they do allow a number of compile-time loopholes that are closed in Java. Java also performs array bounds checking during runtime so that programmers cannot inadvertently wander outside the bounds of an array and corrupt memory in that way.

Secure

Because Java was designed to operate in a networked environment, great care has always been taken to ensure that Java offers security mechanisms that prevent the destruction of a client system through the download of malicious code. The original security model, implemented in the first version of the Java Development Kit (JDK), is known as the sandbox model. In this model, code that is downloaded has very limited and restricted access to the local system. A downloaded applet is presumed to be untrustworthy and can therefore not access the local file system and other key local system resources. Code that originates locally, however, (i.e., loaded from the local file system) has full access rights to all system resources because it is presumed to be safe.

The sandbox model is very effective in preventing harm to the local system from malicious code. However, it severely restricts the flexibility of applications in a networked environment. Therefore, the model has evolved and become less restrictive in subsequent versions of the JDK. The first step in loosening the sandbox restriction was taken in JDK 1.1 with the introduction of the concept of a signed applet. Using public key/private key cryptography technology, a signed applet from a trusted source is treated like local code and has all of the access rights given to local code. Signed applets are delivered in signed Java ARchive (JAR) files. Applets that are not signed by a trusted source are subject to the sandbox restrictions.

This all-or-nothing approach to local system access evolved in JDK 1.2 to allow all applets and applications to be subject to a security policy. With this approach, the system administrator or the individual user can configure various levels of permission for applets from various signers or locations. The two extremes of access control — no local access versus complete local access — remain options. However, the administrator or user can define a variety of different domains, each given varying degrees of local access. Exhibit 3.1 illustrates the evolution of Java security.

Architecture Neutral

Java is neutral to computing architecture, which is another way of saying that it is a platform-independent language. This is largely due to the fact that Java is interpreted, and the code that is generated is the machine-independent Java byte-code. This allows the same applet or servlet code to run on a handheld device, a Microsoft Windows-based PC, an Apple Macintosh, a UNIX or Linux server, or any other platform that supports the Java virtual machine and runtime environment.

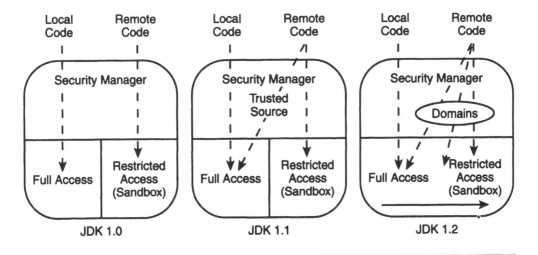

Exhibit 3.1   Evolution of the Java Security Model

Portable

Portability is related to platform independence. Java is portable because the Java byte-code is the same, no matter what the target platform. However, there is another element to portability. C and C++ contain certain implementation-dependent aspects, such as the size and representation of integers and floating point numbers. These languages were created a number of years ago while there was a wide diversity of different platforms with varying computing power. Since then, with the advancement in chip capacities, a certain common denominator of computing power can be assumed. Thus, Java has defined an "int" as always being a signed two's complement 32-bit integer, and a "float" as a 32-bit IEEE 754 floating point number.

Other aspects of portability include the Java libraries and the Java system itself. The libraries define portable interfaces, and there are implementations of the libraries available for all common operating environments. The Java system itself is highly portable. The compiler is written in Java and the machine-dependent runtime is written in ANSI C with a clean portability layer.

High Performance

Sun claims that Java is high performance, while others (e.g., some Microsoft types) claim that Java cannot have high performance compared to code that is compiled specifically for a certain platform. As already stated in the discussion on the interpreted nature of Java, the byte-code-to-machine-language step is normally performed on-the-fly as the program is executing. This extra processing necessarily means that the processor must do more work and can therefore execute fewer instructions per period of time than a language that is already compiled to its native machine-dependent code. As already detailed, the presence of JIT compilers tends to erase the performance gap of Java, assuming that the JIT compiler is relatively efficient and optimized for the target platform.

Multithreaded

Java has built-in support for multithreading. Programs written in a traditional language such as C are single-threaded. Each program is initiated through the execution of the program named `main()`, which maintains control throughout the execution cycle except when it temporarily passes control to subroutines. In a multithreaded environment, on the other hand, a program is broken into separate pieces known as threads. The threads communicate with one another but otherwise are somewhat autonomous units of computing. A thread is the lowest level of work that is scheduled and initiated by the CPU.

A programmer can create a multithreaded environment using a traditional single-threaded language such as C, but the onus for all of the control of the threads and the interaction is on the application programmer. Java incorporates a set of sophisticated synchronization primitives that allows programmers to much more easily incorporate multithreading into their programs. By incorporating these elements into the language itself, the resulting program can be more robust because the language and system take care of the details of the multithreading implementation on behalf of the programmer.

Dynamic

A side effect of Java's interpreted design is that interconnections between various modules and components is made later in the cycle, typically at runtime. This has enormous benefits in making Java very dynamic. In a traditional compile-and-link programming environment, a single object module is created at compile time. All external references are resolved and different modules are linked together. If one module changes later on, the entire program may need to be recompiled and relinked before the changes can take effect.

This can create a serious problem for application developers, particularly if different groups or even different third-party software companies provide the various pieces and components of the overall product. The release of a new version of one piece of the overall product could cause a recompile of all programs that use that piece. Worse still, the interface to that piece may have changed, meaning that all other code that accesses the code may break and need to be updated as well.

In a Java environment, programmers or third-party software providers can freely add to their libraries of methods and variables without impacting existing software that utilizes the objects defined within. This means that the development paths of the various components that comprise an overall solution can proceed independently and without coordination, recompilation, or broken interfaces.

In summary, Java advocates make claims that make Java sound very compelling indeed. There are detractors, of course, and others who delight in pointing out the "problems" of Java. Some of the problems are not unique to Java but rather stem from the fact that yet another language is proliferating that requires its unique development tools and compilers and creates another programmer learning curve. True; but if Java solves real problems, then this is a small price to pay in the long term. Some of the problems of Java often cited (i.e., lack of access to system resources, performance) have been addressed over the five or so years of Java's existence. Java's remaining real "problem" appears to be over the question of the relevance of platform independence (i.e., Sun's Write Once, Run Anywhere) versus platform-specific but language-neutral programs that are efficient and fully utilize the power of the local operating environment (i.e., Microsoft's ActiveX). An organization's collective attitude toward Java may depend on where it stands on this somewhat political and religious issue.

JavaScript

JavaScript was created at Netscape as a means to add dynamic content to Web pages. Before JavaScript, Web pages were either static or they were made dynamic through the use of server-side scripts using the Common Gateway Interface (CGI) standard. With JavaScript, Web pages are made dynamic through the inclusion of script commands embedded and intermingled with HTML and, like HTML, are interpreted and acted upon by the browser rather than the server. Although the Netscape team responsible for developing JavaScript may have modeled some of the syntax of this scripting language after Java, the two languages were developed independently because they each served different purposes. The initial internal name for the scripting language was LiveScript, but the name was changed to JavaScript before its release to leverage the growing popularity of Sun's Java.

The JavaScript code is embedded within a Web page and is interpreted and acted upon by the browser. JavaScripts are delimited by the HTML tags <script> and </script> within a Web page. The script code that is placed between these tags can perform any number of dynamic and interactive functions, for example, change the appearance of a button when the mouse rolls over it, pop up a question box or questionnaire that users need to fill in before they proceed, or expand a list of site navigation options when the mouse rolls over a particular navigation category. The primary advantages of placing these dynamic and interactive functions within the HTML code rather than on a server script is that the responsiveness to the user can be much better, there is no impact to the server in terms of processing and CPU utilization, and the impact on the network is much lower.

While the Java language and JavaScript share certain syntactical similarities, in most environments the people who use the two languages will differ. Java is a full and complex programming language and development environment. Web programmers who are creating new business logic based on Java and its related APIs, components, and platforms will use Java. Programmers who are building new applications using the new generation of Java-based application servers will also use Java. JavaScript, on the other hand, is a relatively simple scripting language that does not meet Java's complexity or its power. As a tool to enliven Web pages, JavaScript will be used by Web site designers and Web page authors.

The Execution Environment

The execution environment is the set of components required, either on a client system or a server system, to execute Java programs, applets, or servlets. The execution environment includes the virtual machine, class libraries required in any Java environment, and possibly JIT compilers and other components. Note that the execution environment is only required for Java programs, not JavaScripts. Support for the JavaScript language is built into the browser, which knows how to correctly interpret and execute the JavaScript statements.

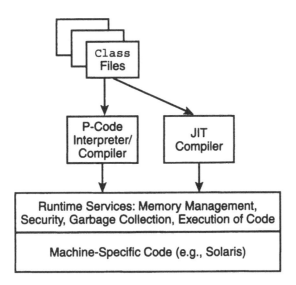

Exhibit 3.2   Basic Components of the Java Virtual Machine

Java Virtual Machine

The Java virtual machine (JVM) is the heart of a Java system. The virtual machine (VM) is the runtime environment that interprets Java byte-code into machine-specific language and executes that code. The VM includes the interpreter for programs that are run as they are interpreted, and it may include a JIT compiler for programs that are compiled when loaded before they are run. The VM is also responsible for implementing and enforcing the Java security model and for providing basic runtime services for Java programs. Exhibit 3.2 illustrates the basic components of a JVM.

Initially, VMs were primarily distributed as a component of a browser. In this model, the VM is implemented within the browser program and it executes Java applets. Exhibit 3.3 illustrates a typical client system with a browser and

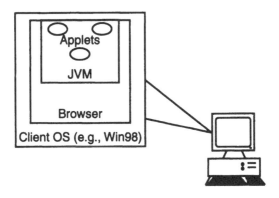

Exhibit 3.3   Client with Browser and JVM

a VM executing Java applets. Since the early days, VMs have been implemented on most server and client operating systems. Any system with a JVM can execute Java programs, applets, and servlets. A VM can also be packaged with Java applications to ensure that the target platform has the requisite VM support, such as might be the case in a specialized Internet appliance.

Java byte-code is stored in a particular type of file called a `class` file format. When one hears about Java class files or class libraries, these are simply individual files or sets of files that contain Java byte-code in a given binary format that is independent of underlying hardware system or operating system. All JVMs must be able to correctly read, interpret, and act upon the code stored in class files. A VM must also be able to manage memory, perform garbage collection on the memory, implement Java security, etc. But in its most basic description, a VM is an entity that reads and executes class files.

The Java language and virtual machine are inherently multithreaded. This means that a JVM must be able to manage multiple threads and the interaction between threads. To do this, the VM manages common data areas and thread-specific data areas during runtime operation. The shared areas of memory include a heap (the common pool of storage from which storage for variables and arrays are allocated) and the method area (a common area that is logically a part of the heap that stores per-class structures that may be referenced by multiple threads). Each time a thread is initiated, a JVM stack for that thread is created. This is a stack that stores local variables and partial results, much like the push-and-pop stacks commonly used in other environments. There are many different types of memory structures managed by the virtual machine.

The JVM dynamically creates, loads, links, and initializes classes and interfaces. Creation of a class or interface is triggered by its reference by another existing class or interface (except the initial class, `void main (String[])`, which is initiated at VM start-up). The class or interface is loaded by locating the representation of that class (i.e., the corresponding class file) and creating an instance of the class in memory. Linking is the process of combining the class with the state of the runtime environment so that the class can be executed. Finally, initialization is the process in which the initialization method for the class or interface is executed.

The Java byte-code executed by the VM consists of an *opcode* specifying the operation to be performed, followed by zero or more *operands* specifying values or variables that the opcode will act upon. For more information on the Java opcodes and operands, refer to *The Java Language Specification*, published by Sun Microsystems.

The VM, as already stated, must also implement memory management, garbage collection, and Java security methodologies. Sun Microsystems does not specify how these are to be implemented — only how they must appear to classes, interfaces, and users. Therefore, these elements of the VM are implementation dependent.

Java Runtime Environment

The Java Runtime Environment (JRE) is a package of elements that allows a platform to support Java programs, applets, and servlets. The current version of the JRE consists of the JVM, core Java classes, and supporting files. The JRE is also packaged with a plug-in that allows common browser platforms to execute Java applets. The JRE does not include development tools such as the Java compiler.

The JRE is licensed by Sun Microsystems and downloadable from the Sun Web site. The JRE license allows third-party developers to package the JRE with their application at no charge so that customers of that software application are guaranteed to have the correct version of the virtual machine and related files. The license agreement indicates that the JRE must be distributed in full, with the exception of certain files that may be excluded if not required for a particular application (e.g., localization files). The JRE can be combined with the application files in a Java ARchive (JAR) file. The advantage of JAR file bundling is that JAR files can be compressed, minimizing the time to download the application if it is distributed over a network.

Java Development Kit

The Java Development Kit (JDK) has been recently renamed the Software Development Kit (SDK) with the introduction of the Java 2 platforms. Whether called a JDK or SDK, this kit is targeted to software developers who are creating Java programs, applets, or servlets. The JDK/SDK includes the components of the JRE (the virtual machine, core Java classes, supporting files) in addition to elements required by Java programmers — specifically, the compiler, the debugger, an applet viewer, all classes and APIs that may be required to create a Java program, and other developer-oriented tools and files.

Although the JDK/SDK is available without charge from Sun Microsystems, the license does not allow organizations to redistribute the JDK/SDK with their application software. This is what the JRE is for. Third-party software providers should use the JDK/SDK internally in the creation of their Java application, and then bundle the application with the appropriate JRE for distribution to their end customers.

Java Components and APIs

The Java language was designed from the start to be object oriented. However, it was a year or more before a component model was added to Java with the 1996 introduction of JavaBeans. A year later, Enterprise JavaBeans was introduced, which extended the object model to the server. A variety of enterprise APIs have also been added over time to allow Java programs and components to communicate with a wide variety of other systems in the enterprise.

JavaBeans

JavaBeans is the original component model for Java. It predates Enterprise JavaBeans, an extension to the component model for server-side components, and the Java 2 platform framework. Support for JavaBeans is available in JDK 1.1 and later versions.

Having said that JavaBeans is a component model, what exactly is a component? A component is a pre-built piece of software that has well-defined boundaries. It can be viewed as a "black box" implemented in software. That is, it has specific and defined inputs, and outputs that are predictable based on the inputs. However, the inner workings of the black box are hidden from the rest of the world. A component is a mechanism by which independent objects can be created and then leveraged as a whole by other programs. That is, a new program can be stitched together using off-the-shelf components, with the programmer focusing on stitching the components together and providing new and unique business logic.

This definition of a component is similar to the description of the benefits of object-oriented models. Thus, a key question is: is any object-oriented model equivalent to a component model? The answer is: no, not necessarily. Object orientation can be viewed as a necessary but not sufficient attribute of a component model. However, object-oriented frameworks do not necessarily lead to reusable code. One of the reasons for this is the very powerful notion of inheritance. Very large frameworks of classes can be built using inheritance. If one of the base classes changes in any substantial way, the effect can be propagated to all subclasses of that base class. The result is a complex, interdependent hierarchy of classes that requires programmers to understand the interrelationships between the classes. This monolithic structure also makes code reuse impractical in many situations and applications.

A component, on the other hand, is a stand-alone element that is not externally a part of a large hierarchy of classes. A component may be very complex internally and be built using class structures and inheritance; but to the rest of the world, the component is only viewed by a clean, external interface that is not interdependent upon other components. Exhibit 3.4 illustrates the difference between an interdependent set of classes and individual components.

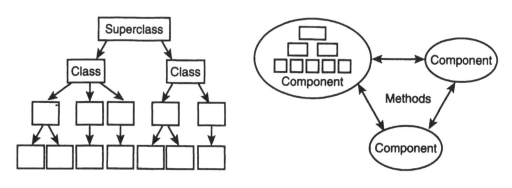

Exhibit 3.4   Interdependent Classes Compared to Components

Component models have been developed over the past decade or so following the paradigm called PME, which stands for Properties, Methods, and Events. PME defines the characteristics, behaviors, and communication interfaces to a component. Prior to JavaBeans, the PME model was implemented by a variety of vendors in a variety of different models, including Microsoft's COM, Apple's OpenDoc, and Delphi's VCL.

In PME, a property is defined as an attribute or variable, together with its value. A property could represent how a component appears, its current state or reading, its display properties, etc. A property is examined or changed by other external agents, such as other components, using Get and Set methods. Methods are the operations upon which the component will act. For example, an address book component may add contacts, display contacts, and make a particular contact part of a group of contacts. Events are the output of the component, the way in which the component communicates with the outside world (i.e., another component) that something has happened. Events can be synchronous, meaning that they are output as the event is occurring; or they can be asynchronous, meaning that they are output some time after the event has occurred. In the address book example, a synchronous event to the *DisplayContact* method may be the output of the particular contact information. An asynchronous event to the *AddContactToList* method may be confirmation of the action of adding a contact to a particular distribution list.

JavaBeans is a component model that implements the PME paradigm. A *bean* is a Java component that adheres to the JavaBeans model. A bean, like a Java applet, can be embedded within an HTML page. Beans can be visual elements that are distributed to users and can be interactive and event-driven. Beans can also be invisible, as would be the case for beans that live on servers. A bean that adheres to the JavaBeans model has the following characteristics, and Exhibit 3.5 illustrates a bean that has these characteristics:

- defined PME
- introspection
- customization
- persistence

Because the JavaBeans model is based on the PME paradigm, beans must have defined properties, methods, and events. A bean must have properties that can be read and modified by external tools or other components. A bean's properties can be defined by the programmer as read/write, read-only, or write-only. The JavaBeans model adheres to the principle that its properties cannot be directly changed or manipulated, but the values of properties can be changed or manipulated (if defined as read/write or write-only). The JavaBeans model supports single-value and indexed properties. Properties can also be either bound, which means that interested parties are notified via events if the value of a property changes, or constrained, which means that interested parties can veto the modification of a property's value. Methods are those actions that a bean will perform. Events are the bean's notification

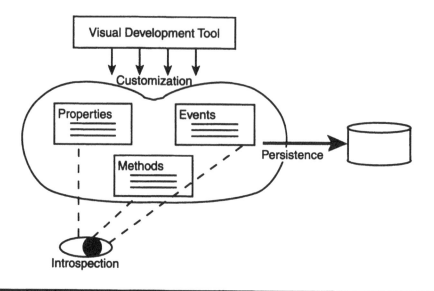

Exhibit 3.5   A JavaBean

to the outside world that something has occurred. In the JavaBeans model, interested parties (i.e., other components) can subscribe to a bean's event, meaning that they will be notified when the event occurs. Using a visual development tool, an event-driven chain of interaction between different beans can be created.

Introspection is the ability for other components and tools to discover the PME interfaces of the bean. Without introspection, the bean interfaces must be published in static form. If the bean changes, then the published interface specification becomes out-of-date. Introspection allows the interfaces to be read or sensed in real-time as the bean is being accessed or incorporated into a program using a visual development tool. JavaBeans have two basic mechanisms for introspection. The first mechanism, known as *reflection*, allows an external entity to discover the signature of the bean's interface in real-time. This is accomplished when the bean adheres to a set of naming conventions by which the bean's methods can be ascertained by the use of common semantics, primarily used for the setting and getting of properties and the sending and receiving of events. The second mechanism involves the use of an explicit class, `BeanInfo`, which is provided by the bean's programmer and provides an explicit description of the bean.

Customization is the ability of a programmer to change the properties of a bean to suit a particular use or implementation. This is really the ability to change the value of the property — not to change the fundamental set of bean properties, as described above. To encourage the reuse of beans, the JavaBeans model enables bean programmers to provide a lot of hooks to the outside world so that potential users of the bean can easily modify the bean through the use of a visual development tool. JavaBeans specifies a `Customizer` class that can be used to provide a wizard-like dialog to interface with the bean or property sheets that allow easy customization.

Persistence is the ability for the bean to maintain state across various executions and requires the ability to store the state of the bean in nonvolatile memory, such as on a hard drive. The bean programmer can make fields in a class persistent simply by defining them as "serializable" up front. Fields that should not be saved are defined as `transient` or `static`. The JDK provides the serialization mechanism and also supports versioning, which allows a newer bean to load state information written by an older version of the bean.

The JavaBeans model was defined from the start with the idea that programmers and non-programmers alike would utilize visual development tools to build applications that utilize the beans. Visual development tools that are "bean-aware" are available from a number of different vendors (e.g., Symantec, Borland, IBM). These tools provide a GUI-based, drag-and-drop interface that allows beans to be easily manipulated and incorporated into programs without having to write code from scratch. The tools present a toolbox and palette interface and allow the programmer to drag-and-drop a bean, modify its appearance, define its interaction with other beans using methods and events, and then create a Java application, applet, or new bean.

There is a difference between a design-time bean and a runtime bean. The design-time bean is the superset that has all of the information needed by the visual development tool, including such things as the property editor, `BeanInfo` class, `Customizer` class, icons, etc. While these items are necessary to allow a visual tool to easily utilize and customize the bean, their presence in a runtime environment adds unnecessary bloat. Beans can (and should) be packaged into separate archives (JARs) for design-time and runtime.

Sun Microsystems offers a JavaBeans Development Kit (BDK) for developers of tools and beans. The BDK is licensed in addition to a JDK. The BDK includes:

- BeanBox test container (i.e., a reference container that demonstrates how a container is built)
- example beans that run within the BeanBox and demonstrate a variety of bean behaviors
- variety of reference source code
- makefile information
- JavaBean tutorial

Since its introduction in 1996, the JavaBeans architecture has been extended with three new APIs intended to facilitate the interconnection of beans at runtime. The first, the Extensible Runtime Containment and Services Protocol (also known as the BeanContext API), allows a bean to interrogate its environment at runtime. Before this API was available, bean introspection and reflection happened during design time only. That is, a programmer using visual development tools was able to determine the properties, methods, and events of a bean through introspection and create a program utilizing that information by interconnecting beans together. The BeanContext API supports a logical containment hierarchy in which beans can be grouped together in a logical and traversable manner. The services API of BeanContext allows beans, during runtime, to discover what services are available from other beans and to connect to those beans to make use of the services.

The second JavaBeans extension, the InfoBus extension, was originally defined by Lotus. InfoBus enables the dynamic exchange of information between different beans. Its name is based on the concept of an information bus between components. The InfoBus specification defines a small number of interfaces for cooperating beans and defines the protocol used for the communication between the beans. All beans that implement InfoBus can plug into the bus and exchange information with any other bean connected to the bus.

The third extension to the JavaBeans model is the JavaBeans Activation Framework (JAF). JAF allows a bean to elicit certain information about data in a runtime environment so that it can act properly upon that data. A common example about the usefulness of JAF is in a helper application that needs to be able to discern the contents of a file in order to display it. For example, a Web browser could determine that a particular stream of data is a JPEG image file and therefore display it properly as a JPEG. JAF determines the type of arbitrary data, encapsulates access to the data, discovers operations available on a particular type of data, and instantiates the software used to operate on a particular type of data.

Development of the JavaBeans model was an important piece in the evolution of Java. With the addition of the JavaBeans component model, Java began to be viewed as a programming environment rather than just a programming language. While JavaBeans was an important development, it was the later addition of Enterprise JavaBeans and enterprise-class APIs that allowed Java to completely fulfill its promise as a total computing framework capable of supporting the enterprise and its variety of applications.

Enterprise JavaBeans

Enterprise JavaBeans (EJB) is positioned as an extension of the JavaBeans model for server-side, transactional-based applications. However, the two frameworks are very different because they are solving very different technical problems and address different markets and requirements. JavaBeans is targeted to the client development community. As such, the focus of the JavaBeans framework is to facilitate the creation of client-based components using visual development tools. Beans developed using the JavaBeans framework typically reside in a single address space, such as on a desktop or handheld device, and are often GUI elements like buttons, viewers, etc. EJB, on the other hand, is targeted to the enterprise, transaction-oriented, multitier application environment. In this environment, the focus is on building scalable enterprise systems that can support thousands or tens of thousands of users.

EJB is a component model for server-side components. Like client-side components, server components are reusable and may be purchased, off-the-shelf elements that an enterprise programmer can use to build unique business applications. The EJB specification defines not only the component interface and how components communicate, but it also defines a complete set of middleware services provided by the EJB server. These services are provided on behalf of the components and include security, transactional integrity, persistence, and other services.

An EJB component is called an enterprise bean. An enterprise bean cannot execute on a server on its own — it requires a container. A container is the environment in which an enterprise bean runs. It provides the middleware services to the enterprise bean, and shields the enterprise bean from direct interaction with the client. When the client application invokes the enterprise bean through a defined method, the container intercepts the invocation to manage security, persistence, and system resources. For example, the enterprise bean does not manage threads, processes, or memory. These are managed by the container. The reason for this goes back to the goal of scalability in a server environment. The container parsimoniously manages scarce system resources to maximize the scalability of the server. Therefore, when a thread is no longer needed or is not being utilized at the time, the container returns the thread and memory to a common pool to be used by active beans. A container may contain one enterprise bean or many enterprise beans.

There are two different types of enterprise beans: session beans and entity beans. A session bean can be viewed as a somewhat transient entity that is created by the client and usually only exists for the duration of the session between the client and the server. Session beans can be stateful or stateless. A stateful session bean maintains state during a conversation with the client that spans multiple methods. For example, a stateful session bean may be a shopping cart that keeps track of a customer's choices and then executes the sale when the shopping session is complete. A stateless session bean is one in which state is not maintained between methods. An E-commerce example of a stateless session bean is a credit card authorization method.

An entity bean is viewed as a persistent entity that represents the back-end resources of the EJB server. In the current EJB model, the entity bean usually represents a hook to a relational database. An entity bean is usually invoked once and persists throughout the duration of many client/server sessions. An example of an entity bean is the concept of a Customer. The entity bean developer would decide which fields of a given set of customer databases are relevant and then would define the methods that could operate upon the Customer bean. Many clients can access the Customer bean identity at any given time, although only one client could manipulate a particular instance of the Customer bean (e.g., Mary Jones). Exhibit 3.6 illustrates the difference between a session bean and an entity bean.

Entity beans are persistent, but there are two types of entity bean persistence: container-managed persistence (CMP) and bean-managed persistence (BMP). As the names imply, the difference between these two models of persistence has to do with which entity manages the persistent data and connection. In the CMP case, the container manages persistence. The bean

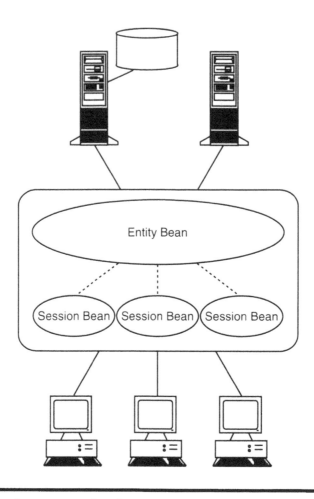

Exhibit 3.6   Session Beans and Entity Beans

developer does not have to write any explicit code to synchronize database queries or updates. The enterprise bean developer simply indicates which fields should be persistent. In the case of a relational database, a persistent field may be associated with a particular column in a table. The container takes care of the synchronization and alerts the bean when fields have been populated with data from the database or when data is about to be written to the database. CMP is not limited to relational databases; CMP beans can be mapped to flat file systems and other legacy data systems.

A BMP bean, on the other hand, synchronizes its state with the database manually (i.e., by the bean programmer). BMP provides more flexibility to the bean programmer but demands greater sophistication on the part of the programmer. Entity beans that need to access several data sources, including perhaps legacy systems, are good candidates for BMP rather than CMP. CMP provides an excellent set of services, but may not meet the needs of all environments; when more sophistication and control is required, BMP may be necessary. The BMP bean manages its own persistence, but the container still provides other services to the BMP bean, such as security and read/write coordination.

The relationship between an enterprise bean (either session or entity) and its container is referred to as a contract. The contract defines an established set of services and a clean interface boundary, allowing beans to reside within the containers of multiple different vendors. The enterprise bean and the container communicate through one of three mechanisms:

1. *Callback methods.* Every enterprise bean must implement several call-back methods that alert the bean to several events. For example, a callback method will alert an enterprise bean when the container is about to remove the bean from memory, write its state to the database, etc. A callback method is a means to allow the enterprise bean to perform housekeeping duties.
2. *EJBContext.* Every enterprise bean must define an `EJBContext` object, which allows the bean to interact with the container to request information about its environment.
3. *Java Naming and Directory Interface (JNDI).* This is the Java enterprise API that allows Java objects to access naming systems such as Light-weight Directory Access Protocol (LDAP) servers and NetWare Directory Services (NDS) servers. The JNDI interface is a fundamental part of the EJB architecture, allowing clients to locate EJB components.

The bean-container contract definition includes the communication mechanisms described above, in addition to a set of rules that defines the operation of the enterprise bean and the container at runtime. The contract is meant to support portability, so that enterprise beans can run in a variety of different containers. Another benefit of the contract is that it simplifies the development of enterprise beans. Because the container manages system resources, persistence, resource location, etc., the enterprise bean can focus on business logic rather than infrastructure logic. The services provided by the container include the following:

- *Life cycle.* The container manages process allocation, thread management, memory management, object creation, and object destruction on behalf of the enterprise bean.
- *State management.* Enterprise beans do not need to implement logic to save and restore state information between method invocations; these duties are performed by the container.
- *Persistence.* The container manages persistent data on behalf of the enterprise bean.
- *Security.* The container authenticates users and checks authorization levels on behalf of the enterprise bean.
- *Transactions.* The container can manage the start, enrollment, commitment, and rollback of database transactions on behalf of the enterprise bean.

The client application interacts with the enterprise bean through two different "wrapper" interfaces. These interfaces shelter the enterprise bean from direct contact with the client and provide the middleware services for the enterprise bean. The first wrapper interface, EJB Home, provides access to the life-cycle services of the bean. Using EJB Home, the client can locate, create, or destroy an instance of an enterprise bean. EJB Object is the wrapper interface that provides access from the client to all of the business methods that are acted on by the enterprise bean. In other words, EJB Object implements all of the methods that are externally accessible for the enterprise bean except the create and destroy methods. The EJB Object for a particular enterprise bean implements either the entity bean interface or the session bean interface, depending on the type of the bean. Exhibit 3.7 illustrates the enterprise bean model with the client wrapper interfaces.

There are two enterprise APIs and sets of services that are a fundamental part of the EJB architecture: JNDI and RMI. The container automatically registers the EJB Home interface in a directory using JNDI for each enterprise bean defined in that container. This allows clients to locate the enterprise bean in order to create an instance of the enterprise bean. Once the instance is created, the container returns the EJB Object interface to the client so that it can then issue methods to the bean.

EJB uses the Remote Method Invocation (RMI) API to handle the communication between the client and the enterprise bean on the server. RMI is the API defined by Java to allow distributed objects to communicate. The RMI compiler creates a stub for the client, which is then either installed on the client or downloaded over the network. This stub handles all the details of the communication with the server. The RMI specification does not specify a communications protocol to be used over this connection. The native protocol, supported in the original EJB implementation, is Java Remote Method Protocol (JRMP). EJB 1.1 has added support for CORBA's Internet InterORB Protocol (IIOP), which will facilitate the interaction between CORBA and Java environments. For example, using the common IIOP protocol, CORBA clients can communicate with enterprise beans and Java clients can communicate with CORBA objects.

Knowing what an EJB server does, it is time to examine where it operates within an enterprise. An organization utilizing EJB servers will still, obviously, have Web servers and browser-based clients. The Web servers (i.e., HTTP servers) still respond to user requests for pages of information. The Web server,

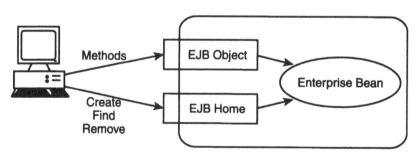

Exhibit 3.7   Enterprise Bean Wrapper Interfaces

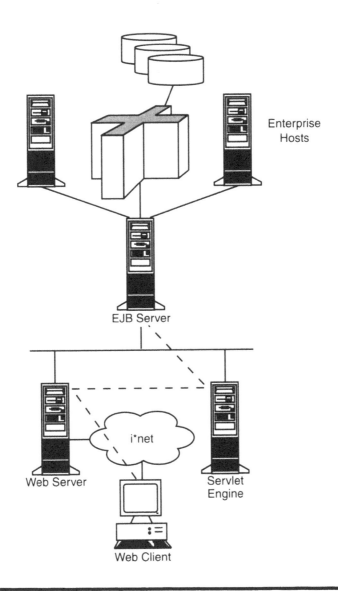

Enterprise
Hosts

EJB Server

i*net

Web Server

Servlet
Engine

Web Client

Exhibit 3.8   EJB Server in the Enterprise

or a separate server, may also be a servlet engine executing Java servlets. The EJB server can be viewed as another layer that sits between the Web/servlet servers and the enterprise databases. Exhibit 3.8 illustrates the overall enterprise server architecture.

The Web clients will usually access the enterprise beans (and the EJB server) via servlets or JSP code. A client applet could, in theory, access the EJB server directly but the applet's browser must be equipped with J2EE, JNDI, and RMI classes. Because this requirement severely limits the number of browsers that can directly access the EJB server, it is recommended that the hooks to the EJB server be coded on a JSP page directly or through the combination of JSP and a regular JavaBean. The JavaBean code becomes an intermediary that allows the JSP code to be quite simple and promotes reuse because multiple JSP pages can rely on the same JavaBean for access to the EJB server.

As of this writing, the current EJB specification is version 1.1, which is the second major release of the specification. Version 2.0, the third major release, is currently out for review and comment but is not expected to be finalized with products implementing it available until some time in 2001 or 2002.

To summarize, an EJB server is an entity that supports the creation of distributed server-side objects in a Java environment. The EJB server and its container provide a number of services to these objects, known as enterprise beans, that facilitate the creation of enterprise beans and promote scalability and security. The EJB server parsimoniously manages scarce system resources on behalf of the enterprise beans to ensure that the server can scale to support thousands or tens of thousands of clients.

How, then, does an EJB server compare to definition of an application server? There is a great deal of overlap, and one could certainly argue that an EJB server, at the current specification level, is a specialized application server that handles database transactions. A more complete application server, however, includes hooks to other types of enterprise applications. A more complete application server also provides sophisticated load balancing and a more complete security model, among other things. The EJB specification will evolve over time, perhaps including these other services. For now, a true application server may include an EJB server engine but then augment that engine with other services and APIs.

Enterprise Java APIs

The EJB specification makes use of some — but not all — of Java's enterprise APIs. The enterprise APIs are intended to provide access to a variety of enterprise resources, including directories, legacy applications, policy servers, and CORBA applications. The list of current enterprise APIs is provided in Exhibit 3.9. This exhibit is followed by a brief description of each of the APIs that has not already been discussed.

Java Authentication and Authorization Service (JAAS)

The initial concept of security in a Java environment focused on the notion that applets are downloaded to client systems. The early sandbox model and its subsequent enhancements are all code-centric security models, in which the user is authorizing code from a particular source to be trusted in part or completely. However, this model does not deal with the security from a server standpoint, in which the user must be authenticated and then authorized to perform a given set of tasks. This is a more traditional view of security from the perspective of enterprise applications.

With the proliferation of server-side Java applications, JAAS provides a framework to allow multiuser applications to authenticate users and assign

Exhibit 3.9   Current Enterprise APIs

Acronym	Name	Function
EJB	Enterprise JavaBeans	The API that specifies the server component model and defines the container-bean contract
JAAS	Java Authentication and Authorization Service	The API that can be used by enterprise applications to grant different privileges to different users in a multi-user environment
JAF	JavaBeans Activation Framework	A standard extension API to determine the type of an arbitrary piece of data, encapsulate access to it, discover the operations available on it, and to instantiate the appropriate bean
Java IDL	Java Interface Definition Language	Java IDL enables seamless interoperability and connectivity to CORBA resources
JavaMail	JavaMail	Provides a set of abstract classes that model a mail system
JDBC	Java Database Connectivity	Provides cross-DBMS access to SQL databases and also tabular data such as spreadsheets and flat files
JMS	Java Message Service	Supports message-based enterprise applications, in which business data and events are exchanged asynchronously
JMX	Java Management Extensions	Extension API that supports the management of Java elements and management within a Java environment
JNDI	Java Naming and Directory Interface	Provides access to naming and directory services such as DNS, NDS, LDAP, and others
Java Servlet and JSP	Java Servlet API and JavaServer Pages technology	Extend the functionality of the Web server through the addition of servlets and scripting pages
JTA	Java Transaction API	Provides standard interfaces between a transaction manager and the various elements involved in a distributed transaction system
JTS	Java Transaction Service	Specifies the implementation of the transaction manager that utilizes the JTA
RMI	Remote Method Invocation	Supports the communication between distributed Java objects

privileges. The JAAS authentication framework is based on pluggable authentication as defined by X/OPEN. With this framework, the system administrator can "plug in" any authentication module that adheres to the PAM standard and that is appropriate to the situation. JAAS extends the existing Java 2 security policy that allows administrators to define which resources are accessible to authorized individuals.

Java Interface Definition Language (Java IDL)

IDL is a concept used in CORBA to define objects and their interfaces (see Chapter 4 for a complete description). Java IDL is an implementation of this IDL to allow Java applications to define, implement, and access CORBA objects.

While Java IDL is still supported in Java 2, the addition of RMI-IIOP has rendered Java IDL somewhat obsolete. As described earlier, RMI-IIOP represents the marriage of Java's RMI with the IIOP used in CORBA. This allows Java objects to access CORBA resources and vice versa. With RMI-IIOP, programmers can write CORBA interfaces directly into their Java applications without requiring the intervening Java IDL.

JavaMail

The JavaMail API provides a set of abstract classes that model a mail system and a platform to build Java-based mail and messaging applications that are platform neutral and protocol independent.

Java Database Connectivity (JDBC)

JDBC provides Java applets and applications access to a variety of existing databases. That access may be direct in the case in which the database vendor has provided a native JDBC interface, or it may be through some driver or middleware that converts the JDBC to some other native format expected by the database. JDBC supports SQL databases as well as tabular data and data found in flat files.

Java Message Service (JMS)

The Java Message Service API facilitates the asynchronous communication between various different applications. A message-based application is not synonymous with an e-mail application. A message-based application shares reports, events, or requests asynchronously with other message-based applications. E-mail is one example of a message-based application. However, JMS facilitates the creation of distributed, enterprisewide applications that asynchronously share events, data, and information to allow each application to track the progress of the enterprise.

Java Management Extensions (JMX)

The JMX specification defines a management architecture, APIs, and management services under a single umbrella. JMX does not, on the other hand, specify a new management protocol. Rather, it works with existing systems and network management protocols such as Simple Network Management Protocol (SNMP). Using JMX, any Java application can be management-enabled with just a few lines of code.

The JMX architecture is divided into three levels: the instrumentation level, the agent level, and the manager level. In addition, JMX provides a number of APIs to allow JMX applications written in the Java language to link with existing management technologies.

Java Transaction API (JTA)

JTA is a service-oriented API that provides a demarcation for transactions. Programmers use JTA to group multiple different operations into one or more logical transactions. JTA provides three types of services: transactional operations in clients, transactional operations in application servers on behalf of clients, and global transactional management in a Java transaction manager.

Java Transaction Service (JTS)

JTS specifies the implementation of a transaction manager that implements JTA and also implements the CORBA Object Transaction Service (OTS). A JTS transaction manager provides transaction services to the parties involved in distributed transactions: the application server, the resource manager, the stand-alone transactional application, and the Communication Resource Manager (CRM).

Java 2 Platform

Sun announced the "Java 2" name in December of 1998, just as it was beginning to release the initial technology for the Java Development Kit version 1.2. Since then, the Java platforms have all assumed the Java 2 branding. There are three platforms — Standard Edition, Enterprise Edition, and Micro Edition — each packaging various Java technologies for a given environment. The Java virtual machine and the Java programming language do not, however, take on the Java 2 branding.

Java 2 Platform: Standard Edition

The Java 2 Platform, Standard Edition (referred to as J2SE), is a collection of the essential Java Software Development Kit (SDK, previously referred to as the JDK), tools, APIs, and the Java runtime. This collection is targeted to developers of Java applets and applications. The platform is not a piece of software; it is the abstract functionality that is implemented in the SDK and the JRE.

The version of J2SE that is shipping at the time of this writing is version 1.3, announced in May of 2000. This release added the Java HotSpot Client VM for increased performance and a smaller footprint on the client. Several enterprise APIs are bundled with J2SE, including RMI-IIOP, Java IDL, JDBC, and JNDI. However, the Enterprise Edition platform is the one targeted to the development and deployment of enterprise application and has the complete set of enterprise APIs.

J2SE is available for license at no charge and the SDK and JRE source and binary code are available on the Sun Web site for download. Platforms supported by J2SE include Solaris, Linux, and Windows (2000, 98, 95, NT 4.0).

Java 2 Platform, Enterprise Edition

The Java 2 Platform, Enterprise Edition (J2EE), is targeted to developers of enterprise-class, server-side applications. It is this platform that forms the basis for Java application servers and also the basis for custom-developed business applications. J2EE is a superset of J2SE. Although J2SE supports some of the enterprise APIs, J2EE includes all of the enterprise APIs including, notably, EJB. With EJB support, J2EE becomes a complete framework for server-based applications. Exhibit 3.10 summarizes the capabilities of J2SE and J2EE.

There are four deliverables of the J2EE platform:

1. *J2EE platform specification:* specifies the Java APIs that must be supported in order to be compliant as a J2EE platform and defines a common way of packaging applications for deployment on any J2EE-compatible platform.
2. *J2EE compatibility test suite:* a suite of tests, provided and licensed by Sun, that allows programmers to test their implementations to ensure conformance to the J2EE platform specification.
3. *J2EE reference implementation:* an implementation, provided by Sun, that is the "gold standard" for adherence to the J2EE platform specification. The reference implementation is not a commercial product and its licensing terms do not allow its commercial use. However, it is available for free in binary form and may be used for demonstrations, prototyping, and research.
4. *J2EE blueprints* (formerly referred to as the J2EE application programming model): design guidelines that represent the best-practices philosophy for the design and building of J2EE-based applications. The philosophy for building n-tier applications is provided in addition to a set of design patterns with a set of examples on how to build the applications.

The model of computing that results from the implementation of J2EE platforms and applications is depicted in Exhibit 3.11.

Exhibit 3.10   Comparison of J2SE and J2EE

Feature	J2SE	J2EE
Basic Features		
Security and signed applets	✓	✓
Collections framework	✓	✓
JavaBeans	✓	✓
Internationalization	✓	✓
I/O	✓	✓
Networking	✓	✓
Language and utility packages	✓	✓
Remote method invocation	✓	✓
Arbitrary-precision math	✓	✓
Reflection	✓	✓
Package version identification	✓	✓
Sound	✓	✓
Reference objects	✓	✓
Resources	✓	✓
Object serialization	✓	✓
Extension mechanism	✓	✓
Java Archive (JAR) files	✓	✓
Java Native Interface (JNI)	✓	✓
Java Foundation Classes (JFC)		
Abstract Window Toolkit	✓	✓
Project swing components	✓	✓
2-D graphics and imaging	✓	✓
Input method framework	✓	✓
Accessibility	✓	✓
Drag-and-drop data transfer	✓	✓
Enterprise Features		
RMI-IIOP	✓	✓
Java IDL	✓	✓
JDBC	✓	✓
Java Naming and Directory Interface (JNDI)	✓	✓
Enterprise JavaBeans		✓
Java Servlets		✓
JavaServer Pages		✓
Java Transaction API (JTA)		✓
JavaMail API		✓
Java Messaging Service (JMS)		✓

Source: Sun Microsystems.

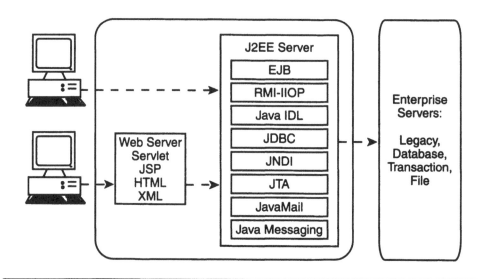

Exhibit 3.11 J2EE Model of Computing

The popularity of J2EE is growing rapidly, in large part due to the fact that the platform provides a great deal of the infrastructure required to build many different types of applications, including:

- distributed object technology
- security
- persistence
- messaging
- transaction interface
- application deployment
- database connectivity
- server middleware and resource management

As a result of the J2EE infrastructure, application programmers are finding that they are able to implement new applications faster. Further, most of the leading application server vendors have licensed J2EE and plan to integrate the platform into their offerings. Chapter 5 provides a complete overview of application servers and Chapter 7 provides a description and comparison of some of the leading application server offerings available in the marketplace.

Java 2 Platform, Micro Edition

The Java 2 Platform, Micro Edition (J2ME), is an optimized Java runtime environment to support consumer devices and embedded systems such as pagers, cellular phones, screenphones, set-top boxes, and car navigational systems. J2ME is designed to support these consumer devices, which often have very limited resources, with the same portability and safe network delivery that is the hallmark of Java technologies. Applications that are written using J2ME can later be scaled upward through the use of J2SE or J2EE.

Final Thoughts

Java has evolved at really a dramatic rate when compared to other computing languages, models, and architectures. In only five years, it has become a complete set of platforms targeted to desktop, server, and consumer electronic systems. The amount of press devoted to Java, the number of vendors supporting Java platforms and technologies, and the exponential growth in the number of Java programmers all attest to its widespread appeal and relevance to implementing E-business solutions.

The original excitement surrounding Java centered on the client. Java applets, downloaded at will and on demand from Web servers, would facilitate the replacement of big, complex, and difficult-to-manage desktop PC systems with a new breed of thin, inexpensive, and easy-to-manage network computers (NCs). Industry leaders and luminaries heralded the end of Microsoft's stranglehold on the industry and the dawn of a new era of thin-client computing.

However, Java applets that had meaningful functionality were very slow to download. JVMs were also resource-hungry and slow. As a result, the NC industry stalled and many early predictions about the dominance of Java-centric thin clients failed to materialize.

Nevertheless, the evolution of Java continued, and server-side Java technologies like EJB and enterprise APIs renewed interest in Java for server-based servlets and applications. Server-based computing is proving to be the brass ring for Java. J2EE, in particular, is allowing the rapid proliferation of the complete set of Java technologies within enterprises. Application servers based on the J2EE platform are now common and are rapidly gaining acceptance.

It is worth pondering the role of standards bodies in the quick evolution and deployment of new, disruptive technologies such as Java. Sun originally indicated that it would hand over responsibility for Java evolution and development to standards bodies. However, it decided against that move and instead has maintained control over Java. It does, however, involve the user and vendor community in providing requirements, input, and reviews through the Java Community Process. Sun has also been very "open" about Java technologies; complete disclosure through documentation and sometimes even the release of source code has been a standard operating procedure.

It can be argued that Sun's stewardship of Java has provided a level playing field for all interested parties. A level playing field is the general reason that user and vendor communities tend to prefer standards bodies to control and define technologies rather than a single vendor with its own agenda and commercial interests. However, the standards process is typically characterized by its glacial speeds. The standards process sometimes creates standards that are bloated and late. Java, on the other hand, has gained a lot of functionality in a relatively short period of time.

The end result appears to be that Java will gain an irretrievable foothold in many enterprise environments. Alas, this cannot be said for some technologies that have complete blessings of a vendor-neutral standards body. For example, CORBA, the subject of Chapter 4, has evolved over a number of years through the leadership of the Object Management Group (OMG). Some argue that Java's success is in part due to the failure of CORBA to quickly evolve to embrace Web technologies. Whether this criticism is fair, it is clear that Java is enjoying wider vendor and user support. Sun must be doing something right in its stewardship of Java.

Note

1. See http://java.sun.com/docs/overviews/java/java-overview-1.html.

Chapter 4

CORBA

Most application servers are built upon a technology base of Java, CORBA, or a combination of the two. This chapter provides a detailed description of the major components and technologies of CORBA. This information serves as a foundation for the following chapters.

History and Overview of CORBA

In April of 1989, eleven companies representing IT users and vendors initiated the formation of the Object Management Group (OMG). The purpose of the consortium was and is to develop and promote commercially viable and vendor-independent technologies for Distributed Object Computing (DOC). The consortium, organized as a not-for-profit corporation, now has over 800 members. The group is responsible for the definition of Common Object Request Broker Architecture (CORBA) and all of its related technologies and specifications. In addition to CORBA, the OMG has specified the Unified Modeling Language (UML) and a number of industry-specific, vertical market application frameworks.

The OMG, headquartered in Needham, Massachusetts, has offices in several countries: Bahrain, Brazil, Germany, India, Italy, Japan, and the United Kingdom. The consortium is organized into three major bodies: the Platform Technology Committee (PTC), the Domain Technology Committee (DTC), and the Architecture Board. Membership is offered at three different levels, reflecting a varying amount of direct input and influence over specifications that a member may have.

The first specification produced by the OMG was the Object Management Architecture (OMA). This architecture specifies an overall object model that is a framework for CORBA and all of the other specifications produced by the OMG. The OMA is comprised of two parts: the Core Object Model and the Reference Model.

The Core Object Model is an abstract model that underlies CORBA. It defines the concepts used by object request brokers (ORBs) to facilitate distributed object computing. The abstract model does not specify or constrain implementations. The Core Object Model is of particular interest to ORB developers rather than application developers. The main goals of the Core Object Model are portability and interoperability. In this context, portability means that applications can be created whose components do not rely on the existence or location of a particular object implementation. Interoperability means the ability of an application to invoke an object without regard to the platform and language its implementation is based on.

The Reference Model is an architectural framework that standardizes the interfaces to infrastructures and services that an application can utilize. The Reference Model provides a means for components to understand what services they can expect to receive from ORBs and other third-party components.

CORBA is a concrete model based on the abstract OMA. CORBA has been evolving since its initial definitions. In particular, it has evolved to specifically embrace the Internet as a transport mechanism and Java's EJB and RMI technologies. The current version of CORBA specification is V2.3, but the end of 2000 will see the early-stage release of products based on the Version 3 specification. Version 3 will bring the following additional features:

- firewall specification for transport-level, application-level, and bi-directional firewalls
- extension of the CORBA naming service to support URLs
- quality of service control
- extensions of CORBA for embedded systems, fault-tolerant operation, and real-time environments
- CORBA components to provide a container environment, integration with Enterprise JavaBeans, and enhanced application distribution
- CORBA scripting maps CORBA and component assembly to several widely used scripting languages

Although CORBA has evolved to incorporate and accommodate the Internet as a transport and to integrate with emerging Java technologies, the goals for CORBA continue to be portability and interoperability. While Java provides a framework for distributed object computing, the Java technologies accommodate only one language — Java. Java interoperates with other distributed object models (i.e., CORBA) by leveraging CORBA's Internet Inter-ORB Protocol (IIOP). Java's portability is based on the fact that the Java language can run on any platform supporting a Java virtual machine. CORBA, on the other hand, has always been both platform independent and language independent. Therefore, CORBA components can be created in a wide variety of programming languages (including Java) and can reside on any native operating system without requiring an additional virtual machine layer.

To fully appreciate the CORBA goals of portability and interoperability, it is useful to reflect on the state of computing at the time the OMG was formed.

1989 was a time in which there was still a great deal of attention and effort in implementing traditional client/server computing. However, as detailed in Chapter 1, the difficulties and shortcomings of the client/server model were being felt. To summarize:

1. Standard programming APIs were available, but not for all types of applications. Many proprietary APIs proliferated.
2. All enterprises had a variety of legacy systems to support and potentially to integrate into the new applications.
3. Enterprises were faced with a variety of different desktop and server operating systems. Porting the client/server programs to each operating system and environment was prohibitively expensive.
4. Enterprise networks did not support a single protocol or architecture.

Distributed object computing was a new paradigm that would solve these problems inherent in traditional client/server systems. This paradigm allowed organizations to architect a total system as a set of relatively independent components that communicate via standard means. Components could be implemented on the system and in the language that was best suited for a particular task or worker skill set. The paradigm also provided an infrastructure that would find and recognize components wherever they were implemented so that the individual programs utilizing those components would not have to contain information about their location. Exhibit 4.1 illustrates the difference between a traditional client/server implementation and one based on distributed object computing.

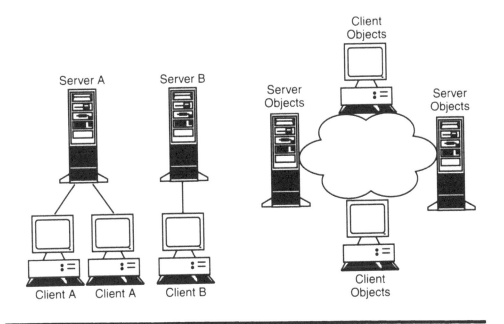

Exhibit 4.1 Traditional Client/Server versus Distributed Object Computing

CORBA was the first specification that defined a complete distributed object computing model. Because it was defined by a large consortium of different vendors and users (the OMG), CORBA met its goal of being neutral to vendor, platform, and language. The only object models that compete with CORBA are Microsoft's COM+ and now Java. Microsoft's model is language neutral but not platform (or vendor) neutral. Java is platform and vendor neutral but not language-neutral. Nonetheless, Java and CORBA are complementary specifications. Enterprises with a great deal of legacy code will look to CORBA as a means of tying together disparate systems, while new applications may be written using Java and its related technologies. Fortunately, the two will seamlessly interoperate, particularly as the newer versions of the specifications become implemented in products and mature in the marketplace.

CORBA Architecture

CORBA is a concrete set of specifications based on the OMG's Object Management Architecture (OMA), described above. CORBA's specifications define the:

- components of a CORBA system
- services provided to objects
- definition of objects
- mapping of CORBA services to particular programming languages
- interoperability between CORBA objects and objects based on other models
- growing set of industry-specific, vertical application frameworks

The CORBA architecture, at a very high level, is based on four different elements that support the goals of portability and interoperability: the Object Request Broker (ORB), the Interface Definition Language (IDL), the client object (or requester of a service), and the server object. CORBA is logically viewed as a bus-based architecture, in which the ORB provides a bus for communication between elements. Exhibit 4.2 illustrates these elements.

Portability, in the context of CORBA, is defined as the transparency of location. That is, the location of an object is transparent to programs that communicate with that object. Location transparency is achieved in CORBA through the Object Request Broker (ORB). The ORB is the heart of a CORBA environment. Conceptually, the ORB is the bus that brokers requests from client objects to server objects.

Interoperability, in the context of CORBA, is defined as the transparency of programming language. Objects can be programmed in any one of a variety of programming languages. The other objects in the system do not need to be aware of the language of the object. Interoperability is provided in CORBA through the Interface Definition Language (IDL). This is a language-neutral definition file that defines the object, its methods, and its attributes. A programmer of a client that uses the object only needs the IDL that defines the object to be able to utilize the object.

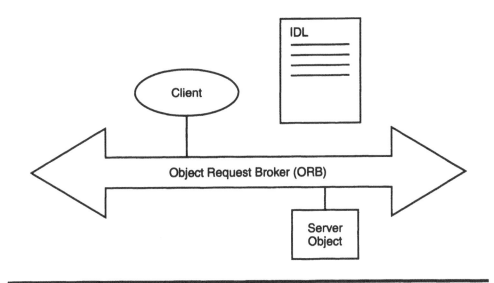

Exhibit 4.2 Major Elements of the CORBA Architecture

A CORBA client object is the entity that is requesting another object to perform some action through invoking a method. The server object is the object performing the method. Note that the terms "client" and "server" are relative to a particular operation or method and simply refer to the role being played by the object at that particular time.

For the client and the server to communicate via the ORB, the IDL is parsed by an IDL compiler, and "stub" and "skeleton" code is created that the client and the server, respectively, link to. The client stub code maps, or *marshals*, the programming language data types into a wire format that is transmitted via the ORB. The server object has skeleton code that performs the reverse process, which *unmarshals* the wire format into the data types appropriate for the programming language that is used to implement the server object. Exhibit 4.3 illustrates the CORBA architecture again, this time with the client stub and server skeleton pieces added.

In addition to this static model, CORBA defines a dynamic interface that allows clients to dynamically build requests for services. There are two interfaces supported by the ORB: (1) the Dynamic Invocation Interface (DII) allows the client to build dynamic requests for an operation, and (2) the Dynamic Skeleton Interface (DSI) is its corresponding object-side interface that allows an object to respond to arbitrary requests.

The OMA reference model specifies a set of services, facilities, and frameworks that extend the overall model. There are four categories of object interfaces: object services (CORBAservices), common facilities (CORBAfacilities), domain interfaces, and application interfaces. The last interface, by definition, is application specific. The OMG has defined interfaces for the other three types of object interfaces.

The CORBAservices specifications define system-level object services that extend the bus. That is, CORBAservices are a set of services implemented by

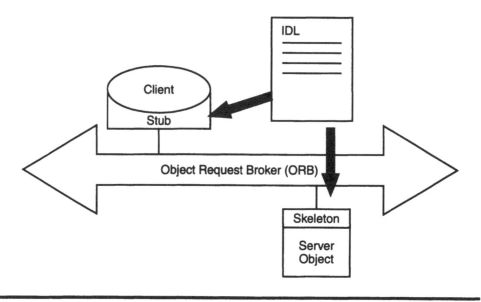

Exhibit 4.3   Client Stub and Server Object Skeleton

the ORB. The CORBA objects know about the services and how to use them because they are defined via an IDL specification. There are currently 16 different services specified:

1. *Collection service:* supports the grouping of objects and the ability to manipulate the objects as a group
2. *Concurrency service:* mediates concurrent access to an object so that consistency of the object is not compromised when it is being operated upon by concurrently executing processes or programs
3. *Event service:* communicates events between objects
4. *Externalization service:* defines the protocols and conventions to allow the state of an object to be saved in a stream of data (i.e., externalized) and later be internalized into a new object
5. *Licensing service:* allows license attributes to be combined and derived to support flexible licensing policy implementations
6. *Life cycle service:* defines services and conventions for creating, deleting, copying, and moving objects
7. *Naming service:* allows names to be bound to objects; name binding is always defined relative to a naming context
8. *Notification service:* extends the event service by allowing suppliers and consumers of events to have better visibility into events and more flexibility in subscribing to events
9. *Persistent object service:* provides common interfaces to the mechanisms used to retain and manage the persistent state of objects
10. *Property service:* supports the dynamic creation and deletion of an object's properties, whereas CORBA attributes defined in the IDL are static

11. *Query service:* supports the manipulation of collections of objects; manipulation in this sense refers to selection, insertion, update, and deletion
12. *Relationship service:* allows entities and relationships between objects to be explicitly represented
13. *Security service:* defines the following security functions: identification and authentication, authorization and access control, security auditing, non-repudiation, security administration, and optional confidentiality
14. *Time service:* allows a user to obtain current time and an error estimate associated with it
15. *Trading object service:* facilitates the offering and discovery of instances of services of particular types.
16. *Transaction service:* supports the concept of a transaction that has the following characteristics: it is atomic, it produces consistent results, it is isolated, and it is durable

The CORBAfacilities (or CORBA Common Facilities) specifications are a set of services that different applications may share. Like CORBAservices, the CORBAfacilities provide an enhanced set of services and are defined by IDL. CORBAfacilities differ from CORBAservices in that they are less fundamental than CORBAservices. There are currently only two facilities that have reached the point of formal documentation, although work is ongoing in the OMG to define more facilities. The current facilities are:

1. *Internationalization and time:* allows data to be localized to a particular locale; the six categories of data controlled by locale are: character classification and case conversion, collation order, date and time formats, numeric formatting (both non-monetary and monetary), and formats of informative and diagnostic messages and interactive responses.
2. *Mobile Agent Facility:* standardizes certain aspects of mobile agent communication to enhance interoperability between mobile agents; and deals with interoperability between agents written in the same programming language, not agents written in different languages.

The OMG is continually refining and expanding its list of domain-specific interfaces. These interfaces are specific to particular vertical markets and provide a framework and set of services for vertical applications. The domains that currently have at least one interface formalized are:

- business
- finance
- manufacturing
- medical
- telecommunications
- transportation

Interface Definition Language (IDL)

The Interface Definition Language (IDL) is the descriptive language used to describe the interfaces that client objects call and object implementations provide. An interface definition written in IDL is complete. A programmer of a client object can, given the IDL file associated with the destination object, make full use of all of the object's methods and access all of the attributes of the object.

IDL is a descriptive language, not a programming language. There are no programming constructs or statements at all. The syntax of IDL is based on C++ but the object can be written in any language for which there is an IDL mapping. The IDL mapping allows the IDL compiler to create the client stubs and object skeletons described earlier in this chapter. It is the IDL compiler that takes care of the conversion from IDL types and constructs to those of the native programming language.

The constructs supported by IDL to describe an object are as follows:

- constants
- data type declarations
- attributes
- operations
- interfaces
- modules

Lexical analysis of an IDL file identifies five types of components:

1. *Identifiers.* Identifiers must start with a letter and be followed by zero or more letters, numbers, or underscore characters. There are no valid punctuation marks within an identifier except for the underscore character. One unusual attribute of IDL is that identifiers are case sensitive, but two identifiers that differ only in case cannot coexist in the same name space. The reason for this is that the IDL may be mapped to a language that is not case sensitive, and therefore in the mapping two identifiers that differ only in case could not be differentiated.
2. *Preprocessing.* Similar to C++, IDL has certain macros that are processed first, before the other lexical analysis is performed. IDL uses the same preprocessing macros as C++: #include, #define, #ifdef, and #pragma.
3. *Keywords.* There are 47 keywords that are reserved and may not be used otherwise, such as for identifiers. Most of the keywords are in lowercase only (except FALSE and TRUE), but identifiers cannot be used that are identical to keywords except for case.
4. *Comments.* There are two styles of comment delineation in IDL. The C++ character combination "/*" begins a comment and "*/" ends it. In addition, the remainder of the current line of text is a comment when preceded by "//". Comments cannot be nested.

5. *Punctuation*. There is a set of lexical rules as to the usage of curly braces, semicolons, colons, parentheses, and commas.

Names (identifiers) within IDL must be unique within a defined name space. In IDL, a name space is defined as those within a given module. The module is identified as one of the IDL constructs and there is usually a one-to-one relationship between module and IDL file.

An interface can be derived from another interface. This is analogous to object inheritance. The *derived interface* inherits the constants, types, attributes, exceptions, and operations of the *base interface*. The derived interface can then declare new elements and even modify the elements of the base interface. An interface can also inherit from more than one interface, resulting in multiple inheritance. Exhibit 4.4 illustrates common inheritance examples. In the case on the left, interface B and C both inherit from base interface A, but B and C have no direct relationship to one another. In fact, B may modify or redefine the elements it has inherited from A, so that B and C are quite different. In the example on the right, interface D inherits from both B and C, which have in turn inherited from the same base class A. This diamond shape of inheritance is legal but references to the various base classes must be unambiguous.

The language neutrality of CORBA forces one limitation upon it not shared by the Java object technologies. CORBA requires all objects to be defined by an IDL. Even objects that are dynamically discovered by client objects using the Dynamic Invocation Interface (DII) must have IDL definition files that are compiled and available in a CORBA interface repository (IFR). JavaBeans, on the other hand, supports introspection and reflection. As defined in Chapter 3, introspection is the ability of other components and tools to discover the PME (Property/Method/Event) interfaces of the bean. Reflection allows an external entity to discover the signature of the bean's interface in real-time. This can be done in the Java technologies because the other components and tools utilize the same language — Java. The APIs for accomplishing introspection and reflection are defined in Java, and any program written in Java can make

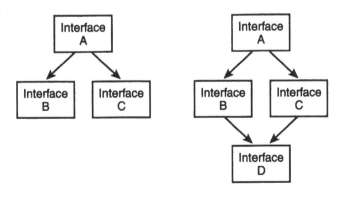

Exhibit 4.4   Single and Multiple Inheritance

use of the APIs. CORBA, on the other hand, assumes that an entire object system can be developed in many different languages and thus requires a language-independent means of describing objects — IDL.

Fortunately, tools are available on the market that will generate IDL on-the-fly, in real-time, directly from an object-oriented language. These tools, combined with the Web distribution of IDL files, will simplify the management, maintenance, and distribution of IDL files. Also, as an organization builds its library of objects, the objects can be added to the interface repository and discovered by client objects in real-time. An IDL file is still required, but it can be compiled and stored in the repository as soon as the server object is created.

Object Request Broker (ORB)

Conceptually, the ORB is the object bus that provides the means of communication between clients and objects. Locating objects and other mechanisms are transparent to the client. The ORB, in essence, is the entity that allows the distributed objects to exist and interoperate without having detailed knowledge about the rest of the environment. The ORB provides a wide variety of distributed middleware services (CORBAservices) and facilities (CORBAfacilities), as detailed earlier in this chapter. ORBs from different vendors can interoperate with one another as long as they support CORBA 2.0 or above.

The ORB has a number of different interfaces to clients, objects, and repositories that allow it to perform its tasks. Exhibit 4.5 illustrates the structure of an ORB.

On the client side, the ORB supports static interfaces via the IDL stubs generated from an IDL compiler. Dynamic interfaces are supported through the Dynamic Invocation Interface (DII). Both the client and the DII have access to an Interface Repository that contains precompiled IDL definitions of objects that the client can invoke and access. The operation of these client-side elements and interfaces is described later in this chapter.

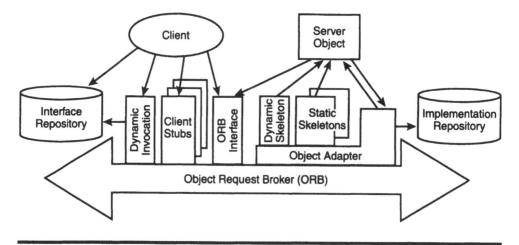

Exhibit 4.5 Structure of an ORB

On the object side, the ORB supports static object definitions by way of the object skeletons that, like the client stubs, are generated by the IDL compiler. The Dynamic Skeleton Interface (DSI) is the dynamic server interface that corresponds to the DII. The DSI handles incoming method calls for components that do not have precompiled skeletons. The object adapter sits between the ORB core and the static and dynamic interfaces. The object adapter accepts requests for service on behalf of the server object. There are two object adapters defined in CORBA: the basic object adapter (BOA) and, new to CORBA 3.0, the portable object adapter (POA). The object adapter has access to the Implementation Repository, which provides runtime information about classes and objects. These server-side elements and interfaces are further described later in this chapter.

In addition to these client-side and server-side specific interfaces, the ORB has a set of APIs (the ORB Interface) that are available to both clients and server objects. Most services provided to clients and server objects are provided by way of the static and dynamic interfaces. Therefore, the ORB Interface contains only a handful of operations that are common to all object types. The types of operations supported by the ORB Interface are:

- convert object references to strings, and vice versa
- obtain information about the ORB services supported
- perform object reference operations common to all objects
- obtain initial object references
- create type codes
- manage threads

The CORBA specifications do not specify how an ORB should be implemented. The ORB vendor is free to design the ORB as a singular process or as multiple components. In practice, most ORBs are implemented as multiple components because a single-process ORB would become a communication bottleneck. A common structure for commercially available ORBs is a structure with two sets of libraries, one linked to each client and one linked to each server, and a daemon process that runs on each host supporting CORBA services. The daemon ensures that all CORBA servers are launched properly and that clients can make connections to servers. Once the client and the server are connected, the communication takes place directly between these two components without involvement of the daemon. This structure enhances scalability of the CORBA servers.

A specific ORB may or may not support all of the CORBAservices and CORBAfacilities defined by the OMG. Because these services and facilities are under almost constant revision and update, it is important for an IT manager to understand which services are supported by the ORB being evaluated or implemented. For example, the OMG Naming Service is evolving into a superset called the Interoperable Naming Service (IONA). With this new specification, load balancing extensions are supported, in which a group of objects can be registered under a single name. The naming service will then allocate client references among the group so that the client load is spread among the group of objects. Other important features that differentiate the offerings of different ORB vendors are system management and configuration, server platform support, development tool support, multithreaded operation, server scalability and performance, server availability and fault tolerance, and security.

Client Implementation and Interfaces

In the CORBA world, a client is a program or process that invokes (server) objects by way of the ORB. The interfaces from the client to the ORB, as already detailed, are the client stubs for static objects and the DII for dynamically discovered objects. A client is, by definition, the requester of a particular operation. Therefore, there may be two objects, A and B, that are peers to one another. Each object invokes operations or methods on the other object. When A invokes methods on B, A is the client for that operation and B is the server-side object. When B invokes methods on A, B is the client for that operation and A is the server-side object. This differs from the traditional client/server paradigm, in which the client and server roles are typically fixed.

The programmer of the client can work in any programming language for which there is an IDL mapping. The programmer writes server object method calls as if they are local calls. The programmer does not need to know the location of the server object or the language in which it is written. When the client code is compiled, either the stub generated by the IDL compiler or the DII access library is linked to the client, depending on whether the server object is static or dynamic. There is a single DII library and one IDL stub for each object type, which is illustrated in Exhibit 4.6.

The client stubs for static objects are typically created at the time the server object is created. The IDL describing the server object is run through the IDL compiler. The server skeleton is created that is appropriate for the programming language of the server object. Multiple client stubs representing multiple different target client programming languages can be created as well. At client compile time, the appropriate stub is linked to the client. There can be multiple

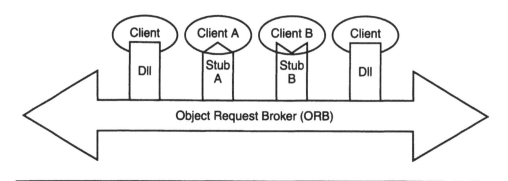

Exhibit 4.6   Client's Interface to ORB

different clients that all invoke the same server object, each written in a different programming language. Their stubs will be different because they will be implemented in the different programming languages. However, the functionality offered each client is the same. The IDL compiler makes sure that the functionality is the same despite the different programming languages.

If the client program uses the dynamic interface rather than the static stub interface, then the DII library is linked to the client program at compile time. Before this occurs, however, the IDL compiler must write the compiled description of the server object to the interface repository. The interface repository can be thought of as a runtime distributed database that contains the compiled IDL information (or *metadata*) for all registered components. Clients use the DII to discover the description of the registered components, the methods they support, and the parameters they require.

Clients can access objects by directly specifying the object and obtaining an object reference from a server. Clients can also access objects by utilizing some of the CORBAservices discussed earlier. For example, a client can request an object by name using the OMG naming service. A client can also request an object that meets a specific set of criteria using the trading object service.

Once the client has obtained the object reference using one of the means described, the client can then invoke methods on the server object. The following call modes for method invocation are available to the client:

1. *Synchronous.* The client sends a request and waits until it receives a reply from the server before performing other tasks.
2. *One-way/poll.* The client sends a request but does not wait for a reply. Instead, it occasionally polls the server until the server responds with the results.
3. *One-way/callback.* The client sends a request and includes a callback object reference. When the operation is complete, the server invokes the callback method on the client.
4. *One-way/event service.* This mode is similar to the previous one but it employs the CORBA event service for notification. The client first asks to be notified by the event service when a completion message is dispatched. It then sends the request to the server. The server sends a completion message to the event service when the operation has completed, and the event service in turn notifies the client.

Server Object Implementation and Interfaces

A *server object*, also called the *object implementation*, is an instance of the object class that has defined methods that other processes or client objects invoke. As already stated for clients, the server object is relative to a particular operation. Therefore, if object A invokes a method on object B, then B is the server object for the duration of that method. The roles of A and B can be reversed in subsequent method invocations.

A server object must have its server interface specified in IDL, as previously discussed. Once the IDL is created, it is compiled and a server skeleton is built in the native language of the server object. This server skeleton performs the reverse process of the client stubs — that is, it translates from the wire protocol to the in-memory data structures of the object. The complete executable server object is created by linking the server program and the skeleton produced by the IDL compiler. It should be noted that the existence of a skeleton does not necessarily imply the existence and use of client stubs. Clients may access a server object using the DII although the ORB accesses the server object through a skeleton.

Object implementations can also be invoked through a Dynamic Skeleton Interface (DSI). This interface allows the object to be reached through an interface that provides access to the operation name and parameters so that the object can respond dynamically to them rather than being tied to a predefined operation through a skeleton. This server-side dynamic interface is analogous to the client-side DII. However, note that a client can access an object through the DSI using either a static client stub or the dynamic client interface, the DII. There is a single DSI per object implementation and there may be multiple skeletons; this is illustrated in Exhibit 4.7.

On the client side, the client has direct interface to the ORB through the client stub and the DII. As Exhibit 4.7 shows, this is not the case on the server object side. Instead, there is a separate piece, the object adapter, that sits between the skeleton/DSI interfaces and the ORB. The skeleton/DSI interfaces do not directly interface to the ORB because different object adapters may be used to suit different implementations.

Besides providing the "glue" between the server interfaces and the ORB, an object adapter is the primary means for an object implementation to access services provided by the ORB. Services that are accessible through the object adapter include generation and interpretation of object references, method

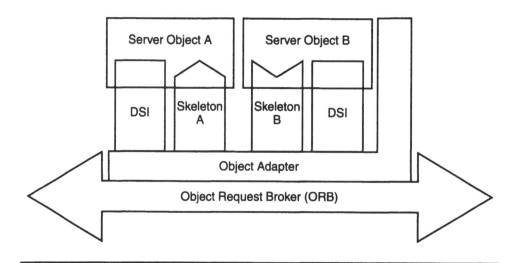

Exhibit 4.7   Server Object's Interface to ORB

invocation, security of interactions, object and implementation activation and deactivation, mapping object references to implementations, and registration of implementations. The OMG anticipated that there would be a few object adapters widely available on the market, with interfaces that are appropriate to a specific set of objects. The OMG has defined two standard object adapters: the basic object adapter (BOA) and the portable object adapter (POA). The POA is a refinement of the BOA and is defined in the CORBA 2.3 specification.

The basic object adapter (BOA) is the mechanism used by the object implementation to inform the ORB when objects come into existence and when running processes are ready to accept incoming requests for those objects. From the client's perspective, the BOA is the mechanism that ensures that a method invocation always reaches a running object that can respond to that method. The BOA launches processes, waits for the processes to initialize, and dispatches requests to the processes. The BOA is logically viewed as being a part of the ORB, but its implementation is usually divided between the ORB daemon, some pseudo-object code, and the code generated by the IDL compiler. The BOA specification, at the time of its adoption, was left intentionally vague because it was not clear at the time how the BOA would be implemented on various platforms. As a result, a number of discrepancies between different vendors' BOAs were introduced. Some vendors implemented proprietary extensions to fill the gaps in the standard.

As a result, the OMG has now defined the portable object adapter (POA), which is meant to replace the BOA. The intent of this new specification is that it is portable across multiple implementations and platforms so that ORBs from different vendors will have the same semantics. The POA specification refers to object implementations as *servants*. The POA is specified in IDL so that its implementation in a specific programming language is relatively automatic using the standard IDL language mapping facilities.

The POA defines standard interfaces to perform the following tasks:

- allow transparent activation of objects
- map an object reference to the servant implementing that object
- associate policy information with objects
- make an object persistent over multiple server process life cycles

The purpose of the POA is to dispatch incoming invocation requests to the correct servant object. The POA specification does not restrict the way in which servants are correlated to a CORBA object identity. POA defines a unique identifier, called an Object ID, that associates a CORBA object identity with a servant. A single servant can be shared by multiple object identities, or a servant can be started and ended for each single method call. This correlation is usually determined using a policy that is defined by the programmer of the CORBA server. This allows the programmer to determine the appropriate range of behaviors for the given implementation.

The POA is the basis for an evolving container model for CORBA components that is analogous to Java's EJB container model. The container model

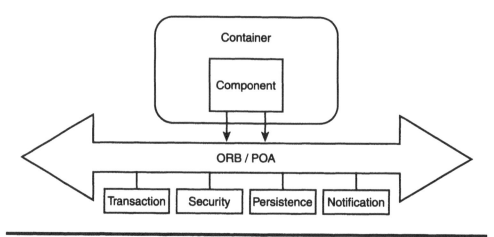

Exhibit 4.8   CORBA Container Framework

will provide a framework for server-based components and provide access to several CORBA services, such as transactions, security, events, and persistence. Exhibit 4.8 illustrates the container framework at a high level.

The current (not finalized) specification for the container model indicates that EJBs will appear to be simple CORBA components. However, the reverse is not true; a CORBA component will not appear to be an enterprise bean to a Java client in most cases. It is anticipated that the next version of the CORBA component specification will detail an EJB-style interface for CORBA components. In the meantime, it is recommended that EJB containers and CORBA containers be implemented side-by-side, with interoperability between them through the use of IIOP. An alternative implementation is to create a CORBA wrapper that surrounds the EJB, although this implementation may be more complex and less efficient. Exhibit 4.9 illustrates these two EJB/CORBA coexistence implementations.

The CORBA architecture recognizes the potential for a system to have several object adapters. However, the POA (and its predecessor, the BOA) is a required element. The OMG states that the POA can be used for most ORB objects with conventional implementations. For extraordinary objects that require a radically different set of services, a unique object adapter must be created.

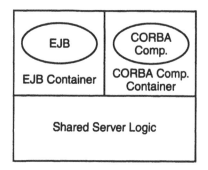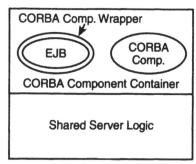

Exhibit 4.9   CORBA Component and EJB Coexistence

The final element on the server side of the ORB structure is the Implementation Repository. This is a storage facility that is proprietary and specific to each ORB and system on which it resides. It contains information on all object implementations defined to that server, and it enables the ORB to locate and activate implementations of objects. This runtime set of information includes data about the classes a server supports, the objects that are instantiated, and their IDs. The Implementation Repository is commonly used as a repository for other runtime information, such as trace information, audit trails, security, and administrative data.

CORBA Interoperability

Because the OMG membership includes a large set of vendors that are active participants, the consortium has always explicitly and tacitly recognized the existence of CORBA products from a variety of different vendors. The group has ensured that the specifications do not favor one implementation over another.

The CORBA interoperability specifications ensure that heterogeneous ORBs can coexist in an enterprise. The set of heterogeneous ORBs in an environment may be from different vendors, implemented on different platforms, and utilizing different native protocols. The goal of the interoperability specifications is to make these differences transparent and to support a common set of services in all environments. The CORBA interoperability specifications include an overall architecture document and a set of specifications that cover particular interoperability products and protocols. CORBA interoperability facilitates the creation of different ORB domains within an enterprise.

Interoperability Architecture

The primary goal of the interoperability architecture is to allow a client on one ORB to invoke an operation of an object that resides on a different and independently developed ORB. The interoperability must allow the two ORBs to interoperate without having any prior knowledge of each other's implementations. The interoperability architecture must also ensure that all ORB functionality is preserved so that there is no loss of function when one ORB interoperates with another.

To meet these requirements, the interoperability architecture recognizes the concept of an ORB domain. A domain is "a distinct scope, within which certain common characteristics are exhibited and common rules are observed over which a distribution transparency is preserved" (CORBA V2.3.1 Specification, Object Management Group, 13-2). Domains tend to be defined or based on administrative boundaries or technology boundaries. For example, administrative boundaries include naming regions, work groups, security domain, or systems management region. Technology boundaries include network protocol, syntax, or distributed computing environment. A single ORB

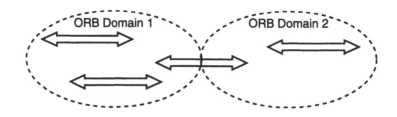

Exhibit 4.10   ORB Domains

can participate in multiple domains, and a single domain can span multiple ORBs. Exhibit 4.10 illustrates the concept of ORB domains.

A single ORB can be viewed conceptually as a multilayered entity, as depicted in Exhibit 4.11. At the lowest level is the ORB core. This is the indivisible and core functionality of the ORB. The ORB core contains the minimal functionality that allows a client to invoke an operation on a server object. At the next level higher is a set of ORB services. This level sits between the ORB core and the higher-level application layer. ORB services are invoked implicitly in the course of application-level interactions and range from fundamental mechanisms such as message encoding to more advanced features such as support for security and transactions. ORB services are different than Object Services in that they are not directly invoked by the application code.

In a single-ORB environment, all of these layers are present on the one ORB. There is no need for any specified mechanism for the various layers to communicate; that is left to the implementer to decide. However, in a multi-ORB environment, the ORB services layer of one ORB may need to communicate with the ORB services layer of another ORB. Thus, the interoperability architecture must define a means to allow the ORB services layers of two or more ORBs, in different domains, to interoperate.

The CORBA interoperability architecture further allows that ORB services can be considered independently and associated with different domains. This means that a single ORB can participate in multiple different types of domains, and each domain can contain a different set of ORBs based on the service it

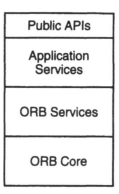

Exhibit 4.11   ORB as a Multilayer Entity

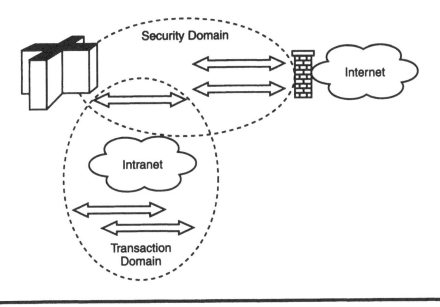

Exhibit 4.12   ORB Domains Based on Different ORB Services

defines. For example, a security domain might include all ORBs located in the corporate data center behind a secure firewall, and a transaction domain might include all ORBs that are used by a particular department of users that are located in both the corporate headquarters and branch locations. Exhibit 4.12 illustrates this concept.

The mechanism defined by the CORBA interoperability architecture to exist on the boundary between domains, mapping or transforming elements of the interaction, is known as an inter-ORB bridge. There are two types of bridges identified by the architecture: mediated bridges and immediate bridges. Inter-ORB bridges are detailed in the following section.

An important element of the interoperability architecture is the set of protocols used to communicate between different ORBs. The most basic and generalized protocol defined by the OMG is the General Inter-ORB Protocol (GIOP). The Internet Inter-ORB Protocol (IIOP) specifies how GIOP messages are carried in a TCP/IP network; both GIOP and IIOP are detailed later in this chapter. The interoperability architecture also accommodates inter-ORB protocols that are specific to a particular environment; these are known as environment-specific inter-ORB protocols (ESIOP). The most common of these is the DCE ESIOP. Exhibit 4.13 illustrates the relationship between these various protocols.

Inter-ORB Bridges

Inter-ORB bridges are entities that reside on the boundary between domains, translating or transforming elements of the interaction. Note that the term "bridge" to define this entity is a rather unfortunate use of terms, particularly

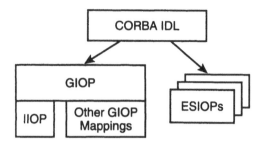

Exhibit 4.13   Inter-ORB Protocol Relationships

to anyone with a background in networking protocols. The reason is that a networking bridge performs no protocol translation; it operates at Layer 2 of the seven-layer OSI networking reference model (refer to Exhibit 1.4 in Chapter 1). An inter-ORB bridge, on the other hand, operates at much higher layers within the stack (Layers 4 through 7) and in networking terms would be called a gateway. Nonetheless, the term "bridge" remains in use because it is what is defined in the CORBA interoperability specifications. Inter-ORB bridges are always bi-directional.

There are two approaches to bridging between two domains. The simplest form is called *immediate bridging*, in which the elements of interaction are transformed directly, from the internal form of one domain to the internal form of another domain. Exhibit 4.14 illustrates the concept of an immediate bridge. Immediate bridging tends to be an efficient and optimal method because the bridge can be specifically engineered for the specific pair of domains. Immediate bridging is most commonly used when the domain boundary is administrative in nature (i.e., there is no change of technology). A single product or process that implements an immediate bridge is known as a full bridge because it implements both halves of the bridging process.

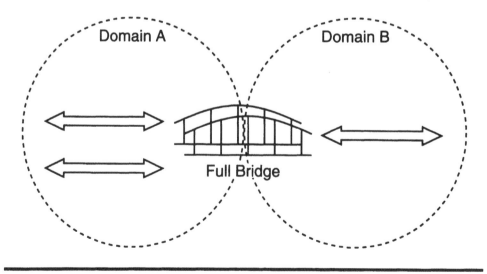

Exhibit 4.14   Immediate Bridging

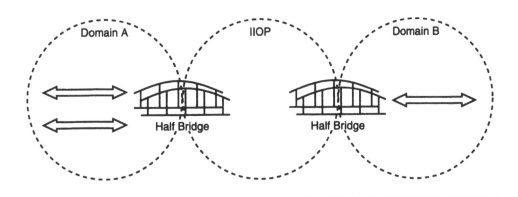

Exhibit 4.15   Mediated Bridging

The second form of bridging is called *mediated bridging*, and is depicted in Exhibit 4.15. In this form of bridging, the internal forms of each domain are transformed into a common, agreed-upon form. The product or process that translates from the internal form of one domain into the common form is known as a half-bridge. IIOP is the common basis for most mediated bridging environments, although this is not a requirement. Two ORB vendors could have a private agreement in which each vendor would implement a half-bridge that is based on a common but proprietary protocol. Alternatively, there could be multiple common forms that are widely implemented, each optimized for a different purpose.

The location of a full bridge or half-bridge is left up to the implementer. Bridges can be separate, stand-alone products that exist outside of any ORB. They can be processes that run on the same server as the ORB. Or, they can be implemented as functions internal to a particular ORB. Bridges that are implemented internally to an ORB are known as in-line bridges, while those that operate outside of an ORB process or system are known as request-level bridges.

In-line bridging is the most direct bridging level because it is implemented entirely within a single ORB. In-line bridging can be used to implement either immediate bridging or mediated bridging. ORB internal APIs must be defined, along with an inter-process communication scheme. The software components that implement the bridge can exist as additional services within the ORB or as additional stub and skeleton code. Note that the construction of an in-line bridge will usually require the programmer to have detailed, potentially proprietary information about the internals of the ORB.

Request-level bridges are built using application-style code outside the ORB to perform the translation or mapping. These bridges use the standard, public CORBA APIs, including the Dynamic Skeleton Interface, to receive and issue requests. A request-level bridge must also, however, implement special-purpose APIs that allow the transmission of ORB service information from one domain to another, as described earlier and depicted in Exhibit 4.12. A request-level bridge can be used to implement either immediate bridging or mediated bridging. The construction of a request-level bridge can be built by anyone who has access to an ORB; internal information about the ORB is not required.

In the CORBA object model, an *object reference* is defined as an object name that reliably denotes a particular object. A particular object name always resolves to the same object, although a particular object could be known by multiple different object names. The object reference, however, is bounded by a name space that corresponds to the domain in which the object resides. This implies that object references that cross domain boundaries must be transformed from one domain to the next. Because domain bridges are bi-directional, the transformation in the reverse direction must always resolve to the same object. The interoperability architecture has dealt with this by defining an Interoperable Object Reference (IOR). The IOR is a data structure that contains information about the object's type, the protocols supported, and the ORB services supported in the invocation. The IOR is used within bridges and is not expected to be used internally within an ORB or to be visible to application-level CORBA programmers.

General Inter-ORB Protocol (GIOP)

The General Inter-ORB Protocol (GIOP) specifies a low-level data representation and a set of message formats to facilitate communication between ORBs. GIOP is designed to work over any connection-oriented transport protocol that meets a minimal set of assumptions. Therefore, GIOP could work equally well over Novell's IPX/SPX, IBM's SNA, or TCP/IP networks. The standard for GIOP over TCP/IP is IIOP, which is detailed in the next section. Exhibit 4.13 illustrates the relationship between GIOP and the various possible underlying networking transports. ORBs that implement GIOP with different transport layers could not directly communicate with one another, but it would be simple and straightforward to provide a gateway that would convert from one networking transport to another.

According to OMG's CORBA 2.3.1 specification, the following objectives were pursued in designing GIOP:

1. *Widest possible availability*. GIOP (and IIOP) is based on the most widely used transport mechanism (i.e., TCP/IP) and defines a minimum set of additional layers to transfer CORBA requests between ORBs.
2. *Simplicity*. GIOP is intended to be as simple as possible while still meeting its functionality goals.
3. *Scalability*. GIOP is intended to support networks of ORBs and bridged ORB domains that meet and exceed the size of today's Internet.
4. *Low cost*. The cost of adding GIOP to an existing ORB should require a small engineering investment to encourage the vendor community to adopt it.
5. *Generality*. GIOP is intended to work with a variety of different network transports in addition to TCP/IP.
6. *Architectural neutrality*. GIOP makes minimal assumptions about the architecture and implementation of ORBs and agents that support GIOP.

The GIOP specification consists of three elements:

1. *The Common Data Representation (CDR) definition:* a transfer syntax that maps OMG IDL data types to wire-level representation (i.e., how the data is represented as it flows across the network) for transfer between ORBs and inter-ORB bridges
2. *GIOP message formats:* a set of messages that is exchanged between GIOP agents (i.e., ORBs and bridges) to facilitate object requests, locate object implementations, and manage communication channels
3. *GIOP Transport Assumptions:* general assumptions that are made concerning any network transport layer that may be used to transport GIOP messages

IIOP adds another element to the GIOP specification — the Internet IOP Message Transport. This element specifies how agents open TCP/IP connections and use them to transfer GIOP messages.

Internet Inter-ORB Protocol (IIOP)

From a simplistic standpoint, IIOP is just one of the legal transports for GIOP that provides support for TCP/IP networks. However, due to the pervasive influence of the Internet, the Web, and Java, IIOP is much more important to CORBA than that. IIOP has become the *de facto* standard for communication between ORBs and also between CORBA and Java environments. Since CORBA 2.0, IIOP has been a required element of all ORBs. IIOP also forms the basis for most implementations of mediated bridges.

Each Interoperable Object Reference (IOR), described earlier, contains one or more profiles. A profile describes how a client can contact and send requests to an object using a particular protocol. All IORs that meet the CORBA standards must have at least one profile for IIOP. The IIOP IOR profile contains four elements: the IIOP version number, a string containing the IP address of the host, the port number on the host, and a key value used by the server to locate the specific object referred to in the IOR record.

Strictly from a CORBA and OMG standpoint, IIOP is a critical piece of the overall interoperability architecture. Its influence and importance has extended beyond the OMG, however, to include the entire Java community. Sun and IBM jointly worked to define RMI-over-IIOP. Remote Method Invocation (RMI) is the Java native means of invoking methods on remote objects in a pure Java environment. RMI-over-IIOP is the basis for seamless interoperability between Java environments and CORBA environments. RMI-over-IIOP allows Java programmers to build distributed applications that interoperate with CORBA ORBs and objects. Prior to the RMI-over-IIOP specification, Java programmers were required to learn CORBA's IDL and to specify their objects using this definition language. Now, with RMI-over-IIOP, programmers can pass Java objects (using the OMG Objects-by-Value specification) between the two environments. This will ease the adoption and increase the acceptance of CORBA interoperability to the new generation of Java programmers.

Proponents of IIOP see it as a key underpinning to the future of Web-based interactions. As detailed in Chapter 2, HTTP is a sufficient protocol for the transmission of Web pages. However, HTTP has several drawbacks when it comes to the programmatic and dynamic interchanges typical in a distributed object computing environment. As discussed in several points of this book, a distributed object environment can offer superior scalability, better programmer productivity, higher code quality, and many other benefits over traditional client/server programming approaches, including the Web browser–Web server client/server approach. IIOP will become another key transport for the Web as the adoption of distributed object applications — built using CORBA, Java components, or a combination of the two — becomes more pervasive over time.

CORBA Interworking

CORBA interoperability specifies how heterogeneous ORBs will communicate. With the addition of IIOP technologies to Java and with Java a legitimate language mapping option for CORBA components, the CORBA interoperability architecture also deals implicitly with the interoperability between CORBA-based component systems and Java-based component systems. What the interoperability specification and architecture do not take into account, however, is the interoperability between CORBA ORBs and other (non-Java) component models.

The only "other" component model that has any significant following and market share is Microsoft's COM (and DCOM and its related technologies). The OMG has defined an entire set of specifications to deal with the integration of CORBA and COM. These specifications define the CORBA Interworking architecture. The primary goal of this architecture is to allow objects from either system to make key functionality visible to clients using the other system as transparently as possible. The architecture specifies support for two-way communication between CORBA objects and COM objects. A CORBA client is able to view a COM object as if it were a CORBA object, and vice versa.

There are many similarities between CORBA and COM that allow the transformation between one model and the other to be relatively straightforward. Both the CORBA and COM models define an object as a relatively autonomous and discrete unit that makes its behavior known to others in the system through the use of a fully described interface. Both models have a definition language that defines objects; in CORBA it is IDL, and in COM it is the Microsoft Interface Definition Language (MIDL). CORBA defines a reference to an object by name, whereas COM supports interface pointers. Much of the interworking architecture simply deals with mapping the syntax, structure, and facilities of one model to the other.

However, there are some critical differences between the models that make the task of interoperability between objects in the two models less than trivial.

Many of these differences are based on the different initial design points of the two models. COM (and its predecessor, OLE) was initially designed to support document-centric objects that promoted the collaboration and sharing of information between different applications on a single desktop. Historically, the domain of a COM object was a single-user, multitasking visual desktop running Microsoft Windows, and operations were primarily defined for the visual manipulation of elements, such as cut-and-paste, drag-and-drop, etc. CORBA components, on the other hand, have been designed from the beginning to be distributed in a heterogeneous networked environment. The CORBA architecture has not been designed with a particular visual or desktop environment in mind. Having said this about the different design points of COM and CORBA, both models are growing and evolving. In particular, COM+ (the recent incarnation of COM) is designed to support a networked model of components.

The basic structure of the CORBA interworking model is depicted in Exhibit 4.16. On the left, within Object System A, is the client. The client can be a CORBA client, a COM client, or an Automation client (i.e., a special type of COM client that supports dynamic invocation). Within Object System A is an object called a View. The View is an object within A, mapped to the vernacular of A, that represents the target object within Object System B. The View presents an interface to A that corresponds to the methods supported by the object within B. The View Interface converts the requests from the client object in A into requests on the target's interface in Object System B. The View is logically a component of A and also of the bridge.

On the right side of Exhibit 4.16 is the server, which can be a CORBA server, a COM server, or an Automation server. In the center of the figure is the bridge, which is the conceptual entity that provides the mapping from one model to the other. Conceptually, the bridge holds an object reference of the target object in B. The bridge is the "glue" that joins A and B and can

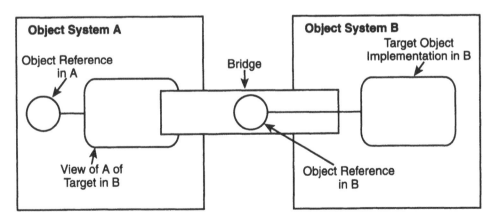

Source: CORBA V2.3, Interworking Object Model, June 1999.

Exhibit 4.16   CORBA Interworking Model

be implemented in any way that preserves all relevant object semantics (e.g., RPC, network shared memory). The interworking model does not constrain the implementation of the bridge. It can be implemented on the client system, the server system, or an intermediate machine.

Language Mappings

There are currently eight different language mappings specified by the OMG. The set of languages covered is diverse and includes object-oriented languages and those that are not. Obviously, the mapping from CORBA/IDL to object-oriented languages is relatively straightforward, whereas the mapping from CORBA/IDL to non-object-oriented languages can be quite complex. Exhibit 4.17 lists the languages for which there is a mapping, along with the version of CORBA that provides that mapping support.

For a system to be considered CORBA compliant, it must implement the CORBA Core plus one language mapping. The language mapping supported can be any of the eight valid mappings. The provision of additional mappings is considered optional; however, all language mappings supported must fully adhere to the relevant CORBA specification for the system to be considered CORBA compliant. The reason that only one mapping is a required element is because the OMG recognizes that only certain languages will be relevant for a particular site or environment. It is not the intention of the group to force products to support all languages when only a subset is required. The list of mappings is quite diverse and most environments will only have a few of the languages in their environment. For example, corporate enterprises will often have COBOL, C/C++, and now Java applications. Research and educational organizations, on the other hand, may have a base of Ada, Lisp, and Smalltalk applications.

The OMG maintains each mapping specification as a separate document. This underscores the fact that the complete implementation of a single mapping specification suffices for a system to be considered CORBA compliant. The details of the individual mappings are not covered here; readers interested in

Exhibit 4.17   CORBA Language Mappings

Language Mapping	CORBA Version Supported
Ada	CORBA 2.0
C	CORBA 2.1
C++	CORBA 2.3
COBOL	CORBA 2.1
Lisp	CORBA 2.3.1
Smalltalk	CORBA 2.0
Java to IDL	CORBA 2.3
IDL to Java	CORBA 2.3

learning about a particular mapping are encouraged to read the OMG spec- ifications, easily found on the organization's Web site. One interesting anomaly, which has particular relevance to the subject of this book, is the existence of two different Java mapping specifications: IDL-to-Java and its reverse, Java- to-IDL. No other language requires two different specifications. Why does Java?

The first specification, IDL-to-Java, is a standard mapping of CORBA's IDL to the Java *language*. Like the other mappings, this specification deals with the details of how IDL constructs map to Java's types, data structures, constants, etc.

The second specification, Java-to-IDL, is the specification that defines RMI- over-IIOP. Essentially, this is the specification that provides interoperability between the Java object model and CORBA. As already discussed, this spec- ification eases the convergence between the two programming communities because it makes it much easier for a Java programmer to write object-based systems that interoperate with CORBA environments. The specification defines a subset of the Java RMI API that is mapped to IDL and can run over GIOP/IIOP.

Final Thoughts

CORBA has been evolving for more than a decade. The ongoing goal for CORBA has been to foster the embrace and adoption of distributed object computing as a model for enterprisewide computing. The base set of CORBA services and facilities has been defined for some time, and now the OMG is working to extend the model, particularly in the areas of Java/Internet inte- gration and the further definition of industry frameworks to facilitate the development of vertical market applications.

The OMG has been incredibly effective in growing its list of members, now numbering over 800, and in keeping the ball moving with regard to CORBA evolution. Many similar consortiums run out of steam after the initial round of specifications. Critics may claim that the OMG is slow and late to enhance CORBA with integration of basic Internet concepts like URL naming and firewall support (although both are coming in CORBA 3.0). They may point to Java as an example of a broader set of technologies than CORBA that has evolved faster than CORBA.

This criticism can be countered with the simple observation that the OMG controls CORBA while a single vendor, Sun Microsystems, controls Java (albeit with an input process known as the Java Community Process). A consortium of competing vendors and end users, each group with its own priorities and agenda, may very well be slower than having a single entity in the driver seat. However, the output of a consortium is almost certain to be vendor- neutral. It is difficult to argue that Sun does not have some advantage over other vendors by maintaining control of Java.

In reality, viewing Java and CORBA as directly competing models is not accurate. The currently available versions of J2EE and CORBA systems are interoperable. Future versions will support even greater integration of the environments, to the extent that a single container will be able to run both types of objects. However, the Java technologies will always be tied to the Java language and therefore targeted as a new generation of distributed object applications.

CORBA's support for a variety of languages, in addition to Java, enables enterprises with legacy applications to build object wrappers or interfaces to the legacy code with relative ease. This is CORBA's real strength. As some CORBA advocates like to point out, in ten years Java may be considered a legacy language. CORBA will support that, as well as a long list of other legacy programming languages, in addition to new ones.

Chapter 5

Application Servers

Application servers are complex products that encompass many different technologies. Often described as middleware, application servers sit in the middle of diverse technologies and provide the glue to create a unified whole. The goal of the previous three chapters has been to provide a brief description of the key technologies with which application servers integrate or interoperate with.

Chapters 5, 6, and 7 focus on application servers. This chapter provides an overview of the market, the architecture, and the packaging of application servers. Chapter 6 describes some of the characteristics that should be designed into an enterprise infrastructure that includes application servers. Chapter 7 discusses some real-world implementation issues, highlights some case studies, and provides an overview of some of the application servers available today.

There is no doubt that application servers are a hot topic. The trade press is filled with articles about application servers. The number of vendors claiming to have an application server product grows almost daily. One Web site devoted to application servers currently lists 66 separate vendors participating in the application server market.

Unfortunately, the term "application server" is sufficiently vague that it could mean almost any server-based platform that supports applications. Indeed, the 66 vendors listed on the application server Web site mentioned offer a very diverse set of products.

One word that is frequently used to describe an application server is middleware. This is an intuitive term because application servers are utilized in three-tier distributed computing environments and represent the middle of the three tiers. The term "middleware," however, has been around since the earlier days of client/server, predating the Web, and has meant many different things, depending on the background of the person or company using the term. For example, middleware has been used to describe everything from a database replication product to a transaction processing monitor.

In Chapter 1, an application server was defined as "a component-based, server-centric product that allows organizations to build, deploy, and manage new applications for i•net users." This definition is more specific than the term "middleware." There are three key aspects of the definition:

1. Application servers are based on a distributed object computing model such as EJB, CORBA, or Microsoft COM.
2. Applications servers facilitate all three activities (build, deploy, manage) related to new application development.
3. Application servers communicate with i•net-based users using the public Internet, a corporate intranet, or a partner extranet. This implies Web-related protocols and client software.

The remainder of this book deals with products that meet this definition.

Market Overview

The application server market is rapidly evolving and growing. New vendors enter the market regularly. The current market leaders are more firmly establishing their lead and growing their market shares, while a number of vendors are carving out their particular niche in the market. Big established companies and smart newer ones are competing on an equal footing. The Java 2 platform in general, and J2EE in particular, is dominating the more established and mature COM and CORBA technologies. Vendors are attempting to differentiate themselves from the pack by offering a range of application servers targeted to different environments and also offering a range of solutions that extend the application server.

Market Size and Growth

The major technology research firms agree on this: the application server market is poised for explosive growth. The actual size of the market may be in dispute, but it is not disputed that the market is growing to become a multi-billion dollar market.

According to the Giga Information Group, a research firm specializing in technology for E-business, the application server market is estimated to have been $585 million in 1999. The firm has estimated that the market will reach $1.64 billion in 2000 and $9 billion in 2003.[1] This estimate indicates the market will grow by 98 percent per year between 1999 and 2003. International Data Corp. and Forrester are apparently not quite as bullish. These two firms apparently predict that the market will be approximately $2.5 billion in 2003.[2]

Without having access to the full research reports, it is impossible to know the reason for these discrepancies. Some of the possible reasons include:

- different definitions of what an application server is and therefore inclusion of a different set of products in the market size extrapolation

- different pricing assumptions, particularly the assumption of the average sales price per unit three years in the future
- different assumptions on the growth of demand in the various world-wide geographies (North America, Europe, Latin America, the Middle East, Africa, the Pacific)

Despite the market size projection differences, the research firms agree that the application server market will be a substantial market in the future. To demonstrate this, take a midpoint estimate that the revenue generated by application servers, worldwide, in 2003 will be $5.75 billion. To estimate the number of licenses this represents, one must make some assumptions about average sales price to the end user (i.e., not to the distribution channel). Today's list prices range from free (unusual) to a high of about $35,000 per CPU. One must consider that as the market matures, there will be some competitive pricing pressure. To estimate unit shipments, use a range of three different average sales prices (i.e., high = $15,000; medium = $7500; low = $3000). The resulting unit shipments are provided in Exhibit 5.1.

Exhibit 5.1   Calculated Unit Shipments in 2003

Market Revenue	Average Sales Price	Units Shipped in 2003
$5.75 billion	$15,000	383,333
$5.75 billion	$ 7,500	766,666
$5.75 billion	$ 3,000	1,916,666

It is obviously critical to get the average sales price assumption right. In this case, the unit shipments range from 383,000 units to almost two million. The "right" number is quite likely near the medium estimate, $7500 average sales price and 767,000 units. Nonetheless, any of these unit shipments represents a very sizable market. Remember that application servers, by definition, are installed on servers — not desktops PCs. The unit shipments calculated are for a single 12-month period, that is, the calendar year 2003. The installed base of units at the beginning of 2003 will already exceed one million units, and perhaps substantially greater than that. Although the precise size of the market in terms of both revenue and unit shipments is in question, the fact that this is an attractive and growing market is unquestionable.

Market Drivers and Customer Requirements

Given the indisputable fact that the application server market is growing, what are the factors driving this growth? The biggest single factor is the furious stampede of organizations trying to achieve E-business.

As described in Chapter 1, an organization's presence on the Web typically evolves in three stages. A static site that merely publishes information about the organization and its products and services using the Web characterizes the first stage. In the second stage, dynamic interaction with the user is added. Scripts and applets are used to achieve the second stage of Web presence. In the third and final phase of Web presence, all of the organization's key business processes are tied to the i*net. Customers, partners, and employees regularly carry out mission-critical interactions with the enterprise using the i*net infrastructure and Web-style interfaces.

To achieve this third phase, which is synonymous with achieving E-business, it is critical that organizations tie their legacy, client/server, and new Web applications together in a cohesive manner. The application server is a platform that enables them to do this. The CEOs and CIOs of almost every major organization have gotten the message — enterprises that do not have a Web strategy will cease to exist, and organizations that stay in the first phase of Web presence will eventually be wiped out by the competition. The very senior level of management understands that the achievement of E-business is essential to the future success of the organization. This is true whether the organization is a for-profit corporation, an educational institution, a nonprofit entity, or a government agency.

As stated in Chapter 1, IBM, a key thought leader in E-business, has defined E-business as "the transformation of key business processes through the use of Internet technologies." This, obviously, is a tall order for any organization, but especially for enterprise-class organizations that have a broad scope of operations and a wide geographical reach. Achieving this wide-reaching transformation places many requirements on the application server, which will be the key platform to allow an enterprise to achieve E-business. The most important requirements are common to most enterprises. These requirements, not particularly listed in order of importance, include:

- *Flexibility.* The application server platform should provide flexibility in supporting a wide variety of different client types, different operating systems and platforms, different legacy systems and application types, and different models of providing dynamic content (i.e., scripting, applets, servlets, server-side objects). It should be adaptable to support the future, as-yet-unidentified needs of the organization.

- *Open standards support.* The support for open standards is an important requirement because it provides flexibility of choice to the organization. If all platforms support open standards, then the organization is free to choose the appropriate platform to suit the needs of a particular task rather than being locked into a single vendor. Open standards support also allows elements from different vendors to interoperate, thus maximizing the value of the whole.

- *Scalability.* Many enterprises have tuned their internal systems to support the full complement of internal users. However, opening up these systems to a whole new set of external users has the potential to vastly increase the pool of users and tax the systems. Application servers must be able to scale to support many concurrent users, and should make parsimonious use of the resources of the systems with which they interoperate.

- *Integration with existing systems and technologies.* The key to an application server is its ability to integrate diverse systems and technologies. The application server platforms selected by a particular organization must be able to support all of that organization's legacy and new systems to allow the organization to transform its key business processes.
- *Support visual development tool of choice.* The key to rapid application development is the use, when appropriate, of integrated development environments (IDEs) that allow a programmer to quickly and easily manipulate visual objects on a screen and create code as a result. Many organizations have adopted one IDE (or perhaps a couple) as their primary tool. An application server should be able to support the organization's tools of choice.
- *Security.* Organizations that are opening their most mission-critical systems to the outside world have a paramount concern for security. If the mission-critical systems are attacked and altered, the organization could be in great danger. The application server platform should support an organization's chosen security policy and work with existing security technologies and solutions.
- *High availability.* If an organization is to depend on a system for all of its key business processes, then that system and infrastructure must be prepared to demonstrate availability figures approaching 100 percent. The application server must support and integrate with technologies and solutions that are designed to allow the infrastructure to survive the failure of an individual component.
- *Speed the development and deployment of new applications.* The "old world order" in which applications took years to build and deploy is over. New applications must be developed quickly, using a combination of off-the-shelf components and tools, and new business logic. They must be deployed easily and automatically, not requiring manual installation or upgrade to each client. The application server platform should facilitate the development and deployment of applications in an i*net environment.
- *Manageability.* In a highly complex n-tier environment, it is critical that problems can be avoided when possible. When they do occur, the problems should be easily diagnosed and resolved. The application server platform should provide visibility and control to the appropriate system and network management tools of an enterprise.
- *Leverage the current skill set of staff.* With the tight labor market a problem for all IT management, the application server should, to the extent possible, leverage the current skill set of the IT staff. Outside, additional training requirements should be minimized.

Each organization will prioritize these requirements differently and will likely add a few of its own. Each organization will also have its own list of specific systems, applications, and technologies that its chosen application server will need to support. Nonetheless, most of the requirements have one thing in common — they support the goal of transforming an organization's key business processes using Internet technologies. That is, they support the organization's ability to achieve E-business.

Application Outsourcing

One major market trend is intersecting with the growth of application servers. This trend is the growing willingness on the part of IT management to outsource certain applications. A whole new breed of service provider — the Application Service Provider (ASP) — has arisen in the past few years to deal with this trend. ASPs host specific applications, such as Enterprise Resource Planning (ERP) systems, and then rent them out to clients on some resource usage, transaction volume, or other pricing basis.

ASPs can utilize any technology they deem suitable to build their systems, including legacy hierarchical or traditional client/server systems. However, because they are in the business of supporting the ever-changing needs of their clients, they will likely look to implement systems that are flexible, expandable, and easily modified. As expressed several times throughout this book, an infrastructure based on a distributed object model enhances the flexibility of that infrastructure. In particular, it allows organizations to more rapidly deploy new applications that can be built from off-the-shelf components.

Quite simply, the application server is a very relevant platform for an ASP. With the growing availability of packaged CORBA or Java components, the ASPs will drive growth and adoption of distributed object-based application servers.

Diversity of Vendors and Solutions

The application server represents the confluence of many different technologies — legacy systems, traditional client/server systems, distributed object systems, and Web technologies. As such, the vendors that have entered and continue to enter the market come from a wide variety of backgrounds. This is depicted in Exhibit 5.2.

Each vendor brings its own unique perspectives and strengths to bear in its application server offering. Some of the solutions are very database centric. Other solutions offer a rich set of hooks to legacy and client/server systems. Still others address a particular niche such as the support of distributed numerical computing services. Some of the solutions are built solely on Microsoft ActiveX/COM technologies, while many others are focused on Java technologies and the J2EE platform. A handful of the solutions offer comprehensive support for COM, CORBA, and Java. Finally, there are several solutions that claim to support enterprisewide deployment with features such as fault tolerance, load balancing, security, and manageability.

The application server market is crowded, and many of the vendors' claims sound similar. Any enterprise planning to deploy application servers needs to

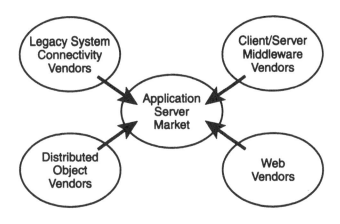

Exhibit 5.2   Vendors Entering the Application Server Market

undergo a careful evaluation, matching up the unique requirements of that organization with the features supported on the current breed of products. In addition, the ability of the potential vendor to support future requirements must be considered as well. For example, the probability that a small startup with excellent database integration capabilities will be able to offer solid and comprehensive support for traditional mainframe applications using old-style 3270 datastreams is pretty small. Chapter 7 concludes with a brief description of the capabilities of many of the current application servers available on the market.

Battle of the Component Models

The working definition of an application server being used in this book includes the term "component-based" as one of the major elements of the definition. An application server, by this definition, must support at least one of today's three common distributed object (component) models — CORBA, Java (EJB), or Microsoft COM.

Until late 1999, it was quite debatable (and heavily debated) which component model would prevail. CORBA is the most mature and complete of the models, and has a huge consortium of users and vendors behind it. Microsoft, as always, has extensive reach into most enterprise environments, and a number of vendors are willing to ride Microsoft's coattails by implementing its technologies. Java, while still very hyped and watched, had lost some of its luster when the network computer, thin-client model of computing failed to meet the expectations set by some of the early advocates. Nonetheless, the release of the Java 2 platform and J2EE has reversed Java's fortunes, particularly for server-side solutions such as application servers.

The Flashline.com Web site[4] maintains a comparison matrix of application server vendors and products. As of this writing, this Web site tracks 28 separate application server vendors. Of these, 27 vendors support the EJB specification in one or more of their products; 15 of the group, representing more than half, are currently J2EE licensees. The tide, at least for now, seems definitely to be turning in Java's favor.

This does not mean, however, that CORBA and Microsoft's COM have become irrelevant. Almost all of the Java solutions support RMI-over-IIOP (or will in a future release) for interoperability with CORBA environments. Some of the top-tier solutions are available from traditional ORB vendors (e.g., Inprise) that have extensively enhanced their products to support EJB and other Java technologies. The top tier of IBM's product line of application servers is built on a CORBA ORB foundation.

Until recently, Microsoft did not offer a stand-alone application server. Its application server functionality had been built into the Microsoft Internet Information Server (IIS) and the Microsoft Transaction Server (MTS). It now has a separate, stand-alone application server product called the Windows 2000 Application Center that boasts features that compete with leading application servers on the marketplace. However, as usual, the Microsoft solution is oriented to a Microsoft COM/ActiveX (only) environment. Some non-Microsoft application server vendors support COM, but usually in conjunction with Java or CORBA. The Microsoft approach and its COM-only product are expected to be widely implemented, especially in small and medium organizations. Larger enterprises that have a diverse set of technologies and a preference for UNIX as an application server platform will be expected to favor CORBA and Java approaches.

Differentiation

As the CORBA standards become more widely implemented and J2EE compliance becomes the norm, application server vendors will need to compete and differentiate their products based on more than just the core functionality defined by these architectures and specifications. Competition will take place on two fronts.

On the first front, application server vendors will augment their products with additional, value-added services such as those discussed in Chapter 6 (security, scalability, load balancing, fault tolerance, and management). The vendors will also craft offerings that are suitable for particular environments. For example, IBM already offers three versions of its WebSphere Application Server at three different price points, representing a low/medium/high amount of functionality. The packaging of application servers is explored in more detail later in this chapter.

On the second competitive front, application server vendors will offer related products that build upon the application server with specific functionality. For example, Bluestone Software supplements its Total-e-Server (formerly the Sapphire/Web application server) with a range of specific solutions such as its Total-e-B2B product, which automates the supply chain, enhances logistics operations, and extends E-business relationships. The set of related products is explored in more detail later in this chapter.

Pricing Models

As briefly mentioned, pricing models for application servers are varied. A few vendors are adherents to the open source initiative and offer their products at no charge. Most IT organizations in large enterprises, however, will prefer to buy their products from established vendors that offer software maintenance and support.

The most common pricing scheme licenses the software per CPU. Therefore, in a multi-CPU system, a customer would purchase one license for each CPU that will run the software. A handful of vendors price their software per server rather than per CPU.

The price targets tend to fall into three different ranges. The lowest pricing range is the sub-$1000 range. These tend to represent the lowest end of a particular vendor's application server product line. For example, IBM's Web-Sphere Application Server Standard Edition (which offers the least functionality of the three different editions of the product) carries a list price of $755 per CPU. The middle pricing range is the $5000-to-$10,000 range. This range is typical for smaller vendors that offer a single product, and for the middle tier of vendors with a multi-product line. For example, BEA Systems' WebLogic Server has a list price of $10,000 per CPU. The final pricing range is the $25,000-to-$35,000 range. This, obviously, represents a high-end product that is comprehensive in its support of component technologies and APIs. The BEA Systems WebLogic Enterprise Server, with a list price of $35,000 per CPU, is representative of products in this upper tier.

The Future of the Market

The application server market is poised both for dramatic growth and for dramatic change. Over the next two years, the number of solutions available will increase. There will be increased standardization of functionality as the J2EE and CORBA 3.0 specifications are implemented. The din of vendors clamoring to get their message out and position their offerings will be loud. Microsoft's solution will gain some traction as its capabilities become more widely known. However, it is doubtful that Microsoft will vanquish Java and CORBA. Just the simple fact that the Microsoft solution is limited to the Microsoft server platform is sufficient to limit its influence, at least within large enterprises. Higher-end UNIX and Linux servers (and even mainframes) are expected to be the usual platform of choice for application servers in large enterprises.

The pool of available Java and CORBA components will continue to grow as independent software vendors provide vertical market solutions and pre-packaged horizontal services. The availability of robust and diverse off-the-shelf components will further spur the adoption of application servers. Traditional integrators will offer customized solutions that are built using many standard off-the-shelf components.

Beginning around 2001, the market will begin to see consolidation as the winners pull away from the pack. It is too early to tell which vendors and solutions will survive, but the survivors selling into the enterprise space will have rich and robust solutions that go above and beyond the basic services detailed in the J2EE/CORBA specifications.

A General Architecture

The second element of the definition of an application server, from Chapter 1 and the beginning of this chapter, states that an application server facilitates three activities related to new application development: build, deploy, and manage. It is a fair question to ask what role the application server, per se, plays in the overall build-deploy-manage process.

IBM and many other vendors identify the build-deploy-manage process as a key application framework for E-business. In other environments, such as the traditional client/server environment or the hierarchical mainframe-based environment, an IT organization must build applications, deploy them, and then manage them in isolated and discrete steps. The deployment process, for example, can be very laborious in traditional environments. Code needs to be installed, usually manually, on each and every system. In a client/server environment with thousands or tens of thousands of clients, this step can be very labor intensive, expensive, and error prone.

The difference between the traditional models and the new model is that these steps are no longer individual and isolated steps. With Web and distributed object technologies, these three formerly discrete actions are all intertwined. At the center of the process is the application server, as depicted in Exhibit 5.3. The build-time tools speed development and deployment of components. These components, through the services of the application server, are made available to clients across the i*net. The management of the component and the application is an integral part of the services offered by the application server.

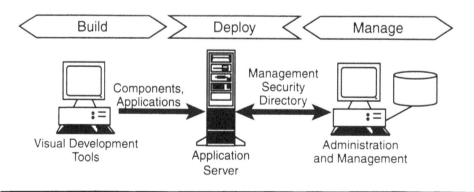

Exhibit 5.3   Application Server in the Build-Deploy-Manage Process

Exhibit 5.4 depicts how the application server fits in the overall enterprise environment. This was introduced in Chapter 1, but now the notion of different computing tiers has been added. The application server is one of the elements in the middle tier in a three-tier environment. This environment is comprised of client devices, an i*net, a Web server (or possibly multiple Web servers), the application server, and finally the external application and data sources that reside on a variety of legacy and other servers. These are the key architectural elements of an application server environment. However, note that this is a logical representation only. Physically, the Web server, the application server, and even the "legacy" data source could all reside on the same piece of hardware. Conversely, there may be multiple levels within each

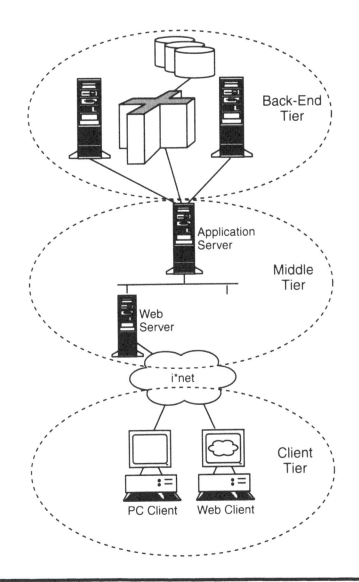

Exhibit 5.4   Three-Tier Environment

of the three tiers (client, middle, back-end). For this reason, some refer to this environment as an n-tier approach.

The following sections look at each of the architectural tiers: the client tier, middle tier, and back-end tier. In addition, the services provided within the network infrastructure are detailed. Finally, an overview of the development tools that facilitate the development and deployment of component-based applications is provided.

Client Tier

The client tier in an application server environment includes the programs that are operating on the client platform (i.e., browser, applet), the protocols used by the client to communicate with the application server, and the client side of the interaction it has with the application server to obtain services.

Client Access

The types of clients interacting with application servers can be very diverse and implement a variety of different technologies. Exhibit 5.5 illustrates an enterprise with many different types of client platforms. The clients access the application server through an internal corporate intranet, an external partner extranet, or the public Internet. Before examining the details of the various technical components of an overall solution, readers will want to examine the various factors and considerations to determine which client-side access technologies are most appropriate for a given situation.

Many of the clients within the intranet will be the usual desktop-based users who the IT department has traditionally supported. These users, equipped with desktop PCs or workstations, use a variety of packaged and custom software to do their jobs. The desktop systems are largely running a variety of the Windows operating system, although Macintosh and UNIX systems are dominant in certain environments. These desktop systems access an application server through a variety of different technologies. As stated in Chapter 2, Java applets and ActiveX controls are often a good fit for these employees because they tend to repeatedly use a small set of applications. The time and network bandwidth to download new applets/controls is minimal compared to the potential benefit of utilizing the client processor to share some of the computing burden, alleviating that chore from centralized servers. These clients will also support client-side components (JavaBeans, CORBA components, and COM components) and standard HTML/XML interaction.

The traditional set of desktop-based users has been augmented over the past few years with a growing set of employees who either travel a large percentage of the time or who telecommute. These users, while having computing needs similar to their desk-bound colleagues, present different challenges to the IT organization. Certainly, they pose a security challenge, but access speed is also a challenge. The traveling and telecommuting workers

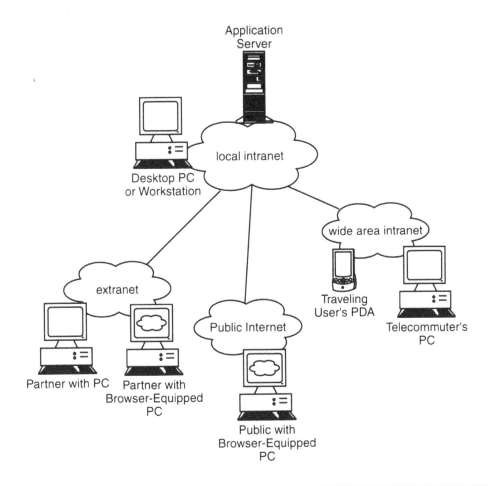

Exhibit 5.5   Clients within an i*net

do not have the benefit of the high-speed internal network. The traveling user may dial in over a 28.8-Kbps line, while the telecommuter may have an ISDN connection. To accommodate the telecommuter and traveling user, the IT organization may need to limit the use of downloadable applets or controls to very specific circumstances. There may be a heavier reliance on server-side scripts/servlets and also on distributed components.

An IT organization also needs to review the type of device used by the telecommuter and traveler. A telecommuter is likely to have a traditional desktop PC or workstation. In the past, traveling users almost always carried laptops, but more and more travelers are forgoing their laptops in favor of PDAs or other handheld devices that may have limited storage, computing power, and display area. These devices can be used for specific functions such as checking e-mail, but also to gain access to certain key enterprise applications. For example, the traveling sales rep may need to check order status and confirm delivery dates using a PDA that accesses an application server. Sun is trying to foster the implementation of the Java Virtual Machine on a variety of handheld devices, so JavaBeans may be common for these devices. For normal Web server interaction, Wireless Markup Language (WML; see Chapter 2) may become a standard wire protocol to these devices.

Extranet users are usually employees at an organization that is a supply chain partner or in some other formalized relationship with the enterprise. Examples of different types of extranet users include:

- auto dealers, independently owned and operated, interacting with the automobile manufacturing company to order cars, check delivery schedules, etc.
- manufacturing suppliers, interacting with the purchasing company using Material Resource Planning (MRP) and related systems
- banks and other loan agencies communicating with credit reporting companies
- retail operations interacting with credit card processors
- E-tailer interacting with express delivery companies to schedule and track package delivery
- two governmental agencies that require the sharing of data

Extranet-based users are in some ways similar to internal users, and in some ways similar to the general public over the Internet. They are similar to internal users in that they can be expected to be equipped with and trained to use PC/workstation systems. They are relatively sophisticated users who repeatedly use a specific set of applications. They usually have some internal help desk or technical assistance available to help resolve technical problems. However, they can also be similar to the general public in the sense that they may access the enterprise over the public Internet or slow direct-dial link. Available bandwidth may be an issue. The level of control that an IT organization has over its extranet users is widely variable. In some cases, the IT organization may be able to dictate equipment and software, as if the users were within the same organization. In other cases, the IT organization may only be able to recommend certain hardware and software, and the assumed common denominator may need to be relatively low (e.g., a Pentium PC with a browser).

It is this final issue — the level of control — that may be the first determining factor in what type of technology can be deployed at the extranet-based client. If there is no control, and cost and complexity need to be minimized, then a simple Web browser using standard HTML/XML may be the optimum solution. With more control over the level of software installed on the client, downloadable Java applets or ActiveX controls may be appropriate. If the organizations are closely related and the interaction is of sufficient volume, regularity, and mission criticality, then a distributed object approach is probably the best solution. The distributed object approach allows the two organizations maximum independence and autonomy while providing the most sophisticated functionality. Therefore, application servers are expected to be regularly deployed to support critical extranet connections.

Users over the public Internet present the IT organization with the widest diversity of hardware and software and the least level of control. Webmasters learned early on that requiring a particular browser level to view a Web site

Exhibit 5.6   Client Access Technologies by User Type

Network	Type of User	Client Device	Network Type	Client Access Technologies
Corporate intranet	Traditional internal user	Desktop PC or workstation	Typically have high bandwidth available	Components, client/server, applets, HTML/XML
Wide area intranet	Telecommuter	Desktop PC or workstation	ISDN connection	Components, client/server, HTML/XML
	Traveling or mobile user	Laptop, PDA, other handheld	Low-speed lines	Components, client/server, HTML/XML, WML
Extranet	High-volume or sophisticated user	Desktop PC or workstation	High-speed WAN connection	Components, client/server, applets, HTML/XML
	Casual business partner user	Browser-based PC	Low-speed line or public Internet	HTML/XML
Public Internet	Consumers	Browser-based PC or handheld	Low-speed, public Internet	HTML/XML, WML

earned the wrath of the public. They soon learned to accommodate various levels on the site and perhaps added the "best when viewed with..." disclaimer to indicate the optimum browser level. Early experiments with downloading Java applets to casual users over the Internet were less than successful, as impatient users abandoned transactions if they had to wait long seconds or even minutes for the download of code. In most cases, IT organizations should assume that the public accessing an enterprise's middle and back-end tiers will do so with only a minimal-level and basic Web browser using HTML. Sophisticated scripts and distributed object components can indeed be implemented within the enterprise, but the output to the client will be basic HTML (and eventually XML) in most cases.

Exhibit 5.6 summarizes the recommended client-side access technologies for the different types of users. These recommendations are generalizations. Unique requirements in a given circumstance need to be taken into consideration.

Client Architecture

The most basic client in an application server environment is a PC/workstation that supports a standard browser using HTML or XML, or a specialty device

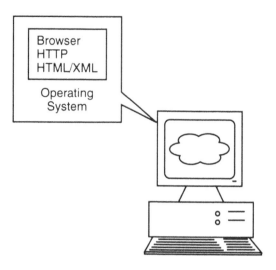

Exhibit 5.7   PC/Workstation with Browser

(e.g., PDA, handheld device) that supports a browser subset and possibly the WML protocol. The architecture of one of these systems is depicted in Exhibit 5.7.

A browser-only device has just two tasks in life: to request that files (i.e., pages) be downloaded from a Web server based on the click of a user's mouse, and to interpret and display or playback the multimedia Web pages that result from the request. However, this does not imply that there is only a simple Web server in the middle tier. The middle tier could be arbitrarily complex, with scripts, servlets, and distributed objects all cooperating and the end result being the simple HTML/XML/WML pages that are sent to the client.

A client system based on the CORBA component architecture may or may not be running a browser. A CORBA component, per se, does not have direct interaction with a browser program. A CORBA client can run any operating system, and the CORBA client program can be written in any language supported by CORBA. It only needs to have a client program with the appropriate stub, and the client component can communicate with ORB-based application servers. Exhibit 5.8 illustrates the architecture of a CORBA client.

The CORBA client must support IIOP to be able to communicate with an ORB. The client uses the services of the ORB (i.e., the CORBAservices and ORB Interface detailed in Chapter 4) to find an object, invoke methods on the object, and receive responses from the object. Because IIOP is now supported by the EJB specification, a CORBA client can also communicate with an EJB server. The CORBA client does not have (and does not need) information about the location of its target objects and the methods they support because everything the client needs to know has been included in the client stub. As detailed in Chapter 4, the client can also access objects dynamically using the ORB's Dynamic Invocation Interface (DII). The middle tier for CORBA clients will consist primarily of CORBA ORBs, EJB servers, and possibly target objects. The middle tier could be simple (i.e., a single

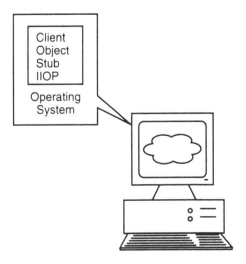

Exhibit 5.8 CORBA Client

server) or complex, but the simplicity or the complexity of the middle tier is transparent to the CORBA client.

A Java client is slightly more complex. The Java client, by definition, must support a Java Virtual Machine (JVM). The client may or may not be running a browser as well, but the most common Java client will be running a browser that contains a JVM. The browser's JVM is used to initiate and run applets and JavaBeans. Exhibit 5.9 illustrates a typical Java client.

The browser interaction with the middle tier will be via one of the standard markup languages (i.e., HTML, XML, or WML). However, once the browser

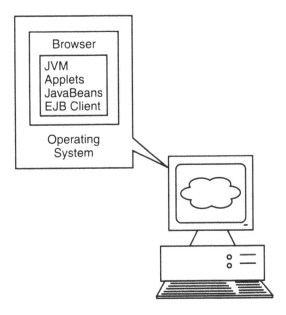

Exhibit 5.9 Java Client

invokes the local applet or bean, the applet or bean is in control. Client-based JavaBeans are usually local entities that represent graphical user interface objects and therefore do not usually communicate across the network. A client accessing an Enterprise JavaBean (EJB) will need to implement RMI in addition to the Java Naming and Directory Interface (JNDI) classes. This requirement will effectively limit the number of Java clients that directly access an EJB; instead, clients will communicate with a servlet using Web pages and the servlet will interface with the EJB. An applet is not limited to HTML/XML, IIOP, or any other single protocol. An applet can utilize any protocol required to communicate with its destination host or server, including a proprietary one (usually over TCP/IP). The middle tier in a Java-oriented environment will consist of standard Web servers, Java applets being stored for eventual client download, Java servlets, and EJB servers. Because of the IIOP-based interoperability between Java and CORBA, the middle tier may also include CORBA ORBs and CORBA-based objects.

A Microsoft client utilizing ActiveX controls and COM+ objects has an architecture similar to its Java client equivalent, except for one big difference: ActiveX controls can communicate directly with the Windows operating system and have direct access to all system resources. Exhibit 5.10 illustrates the architecture of a Microsoft client. This client will utilize Microsoft protocols for communication with a Microsoft-oriented middle tier. A "pure" Microsoft implementation would not include CORBA or Java servers in the middle tier. However, there are plenty of vendors that support products that bridge the gap between a COM environment and a Java/CORBA environment. Indeed, as detailed in Chapter 4, the CORBA specification details such interoperability and calls it "CORBA interworking."

A final possibility for the client is that it is based on a legacy client/server API and therefore does not adhere to any of the component models or rely

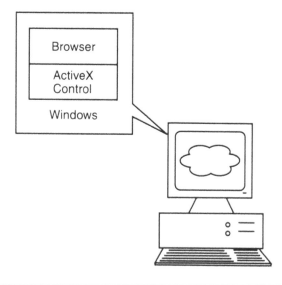

Exhibit 5.10   Microsoft ActiveX Client

on a Web browser. These clients, unless they are to be reengineered from
the ground up, still need to be able to work with a server using the traditional
API and networking approach (hopefully, the possible approaches include
TCP/IP). One example of a common client is one that supports the IBM CICS
client/server interface (the External Call Interface, ECI). Another common
example is a client that makes direct database calls using the standard ODBC
API. These calls may completely bypass the application server, or the application server may support these clients by implementing a gateway specific
to that particular API and protocol.

All of the client systems discussed, with the possible exception of the last
one (i.e., legacy client/server), are assumed to be using TCP/IP as the networking protocol. This somewhat goes without saying because the focus here
is on i*nets that, by definition, are TCP/IP networks. IIOP, HTTP, and the other
protocols mentioned all ride "on top" of TCP/IP. The TCP/IP clients will utilize
a number of different standards and technologies to augment the functionality
provided by the middle-tier servers. For example, TCP/IP-based Domain Name
Servers will be used to locate the Web and application servers. TCP/IP
standards will provide network-based service for security, file and print, IP
address allocation, etc.

Middle Tier

The middle tier of a Web and application server environment is where all the
action is. It is where static Web pages are stored, dynamic Web pages are
created, scripts and servlets are executed, and the applications based on one
or more of the common distributed object models are created and executed.
It is the middle tier that allows IT organization to realize the benefits of thin-
client computing, in which a vast user base spread across an i*net can access
a rich set of enterprise applications that seamlessly integrate the new with the
existing IT resources.

The design focus of the middle tier must start with an architecture that
facilitates change and growth. The distributed object models provide an
excellent starting point, allowing organizations to blend off-the-shelf objects
with new applications and new objects that encapsulate an organization's
unique business requirements. However, the IT organization must also design
in key capabilities to support the mission-critical nature of the new E-business
applications, namely, security, scalability, load balancing, fault tolerance, and
management. These elements are briefly discussed in this section, and then
explored individually in more detail in Chapter 6.

Elements in the Middle Tier

Exhibit 5.11 illustrates the various elements within the middle tier of an
application server environment that services i*net users. The elements within
the figure are architectural and the fact that they are depicted as separate

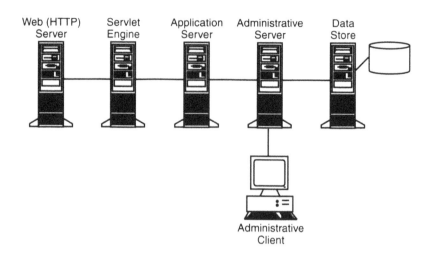

Exhibit 5.11 Elements within the Middle Tier

entities does not mean that they could not or would not all exist on a single server platform.

The first element in the middle tier is the Web server, also often referred to as an HTTP server. This server implements the HTTP protocol and downloads Web pages to client systems. Conceptually, the Web server is a pretty straightforward element. It attaches to the i°net and "listens" for incoming requests from clients. The requests are usually for the download of a Web page, which can contain text, graphics, multimedia files, and even applets.

The client HTTP request can also invoke a script, Java Server Page, Active Server Page, or servlet to initiate a dynamic interaction rather than to simply download static pages. Scripts, JSPs/ASPs, and servlets are all invoked through specifying a URL that equates to a file containing the appropriate type of code. These code files logically reside on and are executed by the element that is identified in Exhibit 5.11 as the servlet engine. The servlet engine is the element that supports dynamic interaction with the user through the use of forms, drop-down boxes, radio buttons, and check boxes. The interaction between the servlet engine and the end user is standard HTTP with one of the standard page descriptive languages (HTML, XML, or WML). Refer to Chapter 2 for further information on the interaction between Web browsers and Web servers and the use of scripts, forms, and servlets.

The third and central element in the middle tier is the application server. This element is based on an architecture that supports distributed objects and thus supports a CORBA ORB, the Java EJB specification and the Java Enterprise APIs, or a Microsoft COM platform. Some application servers available in the marketplace support more than one of these platforms. The application server, beyond supporting the fundamental framework for a distributed object model, also supports a set of common, system-level facilities and services that allow the programmer of the components to focus on creating business logic. The application server can be invoked in a variety of ways. It can be directly invoked by a client program that supports the client side of the appropriate distributed object model (e.g., CORBA client, EJB client). It can be invoked through IIOP (or some other protocol) by the servlet engine, another application server, or some other server in the enterprise.

The application server, in turn, can call a variety of other systems. For example, it can utilize IIOP or RMI-over-IIOP to invoke an object on another application server. It can directly invoke other programs through a standard API. It can also invoke back-end applications through an API, gateway, connector, or other means.

The fourth element in the middle tier is an administrative server and client. The client is the user interface through which the systems management staff controls the environment. Most administrative clients are based on a Web browser interface rather than special client-based software. The administrative server executes the administrative commands, communicates with the other elements in the middle tier, and accesses the administrative data. The administrative element supports configuration and systems management functions. It can implement or communicate with other elements that implement naming, directory, and security services. For example, the administrative server can communicate with a network-based policy server to implement and enforce an organization's security policy.

The fifth and final element in the middle tier is the device or system that stores information relevant to the application server or servers. For example, it can contain all application server configuration information. It can also include information relevant for the location and initiation of objects (e.g., the CORBA Interface Repository). It will usually also be a repository for traces, logs, and other information useful to the system and network administrators. This data store can be accessed via RDBMS calls to a centralized database server, or it can be accessed locally by the administrative server through system calls. Some application servers include a lightweight database management tool to facilitate management of this data.

Web Server/Application Server Design

The previous section discussed the five logical elements within the middle tier of an application server environment that services i•net users. In most enterprises, these five logical elements will be implemented on two or possibly three different groups of servers. These groups will usually consist of multiple different servers that are performing the same or similar tasks. The groups are viewed as a single logical entity because of scalability. Very few enterprises can support all of their Web server needs, for example, with a single server, even a very powerful and high-end server. Instead, they need to pool multiple servers together that function as a whole.

In the first group will be Web and servlet servers. These Web servers will serve static pages and also support scripts, Java Server Pages, Active Server

Pages, and servlets for dynamic content. This first group of servers can support many of the common and routine requests initiated by i*net users and can even directly access a database using a database API such as ODBC. For example, in a retail Web site, these servers will provide the home page and the first level of pages that describe the corporation and its mission statement, list corporate news releases and financial information, provide contact information, and post open employment opportunities. Retail organizations that also offer brick-and-mortar stores usually also provide a store locator facility that provides store location and hours of operation. These servers can support the online catalog viewing that the majority of the Internet users access. They will support the search/query forms that allow a user to search the online catalog for a group of products meeting a specific set of criteria. They will supply the descriptions, images, and pricing of items in the catalog with the help of a catalog database. In short, the Web and servlet servers will serve the majority of the requests of the browsing public on a retail Web site.

It is becoming commonplace that these Web and servlet server "farms" are becoming quite large. Some of the premier consumer-oriented shopping Web sites, for example, may have a data center with hundreds of PC or UNIX servers functioning as Web and servlet servers. Another common trend is to support server farms in multiple, geographically dispersed locations. With this approach, customers in Europe, for example, may be directed to the European server farm, while customers in Australia are directed to the Pacific server farm. This approach helps to speed response times to users and also provides system maintenance windows for the IT organizations supporting them. It is critical, of course, that users are shielded from having to know that there are multiple servers. Users should have a single URL that denotes "The Web Server," and the infrastructure should take care of appropriately apportioning sessions across the pool of available servers. The mechanisms for creating these server pools are detailed in Chapter 6.

The second group of servers in the middle tier is, of course, the application servers. The application servers house the server-side components that represent the new E-business logic. In a Java environment, the application server includes an EJB container and the Java Enterprise APIs detailed in Chapter 3. A CORBA application server is based on an ORB implementation, as detailed in Chapter 4. A Microsoft COM+ application server is based on the COM model. In any case, the application server supports the facilities and services to locate, initiate, and execute server-side components, as well as the ability to communicate with other application servers and back-end data and application systems.

This second set of servers can also support some of the servlets used to access EJBs, COM objects, or even CORBA objects. Recall from Chapter 3 and the previous section that implementing the client EJB interface is not really recommended for the client PC/workstation. The reason for this is that the EJB client uses RMI and JNDI to locate and communicate with the enterprise bean. Requiring these classes to be installed on all potential clients necessarily limits the pool of client machines that can access the enterprise bean. Furthermore, the communication between the EJB client and the enterprise bean is high in overhead; the data must be serialized, transmitted, and then unmarshalled on the other end. This overhead is best kept within the confines of a high-speed internal network rather than over a lower-speed wide area network. Furthermore, if the EJB client and the enterprise bean reside on the same server, the serialization overhead is then avoided because an internal call can be made. As a result, many vendors recommend that an EJB client be implemented on either the same server as the enterprise bean or a "nearby" server (i.e., another middle-tier server). The EJB client is then invoked through a JSP or Java servlet. The interface to the end user's client system is basic HTML/XML.

Similar client location issues exist if the server-side object is a CORBA-based object rather than an enterprise bean. As in the case of EJBs, a CORBA client/server object interaction requires the serialization and marshalling of the data. Therefore, a client proxy object can be implemented on a Web server, a servlet server, or an application server that performs the object-oriented interaction with the CORBA server object. The client proxy can be any program (Java servlet, C++ program, Visual Basic program, etc.) that implements IIOP. As in the EJB case, this approach minimizes network overhead and simplifies the end client, allowing it to support only a simple browser.

In the example of the retail Web site cited above, this second group of servers can support the critical buying processes. Recall that the Web server group is supporting, in this example, the browsing functions — general corporate information, store location and hours, and online catalog search and display. The application servers can be invoked once the customer places an item in the shopping cart. Once this buying behavior is initiated, the components related to the shopping cart, the access of customer records, and the online credit card approval process are called into play. This type of activity is well suited to application servers because persistence is required to complete the total transaction, and the component architecture allows the system to be built with autonomous parts, possibly created by independent programmers or software vendors. There may be ongoing participation by the Web servers because the customer may continue browsing the catalog and adding items to the shopping cart. However, to add to the complexity, most application servers include the functionality of a Web (HTTP) server. Therefore, the application server can, depending on the design (i.e., location of servlets and pages), download Web pages directly to the end user.

As in the case of the first group of servers (i.e., Web and servlet servers), the second group of application and servlet servers should be designed in such a way as to maximize scalability and availability. Thus, in many enterprises, the second group of servers will involve multiple physical servers. Some may be groups of replicated servers in which the same set of servlets and objects are supported on multiple, different physical platforms. In this group there may also be different servers that house different components and different business logic. Therefore, there may be one set of servers dedicated to maintenance of the shopping cart, another that contains the

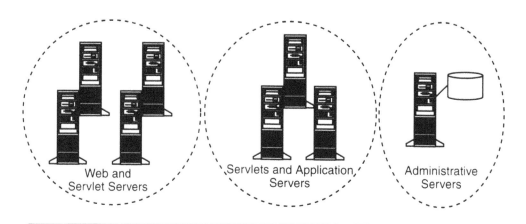

Exhibit 5.12   Groups of Servers in the Middle Tier

component or components related to the concept of "Customer," and another that contains the components and logic to carry out the credit card transaction.

The servers in the second group will each have built-in administrative capability. It is possible, however, that some enterprises will define a separate administrative domain with a dedicated server or servers. The administrative domain will have control over a specific set of Web, servlet, and application servers. Exhibit 5.12 illustrates the three different groups of servers in the middle tier.

Application Server Architecture

The architecture of any application server product necessarily depends on the basic model or framework upon which the product is built. For example, Java application servers are built on the Java-related specifications. Since 1999, that has been synonymous with supporting the J2EE platform. CORBA-based applications servers are built on the basic framework of an ORB and support for at least some of the CORBA services. Increasingly, CORBA-based application servers provide comprehensive support for the J2EE platform as well. Finally, Microsoft COM-based application servers are based on a COM framework. Because the focus of this book is on Java and CORBA, these two frameworks are explored in detail.

Java Framework

When the EJB specification was first published, vendors with products that implemented only that specification called their products Java application servers. Since then, however, the Java server-related specifications have grown and evolved and now encompass much more than just the EJB specification. As detailed in Chapter 3, the Java 2 Enterprise Edition (J2EE) platform specification includes EJB support, JSP and Java servlet support, and a variety of Java Enterprise APIs. The J2EE specification was defined by Sun in 1999 and

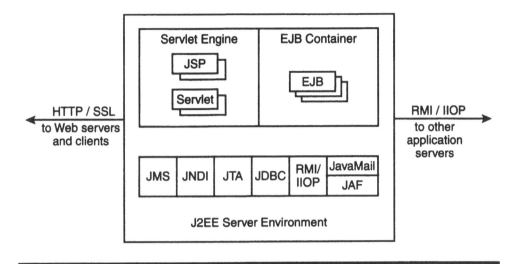

Exhibit 5.13   Architecture of a J2EE-Based Application Server

now provides a baseline of functionality for Java application servers. Full J2EE support is now a minimum requirement to be considered a Java application server. Interestingly, at the core of a Java application server is an ORB. This architectural fact is invisible to the applications that use the application server because the applications only see and use the Java APIs. Exhibit 5.13 illustrates the basic architecture of a J2EE-based application server.

A Java application server provides an engine to execute Java Server Pages and Java servlets. Recall from Chapter 2 that a JSP is simply a Web page that contains both presentation logic, in the form of HTML/XML tags, and application logic. The application logic is identified and delimited by angled brackets, much like HTML and XML code. However, JSP code is dynamically compiled into Java servlets on the server. A Java servlet is a program, written in Java, that runs in the server's Java Virtual Machine. It is similar to a Java applet except that it runs on a server rather than a client. A Java servlet can access an enterprise bean through internal system calls if the servlet and the EJB co-reside on a single system, or it can invoke an enterprise bean through the RMI interface. Because RMI-over-IIOP is considered a strategic interoperability mechanism, servlets should utilize RMI-over-IIOP whenever possible. The added advantage to this approach is that the servlet can then interoperate with CORBA-based object systems as well as EJB-based systems. As described earlier, a common and recommended approach for EJBs is to implement the client EJB interface as a JSP or servlet that communicates directly with the enterprise bean. With this approach, the end-user client machine can be very thin; it does not need to support RMI or JNDI and can run a simple HTML/XML Web browser to interact with the enterprise bean.

The EJB container on the Java application server is the environment within which enterprise beans run. An enterprise bean cannot run without a container. As detailed in Chapter 3, the container provides many of the system services to the enterprise bean and also shields the bean from direct contact with the

EJB client. The container manages memory, threads, and other system resources. The container manages the state of an enterprise bean, saving and then restoring state information between method invocations. It also creates and destroys instances of enterprise beans. It manages persistence, security, and transactions on behalf of the enterprise bean. In short, the container provides several capabilities that the programmer of enterprise beans does not need to track or worry about. Compared to a rich CORBA ORB that implements the full set of CORBA services, the EJB container offers only a subset of services. However, the services that the EJB container provides are more automatic. In most CORBA environments, the programmer must still explicitly write code to create and destroy instances, for example (at least until CORBA 3.0).

The enterprise APIs on the Java application server allow the enterprise bean developer to leverage some key Java services. The full set of APIs is described in Chapter 3. The two most fundamental of these APIs is RMI and the Java Naming and Directory Interface (JNDI), which is the mechanism used to locate the EJB Home interface of an enterprise bean. However, a full-fledged application server also needs to access back-end data and transaction servers, and some of the other enterprise APIs facilitate that access. JDBC support is required to access databases. Java Transaction API (JTA) is important in facilitating the integration of Java application servers with existing transaction-based systems. Java Message Service (JMS) and JavaMail support mail and other applications that share events and data asynchronously.

Sun Microsystems licenses the J2EE platform and also makes its source code available for developers under its Community Source Code program. As stated earlier, more than half of the vendors identified by an application server tracking Web site had licensed J2EE from Sun. Some of these vendors claim to have "the most complete" J2EE implementation, but these statements should be recognized for the marketing hyperbole they are. Over time, the core functionality of many of these J2EE-based Java application servers will become almost identical. The architecture of one of these J2EE application servers — IBM's WebSphere Application Server, Advanced Edition — is depicted in Exhibit 5.14. This product was selected as an example because IBM also offers a CORBA-based application server, called the WebSphere Application Server, Enterprise Edition. The architecture of high-end CORBA-based application servers is presented in the next section.

As Exhibit 5.14 reveals, the IBM WebSphere Application Server, Advanced Edition, is a J2EE-based implementation of a Java application server. The product includes its own HTTP server and will also work with independent HTTP servers. Each application server node includes an administrative server component that is responsible for configuring, monitoring, and managing the application servers running on that node.

CORBA Framework

Today, all major application servers based on a CORBA framework also provide extensive support for the J2EE specification. Therefore, one can view the

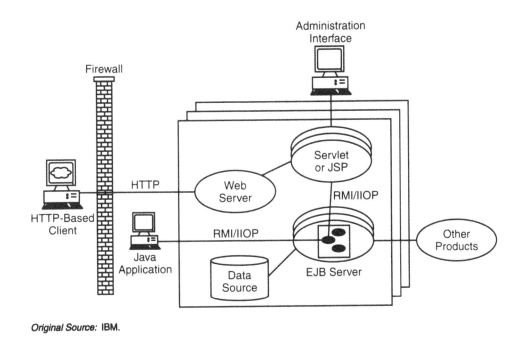

Original Source: IBM.

Exhibit 5.14   Architecture of IBM's WebSphere Application Server Advanced Edition

CORBA-based application servers as providing a superset of capability provided in the J2EE-based application servers. This is because a CORBA-based application server will support components and applications written in Java, but also components and applications written in a variety of other languages. Also, a CORBA-based application server is usually a richer and more complex implementation. For example, a CORBA-based application server usually implements the full set of CORBA services, while a Java-based application server might only implement a handful of these services. Obviously, a product-by-product comparison will yield instances in which a particular J2EE server offers as much functionality as a particular CORBA-based system.

However, two major application server vendors — BEA Systems and IBM — offer a line of application servers, and the high end of the line in both cases is the vendor's CORBA-based system. BEA Systems offers the WebLogic Server, which is based on the J2EE platform. It also offers the WebLogic Enterprise Server, which is based on a full CORBA ORB and full set of CORBA services. Similarly, IBM offers three different editions of its WebSphere Application Server product. Both the Standard and Advanced Editions are based on Java, while the Enterprise Edition is based on the company's Component Broker, a full-fledged CORBA ORB. Inprise also offers a CORBA-based application server.

Exhibit 5.15 illustrates the general architecture of a CORBA-based application server. At the heart of the system is the ORB, which can be viewed as the base structure. On top of the ORB is the application server itself, which provides the complete execution environment for the system. The ORB is the communications

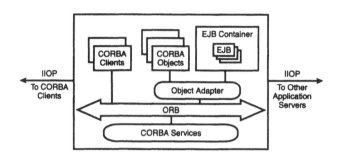

Exhibit 5.15   Architecture of a CORBA-Based Application Server

bus that routes messages and method requests from client object to server object. The ORB also communicates with the outside world through the IIOP protocol (including RMI-over-IIOP). Recall from Chapter 4 that the ORB also provides a long list of services and facilities that support objects. For example, the ORB provides life cycle, naming, security, persistent object, query, event, concurrency, and other basic and essential system-level services.

The application server supports the runtime environment for both CORBA objects and enterprise beans (in most implementations). The application server must support the EJB container as defined in the Java specifications so that enterprise beans can be portable across different application server implementations. The application server will also manage system resources such as threads and memory. The application server (in conjunction with the ORB) also activates and deactivates object instances and maintains persistence and state information across method invocations. A CORBA-based application server can implement the Portable Object Adapter (POA), which (as described in Chapter 4) provides some advanced services, a container model analogous to the EJB container, and better scalability. A CORBA-based system can also support the Distributed Computing Environment (DCE) transaction processing environment, with support for DCE's Remote Procedure Call (RPC).

In summary, both the J2EE- and CORBA-based application servers provide an execution environment and a rich set of services to support components. From an enterprise IT standpoint, which approach is "best"? The answer, of course, is that it depends on the environment. A J2EE approach may be optimal if the environment meets the following criteria:

1. no existing installed base of CORBA objects or COM objects
2. commitment to Java as a development language and environment, with sufficient Java skill sets in-house
3. mainly database back-ends
5. relatively straightforward legacy environment that does not contain a lot of client/server APIs (i.e., distributed CICS client/server, DCE, etc.)

A CORBA-based approach, on the other hand, is likely to be optimal in environments meeting the following criteria:

1. existing CORBA and/or COM object environments
2. rich set of back-ends that include databases in addition to proprietary and standard client/server environments
3. slower evolution to Java, with a significant investment in C++ or other languages
4. requirement for some of the more mature CORBA services (e.g., relationship service, qualities of service)

As stated elsewhere, the Java and CORBA specifications will continue to evolve over time and the gap in functionality between the two will continually lessen. Nonetheless, a fundamental fact of the J2EE approach is that it is tied to the Java programming language. CORBA, on the other hand, is not, and neither is Microsoft's COM. In the end, organizations that are moving to Java should consider J2EE-based application servers; and organizations with a large and continued investment in C++, Visual Basic, Ada, Lisp, COBOL, and other languages should consider CORBA, COM, or both.

Distributed Objects Within the Middle Tier

Many enterprises will, over time, include a variety of different application servers. They can be grouped according to base technology (Java, CORBA, COM), end-user work groups, type of component, or some other criteria. The middle tier will contain application servers that replicate objects and applications in order to support load balancing and fault tolerance. It will also contain different groups of application servers that support different types of objects and applications. This is depicted in Exhibit 5.16.

IBM proposes an architecture for the middle tier that is comprised of three different layers of objects[4]:

1. *Persistent components:* abstractions that map to existing data or procedural programs
2. *Composite components:* new abstractions that represent an aggregation of persistent components
3. *Application components:* new components, accessed by client applications, that focus on business logic and the usage of other components

This architecture of layered components is similar to the concept in the EJB model of session beans and entity beans, except that the IBM model adds a third middle layer. As detailed in Chapter 3, an entity bean is a persistent

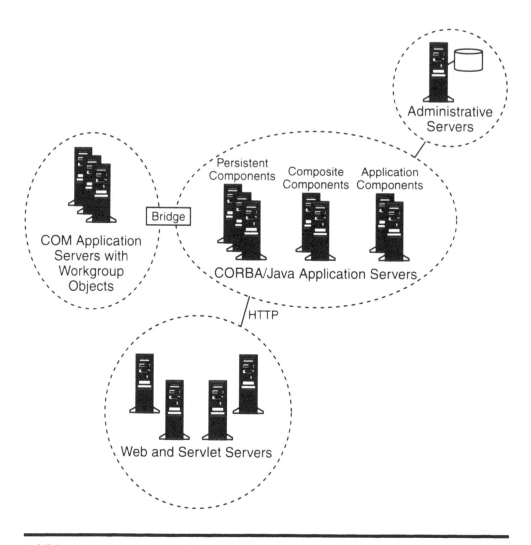

Exhibit 5.16   Groups of Application Servers

entity that represents back-end resources; an entity bean is analogous to IBM's persistent component layer. A session bean is a transient entity created by the client and usually only exists for the duration of the session between the client and the server; a session bean is somewhat analogous to IBM's application component layer. IBM adds the middle layer of composite components to enhance reusability. IBM suggests that all data mappings that are particular to one system should be implemented as persistent components so that if the data mapping ever changes, only the single persistent component needs to change. Composite components, then, focus on aggregating data from multiple back-ends without being dependent on a specific mapping.

Interoperability between different Java and CORBA application server systems will be based on IIOP and RMI-over-IIOP. Interoperability with COM systems will be based on the OMG-defined Interworking Model or on a proprietary implementation of a COM-to-CORBA or COM-to-Java bridge. Some application servers integrate the bridge functionality so that they natively support interoperability with COM objects.

Application Server Platforms

Application servers, of course, must run on some physical server hardware and server operating system. A brief mention of the different choices is in order.

Most application servers will be implemented on a server platform running Windows NT or a UNIX variant. Windows NT will be a logical choice for organizations that have a major commitment to NT and a workforce that is very skilled and adept at managing an NT environment. However, a commitment to NT does not mean that an IT organization necessarily needs to base its application servers on a COM (or COM+) technology base. Quite the opposite is true. Most application server vendors support NT as one of the operating system choices that they support.

Nonetheless, some NT-centric organizations will choose to implement COM-based solutions. As of this writing, Microsoft is offering its application server (called Application Center 2000) for beta testing. This application server's key strength appears, at this time from early information, to be its tight integration with the new NT-based software scaling capabilities, allowing multiple NT servers to be logically viewed as a single entity to promote scalability and fault tolerance. This new capability can address what has been the biggest technical reasons (scalability and fault tolerance) to base an application server on a high-end UNIX system rather than NT.

UNIX is probably the most popular platform for application servers today. However, the UNIX market is highly fractured. The three most prevalent UNIX operating systems in enterprise environments today are Sun's Solaris, HP's HP-UX, and IBM's AIX. Linux, a variant of UNIX, is growing in popularity within the enterprise. Most major application server vendors support all four of these operating systems.

Another server operating system that has some level of support from application server vendors is NetWare. Although the NetWare star has long since dimmed and many enterprises have replaced their NetWare servers with NT or UNIX, there remains a huge installed base of NetWare. Therefore, some vendors do offer application servers for NetWare.

IBM supports some of its application servers on its own OS/400 and OS/390 operating systems as well. OS/400, the operating system of IBM's highly popular AS/400 system, may be a popular platform for smaller organizations or departments that use the AS/400 as the primary system, supporting legacy applications, new applications, and even a Web server. OS/390, the operating system for IBM's mainframe computers, is an interesting option for large enterprises. OS/390 offers the most sophisticated load balancing, high availability, and fault tolerance capabilities of any other computing platform (which is described in Chapter 6). Today's OS/390 comes equipped with a TCP/IP stack and a Web server. Therefore, in some environments, an OS/390-based application server makes a great deal of sense. If there are a great deal of mainframe-based legacy data and applications that need to be integrated with the new application server-based applications, for example, the mainframe might be the best platform for some or all of the components. This design would promote high availability while reducing network overhead.

Back-end Tier

The back-end tier of any enterprise is unique to that enterprise. Each individual enterprise has built, usually over a period of years or decades, a diverse set of systems and applications to run the mission-critical business processes of that enterprise. This tier includes legacy systems that are based on a character interface, client/server systems with proprietary or open APIs, and new distributed object-based systems. There is no single approach that will tie all of these diverse systems into today's application server. Each type of system requires its own approach.

In some cases, the application server supports an API that directly communicates with the back-end server. In other cases, the application server uses object services to communicate with the back-end server. Finally, the application server might utilize a gateway approach, in which another program or server performs the conversion from the API/protocol used by the application server to one expected by the legacy host system. There is no single term for this latter approach; some vendors call the conversion programs "connectors," some call them "adapters," and some call them "gateways." The term "gateway" is used here because it is the most correct from an architectural standpoint. Gateway functionality can be integrated into the application server or it can be provided by a stand-alone product. Several types of gateways were discussed in Chapter 2. The host integration server is becoming increasingly popular. The host integration server is a server-based product that provides generalized access to a variety of different legacy host systems.

Character-based Systems

Many legacy applications based on mainframes and midrange systems still exist today that communicate using character-based data streams. These legacy applications are built around a hierarchical model, in which end users traditionally accessed the applications using dumb terminals. Dumb terminals are simple devices that provide a keyboard and a character-based screen. The user interacts with the application by filling in fields on the screen and pressing the Enter key or a programmed function (PF) key. With the advent of PCs, the dumb terminal has been largely replaced with terminal emulation software that runs on the PC. This software continues to present, in most cases, the character-based user interface to the user. Although dated, the legacy hierarchical systems continue to run some of the most long-standing and mission-critical applications of an enterprise. The investment that has been made in these applications is huge (trillions of dollars worldwide), and IT organizations have found it technically difficult, not cost-effective, or too risky to try to reengineer these applications to fit the client/server or the distributed object model.

Chapter 2 contains a detailed description of the issues and technologies in providing access to legacy systems from Web-based users. Essentially, there are two basic approaches to Web-to-host: client-based applets and server-based conversion programs. In the client applet approach, terminal emulation software is packaged as a Java applet or ActiveX control and downloaded to the user via the browser. Any user with an appropriately equipped browser (i.e., with the proper JVM or ActiveX support) can access the legacy system. Early client-based applets only offered the traditional character-based interface, but solutions increasingly are offering a means of rejuvenating the user interface on-the-fly. Server-based conversion programs and host integration servers can offer greater flexibility and superior rejuvenation of the user interface. A server-based approach can allow a complete revamp of the application flow without changing the legacy application. A server-based approach also allows the user to interact with a new Web-style interface that integrates information from multiple different legacy systems.

Few application servers today integrate a complete host integration server or server-based HTML conversion. One possible explanation for this may be that many application server vendors do not have the expertise or experience to provide this capability. This obviously is not true of IBM, however, and IBM has chosen to integrate its client-based applet with WebSphere Application Server, Enterprise Edition, rather than supporting server-based conversion and host integration. The client-based applet, IBM WebSphere Host On-Demand, is downloaded to users requiring host access. From that point on, the Web-Sphere Application Server has no role in the host access. The client directly accesses the host without going through the application server.

One very likely reason that vendors are not offering extensive legacy host integration features within their application servers is the cycle impact. Server-based conversion of host data streams can be a very costly process in terms of CPU utilization. A single server that is running a full-fledged host integration server in addition to an application server may be constrained to supporting tens or hundreds of concurrent users rather than the thousands of concurrent users that larger enterprises may require. For this reason, many enterprises will implement separate host integration servers to support the legacy, character-based application access.

Databases

The database has been an integral part of the enterprise IT environment since the very early days of business computers. Originally, database systems were accessed in proprietary ways, with a different interface or query language for each system. IBM's IMS, for example, was highly popular and is still being used in many enterprise environments today.

Eventually, in the 1980s, the relational database model became prevalent over the proprietary systems. Relational database management systems (RDBMS) from companies such as Oracle, Sybase, and Informix, accessed using Structured Query Language (SQL) commands, are the norm today. The client/server era was largely based on the RDBMS system. Most client/server applications contain at least some database access. In the client/server world, each RDBMS vendor implemented a unique variation of the SQL command set and a unique protocol and API. This made it difficult for different clients to interoperate with different servers.

The interoperability problems eventually precipitated two changes: the introduction of standard RDBMS APIs, and the introduction of a middle-tier server to communicate with multiple database systems. The standard API widely implemented in client systems and RDBMSs is the Open Database Connectivity (ODBC) API initially developed by Microsoft but now an industry standard. The J2EE platform supports a Java version of ODBC called, appropriately, JDBC.

The introduction of the middle-tier server for accessing multiple database systems marked the beginning of the category of product called an application server. Although today's application server is much more than just a middle-tier device for connectivity to multiple databases, there are still strong ties, to some people, between application servers and database systems. In fact, some analysts, vendors, and writers still position the application server as having a single type of back-end — the relational database system. To these people, a Java application server with JDBC support is all one really needs to access the back-end tier.

One common manner in which application servers access relational database systems is through ODBC or JDBC APIs. The API approach offers a direct interface, which can be very efficient and direct. Legacy databases, such as IBM's IMS, may require a specific gateway (or adapter or connector). Another possible approach is to access the database through a CORBA object implementation or enterprise bean. Some database vendors, for example, have extensively "componentized" their systems so that they are accessible through CORBA ORBs or EJB servers. A final approach is for the application server to utilize its inherent transaction services to access the database system and coordinate between different resources. This is described in the following section.

Transaction Processing Systems

Transactions are really the heart of any enterprise IT infrastructure. Users carry out transactions with legacy character-based systems, with database systems, with message queuing systems, and with a wide variety of other systems. A transaction is a unit of work that has the following properties:

- *It is atomic:* a transaction is the smallest unit of work; all changes to systems are either all committed or they are rolled back.
- *It produces consistent results:* changes to the state of the resource move from one valid state to another.

- *It is isolated:* changes to shared resources do not become visible to others until the transaction commits.
- *It is durable:* changes to shared resources survive subsequent system or media failures.

Early transaction processing systems, like other types of applications and systems, had proprietary and hierarchical interfaces. IBM's CICS is perhaps the most widely deployed transaction processing system, and its original interface was proprietary and largely based on character-based data streams in which the application logic was intertwined with the user interface. With the client/server movement, IBM added a client/server programmatic interface to CICS, and now CICS APIs are supported on a wide variety of client and server systems.

As enterprise environments evolved and more and diverse systems supported transactions, some enterprises deployed a class of product called a *transaction processing monitor*, commonly called a TP monitor. The TP monitor is a piece of middleware that integrates and coordinates transactions that span multiple different systems.

Both CORBA and Java support transaction services, meaning that the CORBA- or Java-based application server can become a coordinator of distributed transactions that span multiple systems. A CORBA application server would need to support the CORBA Object Transaction Service (OTS) specification, and the Java application server would need to support the Java Transaction Service (JTS). J2EE also specifies the Java Transaction API (JTA), an API upon which JTS is built and that is available to programs on application servers that directly communicate with transactional systems. The systems accessed by the CORBA or Java application server could be, depending on the implementation, database systems, legacy systems, message queuing systems, or other TP systems or TP monitors.

An application server that does not support the full OTS or JTS specification can still connect to individual transaction processing systems or TP monitors through a specific gateway (or adapter or connector).

Message Queuing Systems

Messaging and message queuing systems allow two or more applications to communicate asynchronously. E-mail is probably the most common example of a messaging application. However, many other enterprise applications are designed with a messaging interface. Messaging and message queuing systems are often used when the volume of transactions is high, and a very efficient and robust means of distributing and sharing data across multiple heterogeneous applications and systems is required. IBM's MQSeries, for example, is used by a worldwide express package delivery service to track its packages using a variety of different back-end systems.

Messaging and message queuing systems can be interfaced directly by way of a specific gateway (or adapter or connector) integrated with the application server. Clients that require access to the system can do so directly. In the case when the message queuing system is part of an overall larger transaction, the application server, with an OTS or JTS implementation, can coordinate the overall transaction, of which the message queuing is just one piece. Finally, both the Java and the CORBA specifications contain messaging interfaces. The Java Messaging Service (JMS) provides a common Java interface to messaging products. CORBA supports two services, the Event Service and the Notification Service, that facilitate messaging. JMS can even be implemented on top of the CORBA Event and Notification services.

Other Back-end Systems

Enterprise IT environments include a wide variety of other types of mission-critical applications that represent key business processes or provide a critical function in the infrastructure. Some of the applications that may require integration with an application server include:

- *Enterprise Resource Planning (ERP)*. These systems, from companies like PeopleSoft, SAP, and Oracle, integrate the various functional organizations such as human resources, finance, and business process management.
- *Workflow automation and collaboration*. Software, such as Lotus Notes, that promotes workgroup collaboration and automation of workflow between groups.
- *DCE-based distributed processing systems*. Applications based on DCE APIs for distributed transaction processing; the most common of these is the Remote Procedure Call (RPC) API, which provides for a network-transparent communication between processes in a distributed system.
- *Network-based services*. A variety of network-based systems that provide directory services, security, load balancing, and other services.

Many of these systems are based on open and published APIs. Application servers equipped with the appropriate gateway (or adapter or connector) can directly communicate with these systems. In other cases, there may be object-oriented interfaces or implementations of the applications that allow a Java or CORBA application server to access the application using standard object services.

Exhibit 5.17 summarizes the potential back-end connections and systems that can be supported by an application server. Each application server will be unique in the types of back-end systems that the application server natively supports. A bare minimum functionality is support for RDBMS access using ODBC or JDBC. More sophisticated application servers will provide a richer set of APIs and gateways/adapters/connectors. Remember that a host integration server that offloads some of the CPU-intensive gateway and conversion functions to legacy systems can augment the application server.

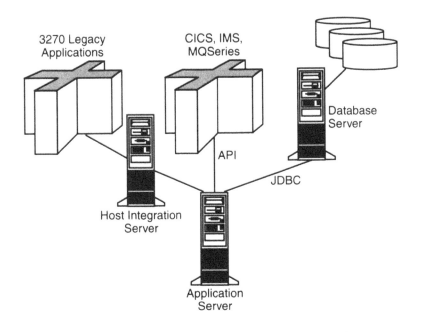

3270 Legacy
Applications

CICS, IMS,
MQSeries

Database
Server

API

JDBC

Host Integration
Server

Application
Server

Exhibit 5.17   Application Server Back-Ends

Development Tools

Recall that the definition of an application server includes the notion that an application server allows IT organizations to *build, deploy, and manage* new applications. The application server cannot do all of these functions alone; it must work with related products to accomplish all three tasks. One of the more important related products is the Integrated Development Environment (IDE) and related development tools used to design and develop the new applications.

One of the promises of distributed object computing is that this model facilitates and speeds the design, development, and deployment of new applications. The distributed object model fulfills this promise, largely through the concept of application reuse and open interfaces to objects and applications. The IDE is a tool or set of tools that can dramatically improve the productivity of software developers by providing an easy-to-use visual interface, automating the generation and deployment of code, and facilitating the test and debug process. The IDE is a category of product that has been evolving over the past decade or so. It is not specifically tied to the development of distributed applications built on application servers. IDEs are used to build traditional client/server and Web server-based applications as well. Popular Java IDEs include IBM's VisualAge for Java, Symantec's Visual Café, Inprise's JBuilder, and Microsoft's Visual J++. These products are commonly used to build client-based Java applets, Java servlets, and JSPs.

Additional tools can be used in an application server environment to model the object environment, map components to resources and applications, and build new business logic that integrates components from around the enterprise.

Different application server vendors approach the subject of development tools differently. Some vendors offer a proprietary tool that works only with their application server and that is supposed to provide all of the functionality an IT organization may need to build and deploy applications using that application server. Others choose simply to provide explicit support for a variety of different IDEs and tools available in the marketplace. The third and most common approach is to provide a bundled tool in addition to support for off-the-shelf IDEs.

Most enterprises will end up deploying multiple tools. This is not because the tools are faulty and there are no comprehensive tools. Instead, it is because there will be different types of individuals, with different skill sets and backgrounds, involved throughout the end-to-end application development process. Web designers, for example, will not care about the great visual modeling and component builder aspects of a tool. Web designers want tools that allow them to easily build sophisticated Web pages. By the same token, a software engineer designing and developing business logic will not care much about the great HTML and XML capabilities of a tool.

An IT organization needs to recognize that there are different tools to suit different jobs. The ultimate goal should be to select a set of tools that supports all steps in the development process: model, design, develop, test, and deploy. However they are packaged within individual products, the following types of functions will generally be required in an application server environment:

1. visual tools for building a GUI user interface (e.g., a JavaBeans customizer)
2. visual modeling tools to model the enterprise deployment of components, applications, and servers
3. visual tools for defining, building, and deploying server-side components
4. visual tools for management of the application server container and core services
5. visual tools for the creation of new business logic that combines multiple components
6. deployment tools for enterprise bean and CORBA object deployment
7. features to map components to back-end resources (e.g., entity beans to databases)
8. code editors for HTML/XML, Java, and scripting languages
9. development kit, which includes compilers (including CORBA IDL compilers with appropriate client support), testing environment, debugging tools, and team development tools

In addition to these development tools, the administrative capabilities of an application server impact the overall development cycle in the sense that these built-in functions can assist in the deployment process. Many application server vendors offer sophisticated administrative interfaces and tools that automatically discover components and services in the environment, which assists in the configuration and ultimate deployment of the application server and its components. These administrative capabilities, while not being considered actual development tools, are a part of the overall development cycle and therefore should be considered in any application server evaluation.

Packaging

The specifications defining Java and CORBA application servers are fairly complete (although evolving over time). The specifications do not get into implementation details, however. Two vendors that each offer fully compliant J2EE implementations, for example, will be able to differentiate their products from those of other vendors by offering specific functionality that extends, enhances, or goes beyond the functionality that is defined in the J2EE specification. One area that Java and CORBA application server vendors are attempting to establish differentiation is in the area of load balancing and fault tolerance. Neither the J2EE nor the CORBA specification directly addresses this key requirement, so vendors are implementing their own solutions to address it. Chapter 6 discusses this in some detail.

Another potential area of differentiation is in how the application server is packaged. Packaging, quite simply, is the combination of features, functions, and products to make a whole offering that is sold to the end user. Vendors can differentiate their application servers by bundling in related tools and products. With this type of differentiation, the vendor can offer a more "complete" product in terms of meeting all related customer needs. This can provide a competitive advantage over other solutions that do not bundle in the same capabilities.

The most common product or functionality bundled with an application server is the Web (HTTP) server functionality. Almost all application servers available on the market have a Web server built in to the product that can serve up standard HTML/XML/WML pages to users' browsers. This is an important capability to be included. Recall from the earlier discussion on Web server and application server design that the application server will very often communicate directly with a browser using standard HTTP. This is because the client object may in fact be implemented as a servlet or a client proxy on the application server itself to avoid the overhead of sending object references across the network. Therefore, having the application server directly communicate with the end user, rather than through a separate and stand-alone Web server, is more efficient. However, just because the application server includes a Web server does not mean that an enterprise should eliminate stand-alone

Web servers. Chances are that the majority of the Web-related i•net traffic will be either static or dynamic scripted pages that do not require the sophistication of an application server. It is best to devote dedicated Web servers to handling this normal traffic, conserving the resources of the application server platform for the more difficult tasks of managing distributed objects and component containers.

Another common type of function bundled with an application server is the gateway functionality for connection to a particular back-end data or application server. As detailed earlier, each application server vendor offers its own unique set of back-end gateways. Some application server vendors bundle in these gateways with their offering. In other cases, the vendors support a standard connector interface and encourage other software development firms to write to their interface. It is expected that, over time, the connector interfaces will become standardized and vendors will offer off-the-shelf connectors that work with a variety of application servers.

Application server vendors also frequently bundle development tools with their application servers. Development tools may be proprietary to the application server or open and applicable to a variety of products. In either case, virtually all vendors that offer some kind of development tool end up bundling it at no additional charge with their application server as a way of providing additional value to their customers and differentiating their product from those of the competition.

An emerging way of differentiation through bundling is in offering complete business object implementations that can be used to build new applications. For example, an application server that is bundled with the business object "Checking Account" and its related methods and properties could significantly expedite the building of new banking applications. This type of bundling is just starting to occur, but one can expect to see more of this in the future. In particular, vertical market object bundles may become prevalent as vendors try to focus on a particular segment of the market.

Vendors can also differentiate their application servers by offering a range of application server products, serving the needs of the small site with minimal functionality at a low price point and the needs of a large enterprise with greater functionality at a higher price point. This type of differentiation allows the vendor to better meet the range of needs in the marketplace while also optimizing revenue. With a single product (and a single price point), an application server vendor might be forced to offer all potential features and functions it has available in that one product. Pricing for this high-end product should be equivalent to other high-end product in the marketplace in order to fund the development for all of the value-added features. However, this may price the vendor out of competing in the departmental environment or the smaller enterprise. Therefore, some vendors already offer two or three different application servers, offering a range of price and functionality. This trend will likely continue.

As an example of this product line approach, IBM offers three editions of its WebSphere Application Server:

1. *Standard Edition:* supports XML, Java servlets, and JSPs
2. *Advanced Edition:* includes features of Standard Edition but adds full EJB and enterprise Java API support
3. *Enterprise Edition:* includes Advanced Edition and also offers EJB engine based on Component Broker (a CORBA ORB implementation) and transaction processing features of IBM TXSeries

Pricing and packaging mechanisms will increasingly be used by vendors to set their products apart from the pack. As more vendors implement the J2EE platform and the CORBA 2.x/3.0 specifications, the products will begin to look more and more alike. Vendors will bundle features or products to augment their products. They will also offer a complete product line that offers a variety of different price points to make sure that they meet the needs of the widest possible set of customers while maximizing revenue.

Related Products

Another way that vendors will attempt to differentiate themselves from the large and growing pack of application server providers is by offering complementary and related products. These may be subsets of the application server that stand alone as products, or they may be related products that build upon and augment the application server to provide a more total solution. This approach is different from bundling because the subset products and the related products are priced and sold separately.

Vendors that offer a subset approach are attempting to maximize the engineering investment they have made in a particular area. As an example of this approach, Inprise offers a variety of different products that each implements one of the CORBAservices. The company sells stand-alone servers for the following services: trading, notification, life cycle, property, collection, concurrency, relationship, and time. The company also sells its ORB separately. These stand-alone servers can augment an Inprise application server environment. However, they can also provide a "foot-in-the-door" to accounts that do not currently implement the Inprise application server. This gives a company the potential to start with a single stand-alone service or ORB and, over time, "sell up" to the full-fledged application server.

The more common approach to selling related products, however, is to sell services that build upon the application server. This elevates the sale from a comparison of features and functions of different application servers to a total solution approach. As most top sales reps will attest, a company that offers a compelling total solution will be much more successful with the core product, in this case the application server. The core product becomes a required infrastructure, and it then does not need to be evaluated against all potential competitive offerings.

The variety of related products that vendors are positioning with their application server products is large and growing. One very common category of product is the E-business suite that offers specific applications and tools on top of the application server. IBM offers its WebSphere Commerce Suite for E-commerce and WebSphere B2B Integrator to support B2B activity with suppliers, business partners, and E-marketplaces. Bluestone Software offers a range of solutions to augment its Total-e-Server application server: the Total-e-B2B, Total-e-B2C, Total-e-Wireless, and Total-e-Global products. BEA Systems augments its WebLogic and WebLogic Enterprise application servers with the WebLogic Commerce Server and the WebLogic Personalization Server. These are just a few examples of the types of E-business extensions available on the market today.

The E-business suites are just the tip of the iceberg when it comes to related tools and products that vendors are positioning with their application servers. Other types of related products include:

1. *Component development tools:* assist in the development and deployment of CORBA or Java components
2. *Business or vertical market components:* prepackaged components that can be integrated with new business logic and other components
3. *Web authoring tools:* support the creation of dynamic and static Web pages
4. *Web site personalization and portal products:* support the concept of a personalized portal through which employees, customers, and suppliers access an individualized view of the Web site
5. *Host integration servers or optional legacy gateways (adapters/connectors):* provide access to specific legacy host and applications
6. *Server and network modeling tools:* allow the IT organization to model the servers and network and anticipate and prevent potential bottleneck points
7. *Site administration and management products:* facilitate the administration and management of the application server and its environment
8. *Network services products:* support the application server infrastructure with directory service, security, load balancing, and queuing technologies and products

IT organizations should take into account the related products offered by a particular application server vendor when evaluating alternatives. Over time, the core functionality of application servers will become very similar. The differences between vendors will become more apparent as the total product portfolio is examined. Preference should be given to vendors that offer total solutions that are required immediately or even possibly in the future, as long as the vendor has committed to providing standards-based solutions. Proprietary approaches that lock an organization into a particular vendor should be avoided. When a particular proprietary solution is required to solve a specific problem, the product should be considered tactical. The base infrastructure should be based on open standards to support future flexibility.

Network-based Services

The application server exists within a network infrastructure that provides multiple services to the i*net and its users. The network was once considered just the plumbing that provided connectivity between sites. Now, with the efforts of enterprise networking vendors like Cisco Systems and IBM, the enterprise network is becoming an adaptive and intelligent infrastructure that enhances overall security, availability, and efficient utilization of bandwidth.

Some of the network-based services are directly called or accessed by the application server, and some are more or less invisible to the application server. Services in the former group include security and directory services. Services in the latter group include network-based queuing and prioritization, filtering and caching, and stand-alone traffic load balancers.

There are a wide variety of different network-based devices that implement one or more facets of an overall security policy. The important subject of security is covered as a comprehensive whole in the first section of Chapter 6. The other four major network-based services are discussed individually in the following sections.

Directory Services

Directory services allow users and programs to discover resources on the network. Like a telephone book, a directory server provides a mapping between a known entity (an element's name) and an unknown entity (the element's address). A directory server also offers the ability for clients (either users or programs) to select an element that matches specific criteria or to browse through a structured tree of resources.

Directory servers are critical to a distributed object environment for the simple reason that components and services are distributed throughout a network. By definition, an application server environment is based on objects that are distributed. The directory server (also referred to as a naming server or service) allows the distributed objects and services to be located.

There are a number of directory servers that are common within enterprise networks. The most common and dominant servers are:

1. *Domain Name Server (DNS)*. As described in Chapter 2, the DNS node is a very common item in a TCP/IP network. The DNS node provides a mapping between a host name and its IP address. For example, a user can request the Web page www.excite.com by typing the URL into the browser window. The browser program will send the request for the IP address of that node to a DNS node. ISPs implement DNS nodes, as do almost all enterprise networks. There is a defined hierarchy of DNS nodes, so if the primary DNS node does not have the IP address of the host, it will find it by communicating with the hierarchy of DNS nodes. Eventually, one will be found that knows the IP address of www.excite.com, and it will return that address to the browser.

2. *X.500.* One of the few technologies from the Open Systems Interconnection (OSI) standards initiative that was ever widely deployed was the X.500 directory standard. X.500 describes an International Telecommunications Union (ITU) standard that specifies the client requesting directory services, the agent which stores the database and responds to requests, and protocols used between them.

3. *Lightweight Directory Access Protocol (LDAP).* The LDAP was defined as a response to some criticism that X.500 was too complex to be implemented. It is based on many of the same concepts as X.500 except it is more streamlined and simpler for vendors to implement. LDAP, which works specifically in TCP/IP networks, is defined by IETF standards. It has become a *de facto* standard for i*nets.

4. *Novell Directory Services (NDS).* NDS is Novell's own directory server. NDS is a mature product that has been around for many years and has evolved to include support for LDAP.

5. *Microsoft Windows 2000 Active Directory.* Active Directory is the newest incarnation of Microsoft's directory services bundled within its Windows server, in this case Windows 2000. It leverages DNS namespaces and LDAP protocols.

CORBA and Java both specify APIs that allow clients to look up and locate objects. These APIs and services work in conjunction with the network-based directory servers described above.

The CORBA Naming Service is sometimes referred to as CORBA's "white pages" because it allows clients to associate names with objects rather than referring to objects using the Interoperable Object Reference (IOR), which is less flexible and scalable. The Naming Service specification supports both hierarchical and federated naming graphs, providing flexibility in the physical and logical organization of resources. The OMG specification does not define the implementation of a naming service. Therefore, this service can be implemented on top of almost any directory server, including an LDAP server.

The CORBA Naming Service is commonly used to locate objects within a department or intranet. For locating objects outside a department or intranet, the CORBA Trader Service is useful. The Trader Service is sometimes referred to as CORBA's "yellow pages" because it allows clients to locate objects that meet specific criteria based on property names and values. Objects that wish to be located by way of a Trader Service can export service offers (collections of property names and values) to the Trader.

The Java API that provides naming and directory functions to Java applications is JNDI. This API has been discussed several times, and it is a requirement for any EJB implementation because it is the means by which enterprise beans are located. Programs written in Java can call the API to look up objects of any type, including remote enterprise beans, JDBC URLs, etc. The API provides methods for performing standard directory operations such as searching for objects by attribute. The JNDI specification, like the CORBA specifications, does not specify the engine that is providing the directory services. Different implementations exist of JNDI on top of LDAP, DNS, NDS, and even CORBA naming servers.

The Java and CORBA specifications are predicated on the fact that modern enterprise networks offer rich and varied directory services. Both distributed object models rely on the existence of such servers to locate specific objects and to search for objects that meet a specific set of criteria. Better yet, both specifications leave the implementation of the API open so that vendors can implement them on top of their already popular and widely deployed LDAP, NDS, or other directory servers.

Queuing and Prioritization

An enterprise network carries a variety of different traffic types. Some of the traffic originates from file transfers; some of it is transaction-oriented data; and some is administrative or management data. A growing percentage of the traffic in the enterprise originates from a Web server located within the corporate intranet or outside it.

Each of the different types of traffic is different and each type of application has a different tolerance for delays and variations in response time. File transfers tend to be very large, but the file transfer applications are tolerant of network delays and variations. In addition, file transfer applications support checkpoint and restart capabilities in order to continue the transfer should it get interrupted for whatever reason. Transactions with legacy systems, on the other hand, tend to be characterized by small transfers of data (a few hundred bytes). However, many transaction systems are very intolerant of network delays and will terminate a session if a response is not received within a specified period of time. In addition, the end users of transaction processing systems tend to be intolerant of response time variations and will likely complain to the help desk if the response time varies from sub-second to five seconds within the same session. Web server traffic, interestingly, exhibits characteristics of both file transfer and transaction-oriented data.

Mixing these various types of traffic on a single network can be problematic. Although bandwidth is simultaneously getting cheaper and growing within the intranet and in the wide area network, it is still a finite resource. Therefore, in most environments there inevitably exists some contention for bandwidth. Consider the case of one user starting a very large file transfer just milliseconds before another user in the same location hits the Enter key to initiate a customer service transaction with a legacy system. If the network had no mechanism to prioritize these two types of traffic differently, the transaction traffic could wait an indeterminate amount of time for the file transfer to complete, and some transaction-oriented sessions would time-out and terminate before the transaction data had a chance to be transmitted. Obviously, this has drastic consequences for network users.

Fortunately, there have been a number of different mechanisms developed to avoid these contention problems and allocate network bandwidth according to some sort of priority. Generally referred to as "quality-of-service" (QoS) capabilities, these mechanisms allow high-priority data to receive a higher quality of service than lower priority data. The mechanisms are varied, but generally rely on the classification of data and the differentiated service provided to data of different classifications.

Data can be classified at the end points or at the intermediate points within the network. To achieve end-to-end quality of service, it is preferable to classify data at its point of origin and then tag or signal the data with the appropriate priority classification. A TCP/IP-based application, for example, can set the IP precedence bits in each of its packets and the network will prioritize the packets accordingly. IP precedence is an IETF-standard way of classifying eight different priorities of data. If not done at the point of origin, classification can also take place within the network. For example, a backbone router can be configured to treat all traffic from a specific interface as high-priority traffic. New mechanisms that identify and differentiate Web users based on browsing versus shopping activity are becoming available.

Once classified, the different classes of data can be treated differently. If there is contention for the bandwidth over a particular segment in the network, data must be queued at the point of ingress. There are a variety of different ways to handle the contention. High-priority traffic can be granted the entire bandwidth until the high-priority queue is empty. Other mechanisms allow for some "fair" distribution of bandwidth so that lower priority data cannot be completely starved of bandwidth. Exhibit 5.18 illustrates the concept of differentiated service based on priority. In this example, the router maintains three different priority queues (High, Medium, and Low) and allocates bandwidth based on some algorithm.

The mechanisms for prioritizing data and giving differentiated service levels to different data are rich and varied. It is important to understand the overall

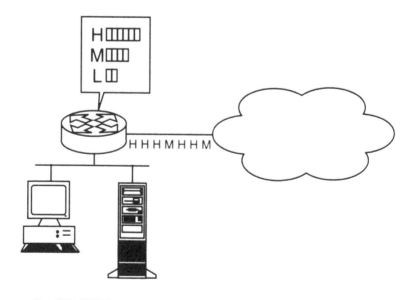

Exhibit 5.18   Differentiated Service Based on Priority

flow of data through an application server before an appropriate policy can be set. For example, an application server may connect to delay-sensitive applications, such as legacy transaction systems, in addition to applications that are not particularly sensitive to delays, such as message queuing systems. It is imperative that the people involved in the implementation and deployment of application server-based components and applications communicate with the networking staff that is setting and implementing network-based quality-of-service mechanisms.

Web Filtering and Caching

Web-related traffic has impacted the networks of enterprises of all sizes. Studies have shown that organizations that implement intranets and Internet connectivity typically experience a huge spike in network traffic and resulting demand on bandwidth. As a result, network administration staffs have implemented a variety of defenses as a way of protecting traditional enterprise application traffic against the ever-increasing demands of Web traffic.

The queuing and prioritization mechanisms described in the previous section can assist in taming Web-related traffic. However, many of these mechanisms rely on classification by application type or port number. They do not have the ability to differentiate between a desirable and an undesirable Web site. An enterprise may have a policy that indicates that only certain Web sites are allowed to download Web pages and information to users. The rest are filtered out. Because an application server is involved in the middle tier, it is important that the application server implementers be involved and aware of the policies being implemented by the Web administration staff.

Another way of managing Web site traffic is in the use of Web caching devices. These devices, which are typically implemented close to the user, save frequently accessed pages and download them directly to the end user, thereby eliminating the need to repeatedly download certain popular pages across the wide area network. Unfortunately, the caching devices can implement policies that are inconsistent with the applications implemented on application servers. For example, a Web caching device might cache (or save) a particular JSP page. If the page changes, the Web caching devices might not automatically detect the update and may download outdated information to the end user. Application server developers should be aware of filtering and caching devices within the enterprise.

Load Balancers

One of the key requirements of enterprises implementing E-business systems is that the infrastructure must scale to support an increasing number of users. Enterprises implement multiple physical servers or multiple software images to allow the environment to scale to support the required number of users. However, it is important that end users be shielded from the implementation within the enterprise. Users must have a single image or view of the enterprise.

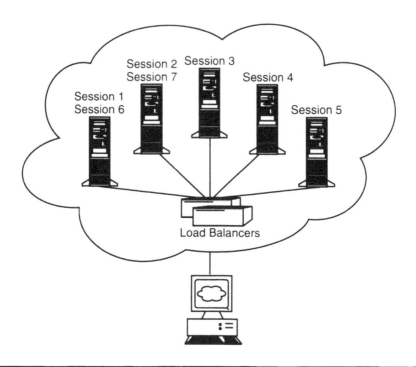

Exhibit 5.19   Round-Robin Load Balancer

Load balancers within the network are a class of networking device that allows a defined set of servers or server images to appear as a single entity to the user base. Clients are able to identify a particular destination as a single entity. For example, all Web clients may see a single Web site name (e.g, www.amazon.com) that actually maps to many different physical systems. A network-based load balancer will serially allocate sessions across the multiple different servers. Therefore, if a particular Web site is implemented on five physical servers, the first session request would be mapped to server A, the second to server B, and so on. Exhibit 5.19 illustrates a multi-server environment that is served by a network-based round-robin load balancer.

Load balancers can either allocate sessions based on the round-robin basis illustrated, or they can allocate sessions based on some knowledge of the loads and capacities of the various servers. In the former example, no communication with the server is required. The load balancer simply keeps track of the last session allocated and moves to the next server in the list on the following session request. In the latter example, a protocol must be implemented between the load balancer and the server that provides information necessary to the load balancer to allow it to make balancing decisions. For example, the server may provide the load balancer with CPU utilization, active session counts, or other metrics upon which the load balancer can make its balancing decisions.

Application server developers should be aware of any network-based load balancers and implement any specific protocols that will be useful in effectively balancing application server traffic across multiple application servers.

Final Thoughts

The application server market is growing rapidly, and more and more vendors are entering the fray. With the more widespread implementation of the J2EE platform and the CORBA 2.x/3.0 specifications, the products will begin to look alike. Enterprises must look beyond the feature/function matrices put out by the vendors and select a product and a vendor that will best serve their needs. IT organizations should give precedence to vendors that demonstrate a commitment to open standards so that their options are left open in the future.

Today's application servers are first differentiated based on the component model supported. Microsoft's COM model is expected to be highly popular, especially in small and medium enterprise environments that have a relatively homogeneous environment. Most large enterprises, on the other hand, need to support a widely diverse and heterogeneous environment. These organizations are more likely to support a Java approach if they do not already have a large base of proprietary client/server, DCE-based, or CORBA-based distributed object applications. For very sophisticated, large enterprises, a CORBA approach, with its multi-language support and very sophisticated and complex services, may be the desired approach. Fortunately, the state of the technology and specifications are such that a large enterprise can quite comfortably implement all of the object models. For example, COM can be utilized in the department to tie together departmental-level objects, while Java can be used for all new component-based applications and existing CORBA systems are left in place. RMI-over-IIOP has become a critical technology for Java–CORBA interoperability, while COM interoperability can be determined by the capabilities implemented within the particular vendor's product.

Once the Java and CORBA standards become more widely implemented, application server vendors will try to differentiate themselves through offering additional services, bundling the application server with tools and additional products, or offering related products. IT organizations should look beyond the feature and function offered in the base application server and consider the product line extensions that augment the application server when evaluating potential vendors.

It is critical that implementers of application servers within the IT organization understand the overall networking environment into which the application servers will go. Today's enterprise network is much more than simple plumbing. Today's enterprise network supports a rich variety of intelligent and adaptive network services. The new applications should take advantage of these network-based services where possible.

Finally, the implementers of application servers need to design the systems for the enterprise. They need to design systems that will protect the enterprise IT resources from intrusion or attack. They need to design systems that support the current and future number of concurrent users. Finally, they need to design systems that exhibit near-100 percent availability to the end user. Chapter 6 focuses on some of these elements of overall application server design.

Notes

1. June 20, 2000, *Business Wire*, Giga Information Group Predicts Application Server Market to Rise to $9 Billion by 2003.
2. January 2000, *Network Magazine*, Application Servers on Parade.
3. http://www.flashline.com/Components/appservermatrix.jsp.
4. *Introduction to WebSphere Application Server Version 3.0*, pp. 33–34.

Chapter 6

Design Issues
for Enterprise Deployment
of Application Servers

The premise of this book is that enterprises of all sizes will deploy application servers to accomplish the goal of E-business. This means that all of the organization's key business processes will be transformed. The public, customers, suppliers, business partners, and internal employees will interface with the organization using Internet technologies. The systems and processes will be tied seamlessly together, providing a different Web-style interface that is appropriate for each audience.

This sounds like a panacea to some, particularly the CEO and CFO. Achieving E-business allows organizations to vastly simplify and streamline what have been cumbersome, costly, manual, and error-prone interfaces. Consider the case of a typical 1-800 call center. In some organizations, these call centers represent the primary point of contact that prospects, customers, and business agents use to interact with the organization. Yet these positions are typified by high turnover rates and high training costs, resulting in uneven levels of service. Worse yet, customers are often unsatisfied with the cumbersome and lengthy call processing interface (e.g., press "1" for account information, press "2" to order supplies, etc.). By Web-enabling the customer service function, an organization can simultaneously reduce costs and increase customer satisfaction. Chapter 7 highlights some real-world examples of organizations that have successfully implemented application servers and reaped significant rewards as a result.

Unfortunately, to the CIO/CTO, achieving E-business can appear risky indeed. These individuals have overseen the evolution and the growth of the enterprise IT infrastructure to support extremely high levels of security, stability, and availability. The thought of opening the floodgates, potentially exposing the mission-critical systems and data of the enterprise to the outside world, is anathema. Another serious concern is the impact on the overall resources of the enterprise network and systems. The internal network, with its years of usage history and trend information, can usually be deterministically modeled. Organizations have been able to effectively plan for additional system resources and networking bandwidth. But by opening the environment to a whole new set of users with uncertain usage patterns, the IT organization has a more difficult time understanding the total impact and planning for upgrades accordingly.

This chapter delves into five different and critical design issues that an enterprise IT organization must face in planning for and deploying application servers:

1. security
2. scalability
3. load balancing
4. fault tolerance
5. management

The application server has innate capabilities that enhance the overall design in these five key design areas. However, the application server cannot act alone in any of these areas; it must work with a variety of other systems, servers, network appliances, and applications to achieve satisfactory levels of security, scalability, load balancing, fault tolerance, and overall management.

Security

The press is filled with stories of computer systems that are attacked and compromised by intentional acts. IT organizations that thought they had a pretty complete security architecture have learned the hard way that they have holes that have been found and exploited by crafty hackers who have a grudge against the organization or who are simply trying to prove that they have the skills to do it. The threats are numerous and varied, and organizations need a comprehensive defense.

Web technologies pose certain security risks. The very open nature of the Web means that the general public potentially has access to any system that is connected to a network that has Internet access. Internal systems should be protected by firewalls and other security measures to prevent unauthorized access and use. Sensitive data should also be protected from prying eyes. Applets and controls should only be downloaded to client systems from trusted sources or they should be prevented from harming the client system. Fortunately, Web security technologies have evolved quickly and are now both effective and pervasive.

The distributed object model poses its own set of security risks. Because new applications are often built using components from a variety of sources, a security hole could intentionally or inadvertently be introduced in one of the components that puts the system at risk. In addition, a single transaction can span several objects or even several different technology domains. End-to-end security measures are required to protect the transaction at each step in the chain. CORBA offers a comprehensive framework for security that individual ORBs and application servers can take advantage of. Java offers a growing set of security-related APIs. Application servers should implement appropriate security while not wasting resources by duplicating security measures that are provided by lower layers such as the network.

Elements of Security

There are three major elements of security that span the session or transaction and therefore involve the two end-points and possibly some intermediate systems:

1. message protection
2. authentication
3. authorization

Message protection ensures that no one has read or tampered with the message. The first facet of message protection is message integrity, in which the undetected and unauthorized modification of the message is prevented. This includes detection of single-packet modification and also detection of the insertion or removal of packets within a multi-packet message. The former type of detection is generally provided by checksum calculations at all points within the network or at the end-points (or both). The latter type of detection is usually provided by the communication protocol. For example, Transport Control Protocol (TCP), the transport layer protocol of TCP/IP, ensures that messages are received in entirety and in the proper order or requests retransmission from the sending point.

The second facet of message protection is encryption. The explosive growth of the Internet and usage of Web technologies have brought this previously arcane technology to the forefront. Encryption is the encoding of data so that it is illegible to anyone trying to decipher it other than the intended recipient. Encryption used to be relatively rare in the IT infrastructure when systems and users were all (or mostly) in-house and wide area links were privately leased, because encryption is an expensive process in terms of CPU utilization. Each message is algorithmically encoded using keys of 40, 56, or 128 bits (or even more) and must be decoded on the receiving end. If performed in software, encryption can significantly impact the end-system. There are a variety of different algorithms that are commonly used and implemented within various end-systems; RSA, DES/TripleDES, and RC4 are among those often implemented. Secure Sockets Layer (SSL), a common security technology used within Web and application server environments, includes encryption as one of the security elements that is negotiated by the SSL-capable end-systems.

Authentication is the element of a security system that ensures that the identity of the user, client, or target system is verified. Essentially, authentication is the process of determining that the client and target each is who it claims to be. In traditional hierarchical and client/server systems, authentication is usually determined by making the user logon to the system using a userID and password combination. In many cases, a separate logon is required for each application because the application-specific data and functions to which users have access may depend on their identity.

Today, the overall authentication process is likely to include the use of digital certificates in addition to traditional userIDs and passwords. The exchange of certificates is a mechanism for authenticating end-systems, not users, and can be used to verify the identity of the target system in addition to the client system. The most common type of certificate system in usage today is based on asymmetric public/private key exchanges, moderated by an external Certificate Authority (CA). A CA is a trusted external entity that issues digital certificates that are used to create digital signatures and public/private key pairs. A digital signature is a unique identifier that guarantees that the sending party, either client system or server system, is who it claims to be. Digital signatures are encrypted using the public/private keys so that they cannot be copied and reused by any system other than the original system, nor decoded by any system other than the intended recipient.

Some systems, data, and applications can be accessed without prior authentication. These resources are available to all users and are known as public resources. A perfect example of this type of system is the public home page that an organization posts on the Web. Most enterprise resources, however, are available only to certain users, and the authentication process establishes end-user or client-system identity. Once a user or system is authenticated, the authorization of that user or system to perform a given task is performed. Authorization can be performed both at system access and application levels. For example, a particular user may be granted access to a particular object that invokes a back-end database application. However, that user may only have the privilege to search and retrieve database records but not update the database. Privilege attributes are often based on logical groupings such as organization, role, etc. Therefore, all members in the human resources department may have access to all personnel records, while department managers only have access to the records of the employees within their particular department.

In a distributed object environment, the ORBs and EJB servers are involved in granting access to users or systems. This is typically done through the use of access control lists that are specified by a security administrator and then enforced through the security services built into the ORB or EJB server. The target application is still solely responsible for granting application-specific privileges and does not gain assistance from the ORB or EJB server to perform the authorization task. These privileges must be specified within each application.

Authentication and authorization within a distributed object environment are complicated by the fact that the initiating user or system of the invocation

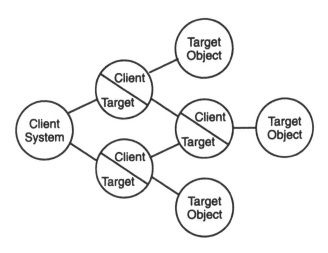

Exhibit 6.1 Delegation in a Distributed Object Environment

or request may not directly interface with the target object. Exhibit 6.1 illustrates the potential chain of calls in a distributed object environment. The distributed object system can support the delegation of privileges so that the objects further in the chain can be granted the same privileges that the initiating principal has. The granting of privileges may be subject to restrictions, so that an intermediate object may only be able to invoke certain methods on certain objects on behalf of the originator.

A security system should implement the concept of non-repudiation. Non-repudiation services provide the facilities to make users responsible for their actions. Irrefutable evidence of a particular action is preserved, usually by the application and not the ORB/EJB server, so that later disputes can be resolved. There are a variety of data that can be used and stored to support non-repudiation, but usually a date and timestamp are crucial. Two common types of non-repudiation evidence are the evidence of proof of creation of a message and evidence of proof of receipt. Non-repudiation often involves the participation of a trusted third party.

In a large and complex enterprise environment, achieving comprehensive end-to-end security can be complicated by the existence of different security domains. Security domains can be defined by scope of policy, environment, and technology. The domains must somehow be bridged or coordinated if end-to-end security is to be achieved. For example, business partners that implement extranet-based business process interaction must coordinate their environments so that each domain is appropriately protected. A large enterprise might implement one authentication technology for dial-in users and another for users within the corporate firewall. These technology domains must be joined to provide a seamless and secure corporate intranet.

The administration of a security policy is a critical factor in the overall effectiveness of the security architecture. It is becoming increasingly common to centralize the administration of security through a security policy server.

By centralizing the implementation of policy, more seamless and airtight security can be implemented within the entire i*net infrastructure. The administration function should include a comprehensive auditing capability, in which actual or attempted security violations are detected. Violations can be written to a log or, for more immediate action and intervention, can generate an alarm to the operations staff.

Java Security

The initial security emphasis in the Java world was focused on providing a secure environment for the execution of applets. This is because the early focus of Java was in supporting the thin-client model in which applications and applets were automatically downloaded over the network to thin clients and executed. To prevent malicious applet developers from introducing viruses or other nefarious code on client systems, JDK 1.0 prevented any applet from accessing client-system resources. Termed the "sandbox model" of security, this model prevented harm to the client system by blocking access to the local hard drive, network connections, and other system resources. Eventually, this model evolved to support a range of different permission levels that varies based on the source of the applet, which is verified through the use of public/private key digital certificates. A security policy is defined that gives different system access privileges to different sources. The current Java applet security model is described and depicted in Chapter 3.

With the shift in emphasis and implementation of Java applications from the client to the server came a new set of Java security technologies. The Java 2 platform now supports three optional APIs for server-side security:

1. Java Authentication and Authorization Service (JAAS)
2. Java Cryptography Extension (JCE)
3. Java Secure Socket Extension (JSSE)

JAAS provides a framework for Java applications (and applets and servlets) to authenticate and authorize potential users of the application. The JAAS specification does not specify a particular authentication and authorization methodology or technology. JAAS is based on the X/OPEN concept of pluggable authentication modules (PAM) that allows an organization to "plug in" modules that support a particular authentication technology that is appropriate to the environment. For example, smart cards could be supported for traveling and remote users, while biometrics devices (e.g., fingerprint or retina scanners) or traditional Kerberos tickets could be used to authenticate users within the intranet.

JCE is a standard extension for use with JDK 1.2 and includes both domestic (i.e., within North America) and global distribution bundles. Like JAAS, JCE does not specify a particular implementation. Instead, organizations can plug in the algorithms for encryption, key generation and key agreement, and message authentication that are appropriate for the environment and consistent with the security policy.

The JSSE API provides support for two client/server security protocols that are widely implemented in Web environments — Secure Sockets Layer (SSL) and Transport Layer Security (TLS). TLS is an enhancement to SSL and is backward compatible with it. SSL has been very widely implemented by a variety of different clients and servers, particularly in Web environments. SSL (and now TLS) is based on a protocol in which a variety of security mechanisms are included or negotiated. SSL/TLS supports data encryption, server authentication, message integrity, and optional client authentication. SSL/TLS supports any TCP/IP application — HTTP, FTP, SMTP, Telnet, and others.

The three Java APIs do not complete the entire Java security roadmap. Future enhancements will include more extensive certificate capabilities, integration of the Kerberos standards, and performance improvements.

It should be noted that the utilization of these Java security APIs is not mandated by the Java 2 platform. Developers of Java application servers and distributed object applications can select whether and which security facilities to utilize. Not all products support the same levels of security. IT organizations should make sure that the platforms and applications they select implement the various security mechanisms that are required within their environment.

CORBA Security

The CORBA Security Services specification is one of the 16 different CORBAservices defined by the OMG. The Security Services specification is incredibly rich and comprehensive. It defines a security reference model that provides an overall framework for CORBA security and encompasses all of the concepts and elements discussed in the earlier section entitled "Elements of Security." The Security Services specification does not, however, specify a specific security policy implementation. Like the Java specifications, it leaves the selection and implementation of specific security mechanisms open.

CORBA security builds on existing security mechanisms such as SSL/TLS. The APIs exposed to the applications do not expose the actual implementation. Therefore, the application programmer does not need to be aware whether authentication is being provided by public/private key pair or simple logon, or whether authorization is implemented with UNIX modes or access control lists.

CORBA security does, however, extend the common security mechanisms to include the concept of delegation. As described earlier, delegation is a security concept that is important in a distributed object environment because it is typical that the initiating user is separated from the eventual target object by one or more links in a multi-link client-object chain. Delegation of privileges makes the implementation of security auditing even more important than usual. The CORBA security specification specifies auditing as a base feature.

As described in the section on "Elements of Security," certain security features are provided by the infrastructure (or ORB in a CORBA environment), and certain security features are dependent on implementation within the application. CORBA supports two levels of security in order to support both security-unaware applications (Level 1) and security-aware applications (Level 2).

With Level 1 security, the CORBA ORB and infrastructure provides secure invocation between client and server, authorization based on ORB-enforced access control checks, simple delegation of credentials, and auditing of relevant system events. There are no application-level APIs provided with this first level of security because it is assumed that the application is completely unaware of security mechanisms. All security mechanisms are handled at a lower level within the ORB, or even outside of the ORB. Obviously, this level of security makes the job easier for application programmers because they do not have to provide any security-specific hooks or logic.

With Level 2 security, the application is aware of security and can implement various qualities of protection. As cited in an earlier example, a database program might allow all authorized users to perform searches and record retrieval, but only allow updates to be initiated by a select group of authorized users. An application implementing Level 2 security can also exert control over the delegation options. Naturally, a Level 2 application must interface to CORBA security APIs, which requires more work and sophistication on the part of the application programmer.

As in the case of Java application servers, different CORBA application servers will offer different implementations of the CORBA Security Services specification. For example, the OMG specification only requires that an ORB implement at least one of the two levels of security to be considered a secure ORB. Non-repudiation, an important concept in an overall security scheme, is considered an optional ORB extension. Interoperability between secure ORBs is defined in varying levels. The security reference model defined by the OMG is very rich and comprehensive, but each implementation will vary in the completeness of its security capabilities. IT organizations need to carefully evaluate CORBA application servers in light of their own specific overall security requirements and architecture.

An Overall Security Architecture

Application servers will be implemented within an enterprise environment that already includes a number of different security mechanisms, technologies, and platforms. Today's i*net would not exist without them because corporations, governmental agencies, educational institutions, nonprofit organizations, and end users would not trust the public Internet to carry confidential financial data, personal statistics, credit card information, and other sensitive data without being assured that sufficient security mechanisms are in place. The new application servers may interoperate with or even leverage existing security services that are already built into the i*net infrastructure.

The first line of defense typically installed when an enterprise connects its internal network with the public Internet is a firewall. The term "firewall" refers to a set of functions that protects the internal network from malicious tampering from outside the firewall. Firewall functionality can be provided in switches and routers, in stand-alone devices, or in server software. Wherever the functionality is provided, the firewall should be placed at the perimeter of the internal network, directly connected to the Internet. With this placement, there is no opportunity for outsiders to infiltrate the internal network. A firewall used to be a simple filtering device that would only allow certain source or destination IP addresses to flow through it. It has since evolved to include very sophisticated features. A firewall can now filter based on application type, hide actual internal user and server IP addresses so they are not directly subject to attack, and perform authentication and encryption services. The CORBA V3 specification will include the addition of a firewall specification for transport-level, application-level, and bi-directional firewall support.

Virtual private networks (VPNs) are another means that an enterprise can use to secure data and communications at the networking level. A VPN is a secure network that rides on top of the public Internet. It is typically implemented by an enterprise with remote users or business partners. It is extremely economical for telecommuters, traveling users, and small branch offices to use the infrastructure of the public Internet for connection to a centralized enterprise campus or data center. However, performing business-critical and sensitive operations over the public Internet is not recommended without implementing security measures. A VPN creates this virtual network on top of the public Internet by implementing encryption and authentication mechanisms. An IETF-standard protocol, IPsec (short for IP security), is often used to implement VPNs. The protocol encrypts either just the data portion of the packet or the entire packet, including its header. Public keys are used to authenticate the sender using digital certificates. A VPN requires software on both ends of the connection to encrypt/decrypt and perform authentication. Each remote client system usually has VPN client software installed on it. At the campus or data center, a router with VPN features or a stand-alone VPN server is implemented. The application (or application server) is unaware of the VPN and needs no special VPN software.

Another level of security often implemented within Web environments is secure communication between Web browser and Web server. The two technologies employed are SSL and S-HTTP. S-HTTP provides the ability for a single page or message to be protected, and is commonly used when individual Web pages contain sensitive information (e.g., credit card information). SSL, on the other hand, provides a secure client/server connection over which multiple pages or messages can be sent. Both protocols are IETF standards, but SSL is more prevalent. As earlier stated, SSL is often a common underpinning for distributed object environments and can be used, for example, for secure communication between a client object and its target object implementation.

A growing area of interest within the enterprise is in centralizing security definition and administration through implementation of a centralized security policy manager or server. A centralized policy server allows IT organizations to centralize the task of defining, distributing, and enforcing security mechanisms throughout the enterprise. A centralized approach allows for a more consistent implementation of security and greatly simplifies the task of managing user identity and authorization and intrusion detection. Policy management is simpler and less error-prone when implemented centrally rather than by individually configuring each router and server. There are a variety of approaches being pursued by different vendor groups. Some vendors advocate integrating the policy management with existing directory services such as LDAP, while others advocate a separate and new approach.

It should be obvious that there are a lot of platforms, products, and servers that can potentially implement one or all of the three major security functions in the path from the client to the new application running on the application server. For example, take the case of encryption. Encryption can be implemented at the client (in VPN client software), at the branch office router, within a firewall, at the campus/data center router, at the Web server, and also at the application server. As indicated previously, encryption is a very expensive process in terms of CPU utilization if performed in software. Therefore, it should be performed only when needed. Encryption within a campus environment that has a high-speed, private, fiber network may be completely unnecessary. Encryption should also be performed only once in a single end-to-end path and therefore the end-points of the encryption process should at least span the entire path that requires data privacy.

IT staff implementing application servers need to be aware of the various levels of security and should be familiar with the overall security policy and architecture. Encryption, authentication, and authorization for application server-based applications need to be coordinated with those services provided within the network infrastructure. For example, if end users are authenticated using digital certificates within the network, that identity can be leveraged by the application server-based applications without requiring a separate logon (unless there is a specific reason to require further validation). IT staff should also be aware of any security policy administration servers within the enterprise and take advantage of the centralized implementation of user identity and authorization mechanisms. Auditing should be a part of the overall security administration. Exhibit 6.2 illustrates an application server within an enterprise that contains a variety of different security mechanisms.

Scalability

The next three topics (scalability, load balancing, and fault tolerance) are related in the quest to design and implement systems that will support many users simultaneously with system availability approaching 100 percent. This is the goal of any enterprise that wishes to integrate its key business processes with the i*net. The three topics for building such an infrastructure are interrelated. In fact, some vendors treat the subjects as all the same thing. However, each of the topics should be individually considered and evaluated during the design

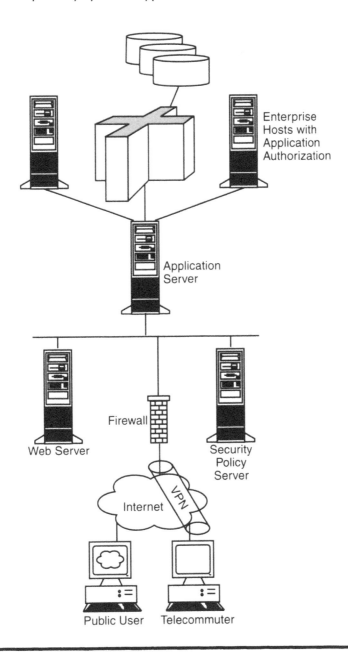

Exhibit 6.2 Application Server in Enterprise with Security Platforms

process. Adding one of the elements without individually considering the other two does not lead to an optimal design and may in fact waste resources.

Scalability Defined

Scalability is a trait of a computer system, network, or infrastructure that is able to grow to accommodate new users and new traffic in an approximately linear fashion. That is, scalable systems do not have design points at which

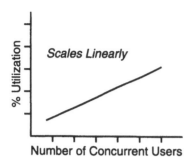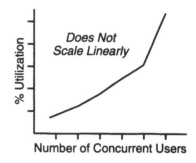

Exhibit 6.3   Scalability Comparison

point the addition of the next incremental user or unit of work causes an exponential increase in relative resource consumption. Exhibit 6.3 illustrates the difference between a system that scales linearly and one that does not.

Scalability within an enterprise requires the examination of the individual elements as well as the overall environment. Any single element will have a scalability limit. But if the overall environment is able to grow through the addition of another similar element, the overall environment is exhibiting characteristics of scalability. For example, a router within an enterprise network will have a given capacity in terms of connections, packets per second, etc. If another router can be added to the environment when the initial router's capacity has been reached and the overall network now has roughly twice the capacity, the network is scalable. Similarly, a single server (even a powerful one) will have a processing limit. A scalable server design allows another server to be added to augment the first server.

Note that any system, network, or infrastructure does have practical upper limits. Today's high-end network switches, for example, support campus backbone links of multi-gigabit speeds. It is not feasible or possible to build backbones that are faster than that. Multiprocessing servers can support multiple high-powered CPUs, but not an infinite number of them. The big question that an IT organization needs to answer is what level of scalability it requires as its design goal. The scalability goal should be high enough to comfortably support today's requirements with additional capacity to support potential future growth.

Designing and implementing a scalable infrastructure involves the identification and elimination of real and potential bottlenecks. This is achieved either through extensive modeling prior to implementation or through implementing a piece of the overall infrastructure and testing the limits. Although modeling tools are getting better and offer a wide variety of capabilities, it is often difficult or impossible for modeling tools to take into account the vast richness and diversity of individual environments. Two enterprises that are identical except for the average transaction size in number of bytes may have dramatically different bottleneck points and therefore different solutions for increasing scalability. Thus, in most large enterprises, there is a group of individuals within IT responsible for performance testing of platforms and systems using the organization's own transactions and usage profiles to estimate the performance of the infrastructure once deployed. Increasingly, networking and systems vendors (e.g., Cisco, IBM) are offering a complete lab environment in which customers can implement, deploy, and test a segment of their actual production environment to identify bottlenecks and quantify the overall scalability of the environment.

There are many different elements within the enterprise infrastructure that impact scalability and that are potential bottlenecks. The multi-tier environment in which an application server resides is very complex and there are a lot of pieces that contribute to the overall scalability of the environment. The next sections identify some of the common bottlenecks and approaches to overcome them.

Network Scalability

Today's enterprise network is vastly superior in terms of raw bandwidth to the enterprise network of a decade ago. In fact, in the 1970s, some of the largest corporations in the world ran networks in which 9.6 Kbps wide area network links connected large data centers and carried the traffic of hundreds or thousands of users. Today's Internet-connected user considers a dedicated, dial-up 28.8-Kbps line a pauper's connection. Of course, the profiles of a typical user and a typical transaction are completely different from what they once were. The typical user in the past was located within a campus and accessed one or a few systems to perform transactions. The transactions were typically a few hundred bytes in size in each direction. Today's user base is literally scattered across the globe and includes employees, business partners, and the general public. Today's transactions typically involve the download of files and Web pages that range from a few thousand bytes to a few million bytes. Therefore, although the total bandwidth of the network has grown exponentially, the demand for the bandwidth continues to outstrip the supply in many enterprise networks. Enterprise IT organizations must build a scalable infrastructure within the campus and, where possible, at the network access points. Once that scalable infrastructure is in place, a second and critical part of building a scalable network has to do with maximizing the available bandwidth.

Today's enterprise network is typically comprised of campus networks, links between campus networks, and a variety of different access networks that connect remote users with one or more campuses. Remote users can be traveling employees, telecommuters, users in branch offices, business partners, suppliers, agents, customers, or the general public. These users can access systems at one or more campuses and connect via either public or private wide area networks. Exhibit 6.4 illustrates a typical enterprise network.

Within the campus network, most enterprises implement LAN switching rather than the shared LANs that were common a decade ago. With shared LANs, each user effectively receives a portion of the overall bandwidth. Therefore, in a 10-Mbps Ethernet shared LAN of 10 users, each user on average

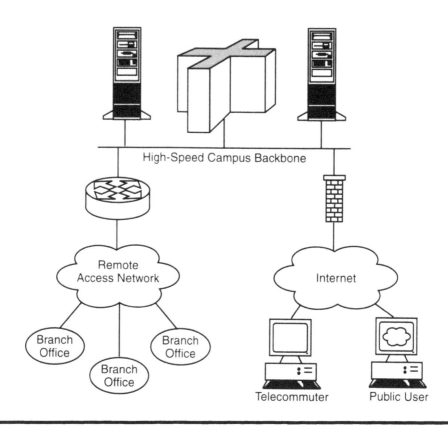

Exhibit 6.4   Typical Enterprise Network

has approximately 1 Mbps of bandwidth available to them. In a switched LAN environment, each user has the full bandwidth of the LAN available to them. Most enterprise campuses are built today with switched Fast Ethernet (100 Mbps) to each desktop and a backbone of Gigabit Ethernet (1000 Mbps). Campus networks, per se, are rarely the bottleneck for effective end-to-end response time and throughput today. Any bottlenecks within the campus environment are likely to be because the servers and legacy systems cannot support the high speeds of the network infrastructure, or because the traffic must traverse a relatively slow system, such as a gateway device or a switch or router that is working at its capacity limit.

Links between campuses are usually implemented (at least in North America) with high-speed private wide area network (WAN) links. These links can be built using a variety of different WAN technologies and protocols, including perhaps Frame Relay, ISDN, or ATM. Private WAN links are leased by the enterprise and thus the enterprise gains full use of the available bandwidth. However, inter-campus links can also be shared or public. In this case, the enterprise is leasing a portion of the total available bandwidth of the link. Because of the volume of traffic that is typical between two campuses, the enterprise normally negotiates for a particular guaranteed quality of service on the link. Bottlenecks within these inter-campus links can occur if either the total bandwidth demand exceeds available bandwidth or if there is contention on the line between different types of traffic. Enterprises that are in the former situation simply need to add more bandwidth on the WAN links. Enterprises that are in the latter situation need to apply bandwidth management techniques to prioritize and shape traffic more effectively.

Remote user access to the campus network is very diverse. In some cases, the enterprise can control the bandwidth and its allocation, and in some cases it cannot. In the case of a branch office (typical in retail, banking, and financial organizations), the link between the branch office and the campus is often a dedicated line (or lines), or a shared or public link that offers a specific quality of service. In these cases, the enterprise has the same level of control and options as in the case of inter-campus links.

In the past, single remote users or small groups of remote users were serviced with dedicated links. For example, a large insurance company would provide a bank of modems and a 1-800 phone number that its base of independent agents could use to dial in to the campus and access the required systems. This remote access structure, while effective, was very expensive due to the high recurring long-distance charges. However, the enterprise was in complete control and could increase service to its remote users by upgrading the modem technology on both ends of the link or by adding more links. With the explosive growth of the Internet, many organizations have found that it is much more cost-effective to service these individual users and small offices through the Internet. As a result, many large organizations have traveling users, telecommuters, and business partners all accessing the campus via the Internet. The users connect to a local Internet service provider (ISP), avoiding all long-distance charges. The difficulty is that no single entity controls the Internet and therefore the enterprise cannot provide a guaranteed level of service to its users. The primary action that an IT organization can take is to ensure that the organization's Internet connections are high speed. Secondarily, the organization can select an ISP that is closest to the core of the Internet, minimizing the number of hops that traffic must traverse.

As with any resource, network bandwidth may be wasted or used inefficiently. Today's enterprise network carries many different types of traffic of varying sizes and priorities. IT organizations should make the most of the total available bandwidth by ensuring that time-critical and high-priority traffic gets through, while low-priority traffic waits until there is available bandwidth. There are a variety of different mechanisms for shaping and prioritizing traffic. The "Queuing and Prioritization" section in Chapter 5 discusses some of these techniques. These techniques can be used to maximize existing bandwidth and support the total goal of network scalability.

Server Scalability

When Web-based computing was first proliferating, a number of experts predicted that the thin-client model of computing would prevail. Web servers would download applets to thin clients, and the client systems would execute much of the new business logic. In this model, the scalability of servers is not particularly critical because the servers simply download logic to client systems. In terms of scalability, this model offers the utmost because the addition of each new user brings the addition of incremental processing power (i.e., the client system). The execution of the logic is not dependent on a single centralized device that can become a bottleneck.

However, the tide has turned and most enterprises are adopting three-tier (or n-tier) environments. In this design, the servers are an obvious and critical piece in the overall scalability design because it is the servers that execute the new business logic comprised of server-side components, servlets, and applications. The scalability of an individual server or a complex of servers is determined by the server hardware, the server operating system, and the applications running on the server.

Server scalability, measured in the amount of work that it can perform in a given amount of time, is obviously impacted by the capabilities of the underlying hardware. It is pretty straightforward to compare the relative scalability of two systems from a hardware perspective. A system based on a 200-MHz Pentium chip, for example, cannot perform as much work as a system based on a 400-MHz Pentium chip. This is obvious and intuitive. However, there is much more than just the raw processing power in terms of MIPS, FLOPS, or some other such measure that determines the potential power of a server. Other factors that help determine its overall scalability are the amount of RAM, the type and processing speed of the internal bus, the type and speed of the permanent storage (e.g., disks, tapes), and even the network interface adapter used to access the enterprise network. Any of these is a potential bottleneck and should be considered, along with CPU power, when comparing two similar systems.

The choice of operating systems running on the server is critical in determining the scalability of a server system. Quite simply, some operating systems are more efficient and can handle more work of a given type. A proprietary server operating system designed to support a single type of work, for example, will probably do that work more efficiently than a similar system based on a general-purpose operating system. Nonetheless, a general-purpose operating system is a better choice for most applications for reasons unrelated to scalability (e.g., time to market, cost, support).

Many server systems have multiple CPUs, and some operating systems are much more efficient than others in multiprocessing environments. For example, Windows NT and UNIX both support symmetric multiprocessing (SMP), in which a system with multiple CPUs allocates individual processes to any available CPU. However, it is widely believed that UNIX systems scale better and support more users than NT systems. In many types of multiuser applications, a high-end UNIX system will support thousands of concurrent users, while a Windows NT system running a similar application will support hundreds. Obviously, this is an area of contention, and advocates in each camp will point to the superiority of their respective system. IT organizations that are evaluating the scalability of systems based on UNIX/Linux or Windows NT/2000 should evaluate those systems using applications that will reflect the planned production environment.

There is another hardware platform that large enterprises should evaluate for hosting new i*net applications: that is, mainframes. The enterprise application platform of a generation ago has changed dramatically in the past few years and now exhibits a price/performance ratio that is very competitive. Mainframes have also benefited from decades of effort in which IT organizations have created the processes and procedures to support fault tolerance and disaster recovery that is unparalleled in other systems. In addition, mainframe operating systems have always been architected to support multiprocessing and to efficiently handle a large or even huge base of users. The latest mainframes, coupled with the latest IBM mainframe operating system (OS/390®), can often support tens of thousands of users simultaneously.

The applications that run on the servers, whether traditional applications written in C/C++ or Java applications leveraging the EJB distributed object approach, must be written to take advantage of the sophisticated multiprocessing capabilities of the underlying operating system. A corollary to that statement is that just because a server operating system supports SMP does not mean that the applications can or will take advantage of that capability. Applications that implement multithreading break up the program into individual and autonomous units that can be allocated to different CPUs for simultaneous execution and therefore take advantage of SMP systems. Applications that do not leverage SMP and do not implement a multithreaded architecture will only utilize a portion of the available power of a multiprocessor system.

The scalability of a single server, in terms of its raw hardware throughput and power and sophisticated software abilities, is only one piece in the overall server scalability puzzle for enterprises. The demands have become so great that a single server, even a powerful one, cannot handle all of the throughput, transactions, or processing ability that an enterprise requires. This has led to the development of server clusters, in which several physical servers are viewed logically as a single entity. This development has led to an increased sophistication in operating systems, because they are the entity that must create a unified whole out of the individual systems. For a server cluster concept to be effective, the user/client community must view the cluster of servers as a single entity. This creates a requirement for load balancing and fault tolerance capabilities, which are explored in detail in subsequent sections.

Application Server Scalability

Application servers are software systems that reside on a physical server. Like other server-based applications, the application server software can dramatically impact the scalability of that server in terms of the number of users supported, the number of transactions performed, or some other metric. The fundamental architecture of the application server software determines its scalability.

An application server must simultaneously manage transactions and sessions with many users. Some of these sessions or transactions may involve persistent components, and some will not. The manner in which the application server manages threads, memory, and other key system resources will, to a large extent, determine its scalability. An application server that is parsimonious in its use of system resources will offer better scalability than one that is not. For example, an EJB container manages the system resources on behalf of the enterprise beans (see Chapter 3). The EJB specification does not detail exactly how the EJB container is to manage those resources. Therefore, different vendors' implementations will manage the system resources differently, and some implementations are bound to be more scalable than others. The same thing is true of CORBA ORB-based application servers. The OMG specifications do not specify implementation, and therefore some implementations will be better than others in terms of inherent scalability.

Some application servers also support the creation of clusters of servers so that multiple CPUs and multiple servers can share the workload. The servlets, EJBs, and CORBA objects are defined as belonging to a group or cluster of application servers with a common configuration. Once again, the implementations will vary. Every application server vendor makes great marketing claims about the scalability of its implementation, but the only way to know for sure is to run an evaluation with traffic that is representative of the enterprise's production environment.

Also impacting application server scalability is the overall design and placement of clients or client proxies, object implementations, and servlets. The communication between an EJB client and its enterprise bean, for example, requires serialization of the data and unmarshalling on the other end, which can create high overhead on the network and work at the two end-points. If these entities co-reside on a single server, then the overhead can be avoided because internal calls will be used instead. However, running the EJB client code on the application server platform will obviously cause extra work for the application server platform. Therefore, there is a trade-off between client and network overhead versus application server scalability that must be examined in light of the particular environment and goals.

Overall Scalability in Multi-tier Environments

The typical enterprise environment into which the application server is placed is very rich and diverse. There are many different platforms and services that are potentially involved in a session or transaction. Overall scalability of the environment can be impacted by various different potential bottlenecks. IT organizations need to understand the complete path of a session or transaction, starting at the client and moving through all systems until the session or transaction path is complete. Any product or platform that processes data or even moves traffic is a potential bottleneck. Some of these potential bottlenecks include:

- points of encryption/decryption
- directory and name servers

- firewalls
- policy servers
- back-end data and application hosts
- gateway devices or software
- load balancing devices

An IT organization that understands the scalability of each and every platform and product within the overall path is equipped to respond to an increased demand for service or additional users. An organization that does not understand the entire path is doomed to fight fires, chasing one bottleneck point after another and usually spending more money in the long run than one that has a more orderly and better planned approach.

Load Balancing

Load balancing is the act of allocating sessions or transactions across a group of servers able to perform the same work. For example, a group of UNIX and NT servers may be running Web server software. Each server contains the same Web pages or has access to a Web page storage complex that is reachable by all the servers in the group. To the clients accessing these servers, it appears that there is a single destination server. A load-balancing platform or piece of software hides the fact that there is in fact a pool, cluster, or complex of servers grouped together to service the users. The load balancer allocates the sessions or transactions on a more-or-less equal basis so that all of the servers maintain a roughly equivalent load.

Load balancing allows organizations to maximize their server resources because it avoids the situation in which one server is overloaded with requests while others are nearly idle. Load balancing also helps achieve the goal of server scalability because it facilitates the formation of server complexes. Without load balancing, client systems may need to be configured for multiple possible destinations or end users may need to be aware of the multiple destinations. If one server destination does not respond or is too slow, the client system or the end user would select another one in the list. Obviously, this is not an optimal approach. It greatly complicates the client system configuration task and demands too much on the part of the end user. With load balancing in place, server complexes can be transparently created, changed, and administered without requiring coordination with the end-user population.

Geographic and Local Load Balancing

Having discussed the fact that organizations deploy clusters of servers to promote scalability, the implication is usually that these servers are all in the same location. Typically, the servers are all in a single data center and are connected to the same high-speed internal network. Load balancers in this type of environment make load-balancing decisions that are based on a particular allocation scheme or server load. They do not make load-balancing decisions based on server location or network connectivity because these are assumed to be the same for all servers.

However, many enterprises replicate server functionality in different geographical locations. They do this when they have a potential user base that is geographically dispersed. By locating a set of servers physically close to the users, the users receive better response times and lower telecommunications costs. The most common example of the geographic dispersion of servers is with Web servers. Many enterprises with a worldwide Web audience have Web server farms located in several major geographic areas. For example, an E-tailer might have Web server farms in Tokyo to support the Far East, in Brussels to support Europe, in Tel Aviv to support the Middle East and Africa, in Mexico City to support Latin America, in Boston (Massachusetts) to support eastern North America, and in San Jose (California) to support western North America.

Geographic load balancers are a specialized type of load balancer that specifically deal with geographically dispersed servers. These products make their load-balancing decisions based on some metric that attempts to measure geographical proximity. For example, Cisco Systems' DistributedDirector system uses routing protocols to determine client-to-server proximity and also uses measured link latency to determine client-to-server round-trip response times. DistributedDirector makes its load-balancing decisions based on these metrics and returns either a DNS or HTTP response to the client, directing it to the "best" server. Exhibit 6.5 illustrates a geographic load balancer.

A geographic load-balancing approach would not work in a local environment such as in a case in which all servers are located within a single data center and connected to the same high-speed network. The test for client-to-server proximity would not lead to any differentiation between the servers because all servers would be the same number of hops away from any client. The test for link latency would also (usually) fail to distinguish between the servers because the round-trip response time would be approximately equal for all servers. Within a campus or data center, a local load balancer is needed, one that makes its load-balancing decisions based on some other metric or factor. Local load balancers that balance traffic between co-located servers are the focus of the remainder of this section.

Load-balancing Approaches

Load balancing for server clusters can be performed by an entity that is outside the server cluster, or it can be performed by software that is running on the servers. External load balancers are usually either special-purpose network appliances or software that runs on a server that is outside the server complex.

External load balancers can make their load-balancing decisions completely transparent to the server complex. That is, the server complex has no awareness of and no participation in the load-balancing decision. In this type of approach,

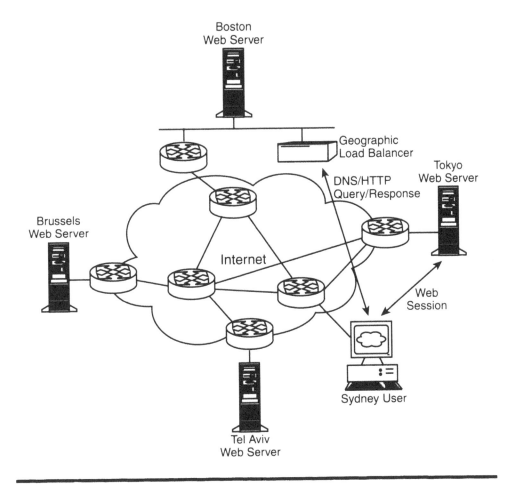

Exhibit 6.5   Geographic Load Balancer

the load balancer can balance traffic to any type of server for any type of application (except that the system must be based on TCP/IP) because there is no dependence on the server for providing input to the load-balancing decision.

The most common type of external load balancer that is transparent to the servers is the DNS round-robin approach. This is a simple and straightforward approach, and load balancers have been around for almost a decade that are based on this approach. The load balancer appears to be a standard Domain Name Server (DNS). A DNS provides a mapping between IP host name or URL and IP address. A DNS round-robin load balancer maintains a list of IP addresses that all map to a single host name or URL. Each IP address corresponds to the unique IP address of one of the servers in the complex. The first client to request the host name would receive the first IP address in the list; the second client would receive the second IP address; and so on until the end of the list of IP addresses was reached. The round-robin load balancer would start again at the beginning of the list, giving the next client the first IP address. Each server in the complex would be allocated approximately the same number of sessions. A weighted round-robin approach is a slight modification that allows a network administrator to weight each server differently. If one server in the complex can support twice the number of sessions compared to the other servers in the complex, it should receive twice as many session allocations. A weighted round-robin load balancer allows this information to be configured.

Some early round-robin DNS products maintained no awareness of the status of the various servers and could therefore send a client an IP address for a server that had just failed. If the user responded to this by trying to re-connect right away, chances are good that the user would get connected because the second attempt would yield a different IP address. However, for many users, this would result in a call to the help desk. To circumvent this problem, some round-robin DNS products implemented a heartbeat mechanism in which the load balancer would occasionally "ping" each server in the list. If a response did not come back from a server within a given amount of time, that server would be removed from the list. This approach did not entirely eliminate the problem, because a server could respond to the ping and then immediately crash; the crash would not be detected until the next ping was sent.

There are other issues with the DNS round-robin approach that became evident over time. If one of the applications failed or hung but the server was still active, the DNS round-robin load balancer would continue to allocate sessions to the failed application. If some client requests initiated a great deal more work on the server than others, then some servers could still become busy while others were underutilized. If client systems cache an IP address after a DNS name resolution (and many do), then that client will continue to access the same server on subsequent requests until the caching timer expires. Finally, the DNS round-robin approach ignored the fact that Web "sessions" are often comprised of many individual HTTP requests/responses. A particular Web user should continue to be sent to the same server from one HTTP request to the next in order to maintain client-to-server persistence. For example, an online shopper will browse the catalog, add an item to the shopping cart, browse some more, add another item to the cart, etc. All of these individual HTTP requests should be serviced by the same Web server to maintain a persistent session and carry user information from one HTTP request/response to the next.

To address these limitations of the DNS round-robin approach, several new approaches have been devised that incorporate some sort of feedback from the server to the load balancer in order to help the load balancer make the appropriate decisions. The feedback may include application status, CPU utilization, or any other important metrics. The feedback is delivered to the load balancer via some protocol. There are no standard load-balancing pro-tocols at this time; thus, all solutions are necessarily proprietary.

As briefly stated earlier, a load balancer can be implemented externally or on one or all of the servers within the complex. Internal load balancers are usually an integral part of the operating system that manages server clusters. The obvious advantage of a load balancer implemented on the target server complex is that the load balancer has access to all sorts of internal server-level information and therefore, it is presumed, can make the optimal load-balancing decisions. To span multiple different server nodes, the server operating system will need to implement a feedback mechanism and protocol similar to those implemented on external load balancers. The downside, then, of server operating system-based load balancing is that it is only effective in homogeneous server environments. To support a mixed environment of heterogeneous server operating systems, one must implement an external load balancer.

The load balancer, whether implemented within a server or in an external device, must support the existence of multiple load balancers. This is to prevent a single load balancer from becoming a single point of failure. If only one load balancer is implemented and it fails, then no clients can reach the servers — undoubtedly a worse situation than if there was no load balancer and users had to serially try to connect to individual servers. Most commercial load balancers support the existence of at least a pair of balancers, and sometimes they support unlimited pooling of balancers and interoperability between local load balancers and geographic load balancers. Cisco offers a local load balancer, LocalDirector, that can interoperate with its geographic DistributedDirector. IBM offers a single product, the WebSphere Edge Server, that can perform both local and geographic balancing.

Application Server Load Balancing

Application servers can be implemented on servers in which the operating system performs server clustering and load balancing. The application server is just one of the many applications on the server that can take advantage of this system-level capability. Nonetheless, many application server vendors have implemented a load-balancing capability at the application server level. Exhibit 6.6 illustrates server clustering and load balancing at the system level and the application server level.

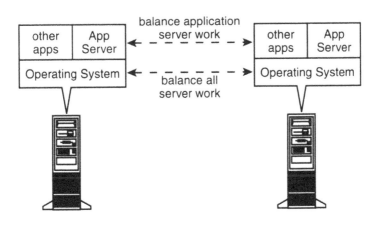

Exhibit 6.6   Load Balancing at System Level and Application Server

The reason that it may be preferable to load balance at the application server level is that the application server can make load-balancing decisions that take into account the location of the object so that the number of hops is minimized. The application server can also permit the dynamic relocation of EJBs, Java Server Pages, and servlets across multiple application server platforms. In most implementations, the individual application servers are defined as belonging to a group of application servers that have a common configuration. Some implementations even support the ability to dynamically add and remove application servers from the group.

Fault Tolerance

Fault tolerance is the ability of a system to gracefully tolerate the failure of a hardware or software component. In terms of the enterprise environment, fault tolerance is the ability of the overall infrastructure to tolerate the failure of an element and still provide service to users. Fault tolerance is thus related to overall availability. To achieve high availability (i.e., approaching 100 percent), it is necessary to implement fault-tolerant designs. The primary way that this is done is through the elimination of all single points of failure.

A single point of failure can be introduced almost any place in the infrastructure — from the remote location all the way to the campus data center. For example, if an enterprise relies on a single DNS to provide host name-to-IP address translation, the failure of that DNS could mean the disruption of all new IP session attempts. If the link between the remote branch office and the campus data center is a single path with no backup defined, then the failure of that link could disrupt all branch-to-campus sessions and traffic. If the enterprise beans that represent a mission-critical application reside on a single application server, then the failure of that server will render the application unavailable to all users.

Fault tolerance is related to the previous two topics of scalability and load balancing because the ability to cluster and balance between servers is one key means of achieving fault tolerance. The server clustering technology must also support a means of detecting the failure of a single server and prevent new session or object invocation attempts from being assigned to a failed or removed server. Eventually, the specifications and implementations may support complete failover of individual sessions and transactions, so that in-process sessions and transactions can be seamlessly transferred to another server when one server fails. To date, this level of fault tolerance is not yet supported except in the case of some mainframe applications.

Network Fault Tolerance

The first step in building fault tolerance within the network infrastructure involves the implementation of multiple paths from any client to the destination servers. Exhibit 6.7 contrasts two similar networks: one network has no multiple

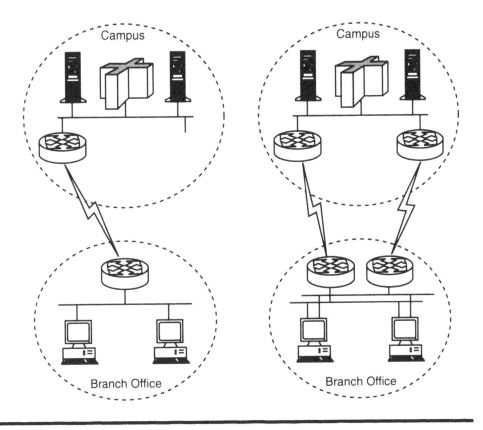

Exhibit 6.7 Non-redundant and Redundant Branch Office Designs

paths while the other has multiple paths. Both networks show two remote branch offices connected to a campus data center over wide area network links. In the case of the network on the left, the single router at the branch office is connected over a single link to a single router in the campus. If any one of these three elements fails, the branch office can no longer communicate with the campus. In the case of the network on the right, redundant designs are put in place within the branch, on the wide area network, and within the campus. The branch office not only has redundant routers but a redundant LAN and two LAN interfaces per client. The branch office is no longer vulnerable to the loss of a single element. Even the loss of a single network interface card in the client systems or the router will not disrupt even a single session. TCP/IP routing protocols will handle the routing around any single failed component.

Exhibit 6.7 represents the extreme cases of no redundancy versus complete redundancy. Many enterprises will determine that the cost of providing complete redundancy at all points in the network exceeds the potential benefits. Therefore, they are likely to target their spending on redundancy within the backbone and within the campus/data center because failures in these places impact the largest number of users. They may, for example, maintain a single router in branch locations based on the experience that simple branch office routers seldom fail, but equip each router with two WAN connections so that a backup link can be activated if the primary link fails. Within the campus/data center, redundancy may be provided by building a campus backbone that is meshed so that the loss of one node does not impact the whole, and also by implementing redundant and hot-swappable network interfaces and power supplies on networking equipment.

It is important to look beyond the switches, routers, WAN links, and LANs that comprise the network infrastructure to include network-based services and the platforms providing them in an overall fault-tolerant network design. As mentioned earlier, it does no good to provide a completely fault-tolerant network and then implement a single load-balancing node for users to access a server complex. The failure of that single node will compromise total system availability. The types of platforms to consider in an overall fault tolerant network design include:

- directory servers
- DNS and name servers
- load balancers
- firewalls
- user authentication and authorization servers
- network-based gateways

Server Fault Tolerance

Single servers can be equipped with certain features and capabilities that enhance the fault tolerance of the system. Certain hardware components that may exhibit a fairly high failure rate can be mirrored for redundancy. The most common mirrored or redundant elements in a server are the power supply, disk subsystems, and sometimes the network interface card. Multiprocessor-based servers can enhance fault tolerance because software programs or subsystems that crash need not impact the entire system, only the processor on which they are running at the time. Obviously, another approach to increase fault tolerance is to make systems redundant, such as in the case of server clusters. Recall that a cluster of servers has a single image to the user base.

Nonetheless, one could implement server clusters that do not have fault tolerance features such as the identification of failed components and the removal from service of the failed component(s). Server clusters without built-in fault tolerance mechanisms are of marginal utility to an enterprise that is entrusting mission-critical applications to the cluster. For the server cluster to be fully fault tolerant, it must support redundancy of four elements: processors, networking, storage, and applications.

Processor redundancy is achieved by the very act of creating a server cluster. By combining several separate server nodes together in a cluster, the overall cluster has redundancy of processors available to it. Redundancy of networking is achieved by connecting the servers to redundant network connections. For example, each server may have two Fast Ethernet network interface cards. Each connection is attached to a separate Fast Ethernet LAN

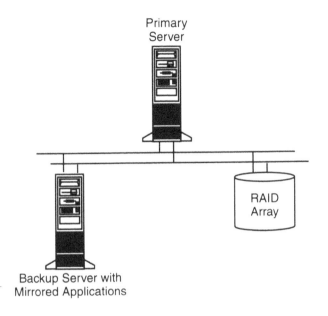

Primary
Server

RAID
Array

Backup Server with
Mirrored Applications

Exhibit 6.8　Fault Tolerant Server Cluster Design

segment so that the network is available even if one of the network interface cards or LAN segments fails. Redundancy of storage is achieved by implementing mirrored or redundant storage devices such as RAID (Redundant Array of Inexpensive Disks) storage subsystems. Note that storage should either be mirrored across multiple servers or shared in order to promote fault tolerance. Storage area networks (SANs) are becoming a common way to support shared storage to network-based servers. Redundancy of applications is the technically most difficult aspect of providing total server cluster fault tolerance because providing it involves the utilization of some very sophisticated mechanisms. Exhibit 6.8 illustrates a fault tolerant server complex design that supports redundancy for the four required elements.

Redundancy of applications is provided at different levels. At the lowest level, the same application (or component, servlet, etc.) is available on multiple different servers. If one application fails, then the complex directs future transactions or sessions to the remaining application images that could reside on separate servers. At this level, all sessions or transactions that were in process on the failed application are lost. Users must logon and start again. Transaction processing systems will take care of the rollback of the in-process transaction so that the incomplete transaction does not compromise the state of the enterprise data.

At a higher level of application redundancy, the failure of one application is completely transparent to the outside world because all in-process sessions and transactions are seamlessly transferred from the failed component to an active application. Obviously, this level of application redundancy offers the best protection. No application transaction or session will ever be lost, and end users will perceive the application to be available 100 percent of the time.

However, this level of redundancy and fault tolerance is very difficult to achieve and comes at the cost of performance because all sessions and transactions must be mirrored or logged in real-time. This level of redundancy is currently only provided by a select group of high-end server products.

The redundancy and fault tolerance provided to applications and server-side components differ from operating system to operating system. The redundancy and fault tolerance capabilities of the three most common enterprise operating systems — Windows 2000, Sun Solaris, and IBM OS/390 — are briefly described in the following sections.

Windows 2000

Windows 2000 supports a cluster service that is technically designed as a set of capabilities that is built on top of the Windows 2000 operating system. Therefore, the cluster service is not an innate part of the operating system, although the operating system required some basic changes to accommodate the cluster service. The cluster service supports two-node clusters with Windows 2000 Advanced Server and up to four-node clusters with Windows 2000 Datacenter Server.

Each of the nodes in a cluster contains an element called the Node Manager. Each Node Manager maintains a list of nodes within the cluster and periodically sends messages (known as heartbeats) to each of its counterparts. If one of the Node Managers detects a communication failure with another cluster node, it broadcasts a message to each other node in the cluster. This step ensures that all active Node Managers have an up-to-date and accurate view of the status of the cluster. Each node in the cluster maintains ownership over resource groups, which can contain applications, disks, and other resources. Once a particular node is determined to be unavailable, the remaining Node Managers selectively distribute the resource groups previously owned by the failed node among the surviving nodes. The factors used in determining which node or nodes will gain ownership of the resource groups include node capabilities, current load, application feedback, or a configured node preference list. The Node Managers communicate using the services of a Communications Manager. This element communicates with its counterparts using Remote Procedure Call (RPC) mechanisms.

Applications must be cluster-aware to take full advantage of the cluster service. According to Microsoft, the following applications are cluster-aware as of this writing: databases such as Microsoft SQL Server 7.0 and IBM DB2; messaging servers such as Microsoft Exchange Server 5.5 and Lotus Domino; management tools such as NetIQ's AppManager; disaster recovery tools such as NSI Software's DoubleTake 3.0; ERP applications including SAP, Baan, and PeopleSoft; and JD Edwards' TCP/IP services such as DHCP, WINS, SMTP, and NNTP. The new Microsoft Application Center 2000 application server is cluster-aware.

The cluster service in Windows 2000 does not prevent loss of session or transaction. It is also relatively limited in the number of nodes that it supports (two or four). Small- to medium-sized businesses may find the current clustering capability sufficient, but large enterprises will find the current limitations somewhat confining.

Sun Solaris

The Sun Solaris operating environment (the company does not refer to it as an operating system) supports Sun Cluster software. This software, a separately licensed software program that supports a variety of Solaris release levels, supports clusters of up to four Solaris nodes and up to 256 processors. It also enables nodes to be separated by up to ten kilometers, which facilitates a disaster recovery scenario because the nodes can be placed in different locations.

There are some similarities between the Microsoft and Sun implementations. Each node in a Sun Cluster passes a heartbeat to every other node in the cluster to continually determine the health of the other nodes. Each storage subsystem is owned by a single node, but that ownership can be passed to another node when the primary owning node fails. When a node fails, the remaining nodes will automatically take over and pick up the workload. However, while the Microsoft solution supports only a single cluster topology (shared-nothing), the Sun Cluster supports a variety of different cluster topologies (clustered pairs, N + 1, fully connected, shared-nothing).

Applications take advantage of the Sun Cluster technology by supporting a high-availability (HA) agent that communicates with the Sun Cluster high-availability API. Two HA agents are included with the latest release of Sun Cluster: HA-NFS and HA-DNS. There are Sun HA agents for a number of different applications: Oracle, Informix, NetBackup, Sun Internet Mail Server, SAP R/3, Lotus Domino, Tivoli, Netscape, Netscape LDAP/Directory Server, iPlanet Web Server, iPlanet/Netscape Mail/Messaging Server, Oracle Parallel Server, and Informix XPS. Third parties sell additional HA agents, including Sybase, Open Market Transact, JD Edwards One World, IBM DB2 EE and EEE, and BEA Tuxedo.

The Sun Cluster technology will not prevent the loss of session or transaction. Although it is limited to four nodes, it supports up to 256 processors within the four nodes. With the scalability inherent in Sun servers, a Sun Cluster will scale to support a pretty impressive number of users/transactions.

IBM OS/390

For the "true Rolls Royce approach" to non-stop operation and complete fault tolerance, one should look to the IBM mainframe and its operating system, OS/390. OS/390 supports a strategic server clustering technology called Parallel Sysplex. This technology, which was first made available in 1994, has evolved and now supports unsurpassed scalability in terms of number of processors and nodes supported, nonstop operation and the protection of sessions and transactions, policy-based load balancing between multiple instances of an application, and disaster recovery support for distances up to 40 kilometers between nodes in the cluster.

Today's mainframe computers are quite a departure from the huge, water-cooled monsters of the past that took up large portions of a data center. The most recent mainframes, based on CMOS technology, are trim and compact and can support from one to twelve CPUs within a single machine. Parallel Sysplex supports up to 32 mainframes in a single cluster. Therefore, using Parallel Sysplex and the latest mainframes, one can support a mind-blowing 384 CPUs. The scalability of Parallel Sysplex is unsurpassed, especially when implemented on the newest mainframes. Nonetheless, Parallel Sysplex does support older generations of IBM mainframes and non-IBM mainframes as well. Therefore, a single Parallel Sysplex cluster can support a mix of different mainframe systems.

Through a variety of different features and capabilities within Parallel Sysplex, OS/390 is able to offer complete non-stop operation for all sessions and transactions. Like Windows 2000 and Sun Solaris clustering technologies, Parallel Sysplex employs a heartbeat monitor to detect the failure of a CPU or a node in the cluster. Unlike Windows 2000 and Sun Solaris, however, Parallel Sysplex continually maintains session and transaction state information in a central resource. Therefore, if a node, a CPU, an application subsystem, or an individual application fails, the components of Parallel Sysplex will work together to recover all sessions and transactions that were in process at the time of failure. The end user will not even be aware of the failure and will not even have to re-enter any data. Parallel Sysplex is able to do this because all CPUs and nodes are interconnected by a Sysplex Timer that keeps all of the elements in sync. All session interactions are written to a central journal, and this information is used to seamlessly take up the session in the event of the failure of one component. Exhibit 6.9 illustrates a high-level overview of Parallel Sysplex.

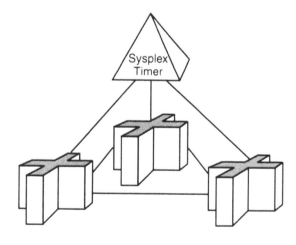

Exhibit 6.9   High-level Overview of Parallel Sysplex

The Workload Manager is a key component of the Parallel Sysplex environment. Working with a feature called Generic Resources, the Workload Manager hides the fact that there are multiple different instances of an application subsystem or application. The user population sees a single destination (e.g., CICS) even if there are 50 different instances of the application (e.g., CICS1, CICS2, ..., CICS50). The Workload Manager balances the sessions across the active and available processors, nodes, application subsystems, or applications, based on some defined policy and on the determination of an optimal load-balancing decision.

Parallel Sysplex was once only available to applications that used the IBM SNA networking protocol. It has recently been extended to include mainframe-based TCP/IP applications, but not all of the features are available to TCP/IP applications. Sadly, the one feature missing is the element (called MultiNode Persistent Sessions) that ensures non-stop session operation. Therefore, if a TCP/IP application (e.g., the WebSphere Application Server) fails, then the user will need to reconnect to reestablish the connection. Nonetheless, the scalability and load balancing are preserved so that the WebSphere Application Server implemented on an OS/390 cluster can easily support tens of thousands of users. In reality, the more typical configuration for an enterprise is to implement WebSphere Application Server on a high-end UNIX platform that front-ends the Parallel Sysplex-based mainframe complex in addition to other back-end data sources. The legacy applications and mainframe systems will be able to leverage MultiNode Persistent Sessions and exhibit 99.9999%+ availability.

For the ultimate in scalability and fault tolerance, the mainframe cannot be beat. The technologies for supporting non-stop, mission-critical operation have been developed and refined over decades. Although PC and UNIX servers are beginning to gain some of the high availability and scalability characteristics of mainframes, the mainframe is still in a class of its own.

Application Server Fault Tolerance

As stated earlier in the load-balancing discussion, many application servers support some form of clustering and load balancing. Application servers are typically defined, using the product's administrative agent or console, as belonging to a group. Each server in the group shares a common configuration. The group may dynamically relocate EJBs, JSPs, servlets, or CORBA objects across the individual machines within the group. The product may support the ability for application servers to dynamically enter and leave the group as well.

To date, the fault tolerance of application servers is limited to the ability to replicate components and applications across multiple servers. The level of automatic fault detection and recovery provided by most applications servers is still somewhat embryonic. However, some are beginning to provide automatic failover for stateful session beans and components. It is clear that fault tolerance capabilities will be a big area of future differentiation between solutions, particularly among the market leaders. IT staff should press any vendors with application servers under consideration to detail the current and future fault tolerance of their products.

Management

Management and administration of a three-tier or N-tier environment is obviously complex. There are so many different platforms, systems, operating systems, and types of programs to manage. There are complex security schemes and policies that must be administered. There is no single tool that will provide all of the modeling, analysis, design, implementation, deployment, configuration, and fault management needs of an organization. Nonetheless, it is important to try to select tools that provide a comprehensive set of capabilities for at least one key aspect or area of the enterprise. It is also important that the products that are implemented within the enterprise provide sufficient management information using a standard such as Simple Network Management Protocol (SNMP) so that the operations staff is not locked into one set of tools.

Application Server Administration

All application servers will have some built-in, native administrative interface. As discussed in Chapter 5, in most cases the administrative component is split into a server component that runs on the application server or a stand-alone server and an agent or client interface through which the operator interacts with the application server(s). Agents are available in a variety of different technology bases.

Some administrative agents are stand-alone programs that run on a standard PC. These programs implement the complete graphical user interface that is used by the operator/systems manager. The program can be written in any language and packaged for a specific operating system, although the trend in stand-alone programs is to be written in Java so that they can run on a variety of systems. Other administrative agents are written as tools that run on top of one of a handful of standard management platforms, such as HP's OpenView or IBM's Tivoli®. This approach has the advantage of leveraging a powerful management interface and the potential of integration with other tools supported by the platform. A final approach is to provide no client; the client is simply a Web browser, and the server-to-agent requests and responses are carried within standard HTTP/SSL.

The administrative server can either directly control the application server and its elements, components, objects, and applications via system calls or it can be based on a distributed object model. In the latter case, the administrative server communicates with the resources using standard component interfaces. For example, in IBM's WebSphere Application Server, Advanced Edition (the EJB-based version), resource beans are represented as container-managed persistent (CMP) entity beans. Administration takes place by method calls to the repository server, which in this case is managed by the IBM DB2 relational database package that is packaged with the Advanced Edition server.

The list of potential features provided by the administrative component is long, and not all of the potential features are required in all environments. A partial list of potential administrative features includes:

1. *Provide a graphical management interface.* Today's modern administration tools all utilize easy-to-use graphical interface to provide more information at a glance and ease the operator's administrative tasks. For an application server, the interface may provide graphical depiction of the state and location of objects, servlets, and other resources and allow the operator to manipulate the resources using a graphical rather than textual interface.

2. *Configure application servers.* The administrative server must, at a minimum, provide complete configuration of the application server and all of its resources.

3. *Deploy servlets, EJBs, CORBA components, JSPs.* The administrative server may allow for the easy deployment of these resources within individual servers and also between servers in a cluster.

4. *Start and stop resources.* The administrative interface must provide operator control to start and stop the server, servlets, containers, components, and applications.

5. *Add and remove application servers from a cluster or group.* If the application server supports clusters or groups, the administrative interface must provide a means of adding and removing individual application servers from the cluster or group, preferably dynamically without requiring any systems to be restarted.

6. *Configure security.* The administrative interface should allow the administrator to specify security levels, authentication information, and access control lists or other authorization mechanism, either directly or by interfacing to an external security policy administration server.

7. *Debug and test tools.* The administrative server should provide appropriate tools and test facilities to assist in diagnosing faults.

8. *Tracing and logging.* The administrative server should trace and log important security and fault/configuration management information under the operator's control.

9. *Generate events.* The administrative element should generate appropriate alerts and other management events.

10. *Communicate with repository.* The server should communicate with the management repository to access, define, or modify resource information (*note:* the repository may be centralized, but all administrative servers should equally have access to it).

11. *Communicate with other administrative servers.* If the application server supports clusters or groups, the administrative servers will communicate to delegate tasks or respond to requests.

End-to-End Management

Of course, the application server is just one element in the overall enterprise three-tier environment. It is a key platform that touches on many other technologies — security, naming and directory, Web servers, client access, and back-end systems. The enterprise IT organization must define tools and processes to manage the entire environment, comprehensively and seamlessly, or else there will be disjoint information, security holes, incomplete problem determination information, etc.

Total network and systems management includes five elements and is often referred to as FCAPS: fault management, configuration management, accounting/billing, performance management, and security management. Some organizations focus almost exclusively on configuration management and fault determination (i.e., event isolation and correlation) because these are the real-time, "fire-fighting" management tasks. Security management is beginning to take center stage as organizations implement E-business solutions.

However, in an increasingly complex and mission-critical E-business environment, operations staff should begin to place more emphasis on proactive performance management. Once an organization begins to implement E-business solutions, the demand for bandwidth can immediately escalate. Bottlenecks can appear suddenly, choking off important E-commerce transactions or critical business partner transactions. Tools that allow an IT staff to model and monitor the performance of all components of the network should be a priority.

There are a number of different items that need to be managed by the enterprise staff and the tools they use. The FCAPS framework should be used to evaluate the effectiveness of an overall management infrastructure for all of the elements within the end-to-end path of three-tier applications. Exhibit 6.10 is a matrix that an IT planning or operations staff should use to evaluate the current management infrastructure. In each of the cells of the matrix, staff should fill in the tool or tools that provide that particular element. Holes in the overall management scheme should be immediately apparent. Once the holes are filled, staff can use the matrix again to indicate, through shading or arrows or some other visual scheme, which tools are communicating with others and make sure that there is a seamless flow of information and no duplication.

Final Thoughts

CIOs today might look back on the enterprise IT problems of a decade or two ago with some sense of nostalgia. Everything is so much more complex now. The IT infrastructure is no longer primarily for internal use. Now, it is connected to the rest of the world. Any mistakes and security holes are amplified, and the risks are much higher than ever before. The infrastructure is infinitely more complex and supports a huge variety of applications, systems, networking devices, and network-based services.

Exhibit 6.10. Evaluating Enterprise Management Using FCAPS Framework

Elements Within the Enterprise	Elements of Management				
	Fault	Configuration	Accounting	Performance	Security
Client					
Wide area network					
Firewall					
Campus network					
Security policy servers					
Naming servers					
Load balancers					
Web servers					
Servlet engines					
Application servers					
Back-end data servers					

On the other hand, the systems of today are so much more capable. The "holy grail" of a decade ago — a common graphical user interface — has been achieved through the simple Web browser. Although the user interface is deceptively simple, today's i*net-based users armed with a Web browser can access a very sophisticated set of enterprise systems and applications. The application server is one key platform that helps to make that possible.

However, there are some key enterprise design issues that must be faced in designing today's Web-oriented, three-tier environments. First and foremost, the security of the overall environment must be rock-solid. No enterprise will risk its mission-critical systems and key business processes to an environment that is vulnerable to attack by a wily hacker. The overall infrastructure must scale to support an ever-increasing pool of users and demands for processing and bandwidth. Systems need to support load balancing and fault tolerance so that end users perceive that the systems are available nearly 100 percent of the time. Finally, the entire complex environment must be effectively administered and managed using a new breed of sophisticated tools.

This chapter has touched on some of the issues that an IT organization must face and the technologies it must accommodate or integrate to be able to build a three-tier, distributed object-based infrastructure that is secure, scalable, manageable, and available 24 × 365. To be sure, the task is not for the faint of heart. However, as the reader will see in Chapter 7, several pioneers have led the way and demonstrated that it is possible to build such an infrastructure. The pioneers have also demonstrated that the rewards are great for those who persevere.

Chapter 7

Tying It All Together

As the wide-ranging set of technical topics covered by this book attests, the application server is the centerpiece of a complex yet extremely powerful infrastructure. It is the linchpin of the new, Internet-connected and Web-interfaced set of applications that facilitate E-business. Through the application server and its Web server companion, IT organizations can fashion a completely new interface that allows employees, business partners, and customers to efficiently carry out essential transactions and interactions with the organization. And, because the new applications built on the application server are based on reusable component technologies and leverage sophisticated visual development tools, the new applications are built more efficiently and more quickly than was possible with traditional hierarchical or client/server applications that were based on procedural programming techniques.

The application server market has been building slowly since the OMG began to finalize and publish the CORBA specifications. Early application servers, based on CORBA ORBs, provided a rich set of services and supported a wide variety of languages, allowing organizations to build very sophisticated distributed object-base systems. However, it is the dominance of the World Wide Web that has propelled the application server market to dramatic growth. The Web has forced organizations of all sizes and in all industries to reengineer their very basic business processes to provide easy, yet secure, access via the Internet to a wide variety of users. This has meant a fundamental change in the "front end" of an enterprise IT infrastructure. However, the "back end," representing the mission-critical systems that keep the key business processes of the organization running on a day-to-day basis, cannot be simply thrown away. The application server provides a way to relatively easily tie together the new front end with the back end, and support the creation of new business logic based on distributed object technology.

However, it is not just the existence of the Web and the need to tie together a Web front end with existing systems that has propelled the application server market to its current exponential growth. The Java technologies — in particular, the Enterprise JavaBeans specification and enterprise Java APIs that are a part of the J2EE platform — have brought the application server to the mainstream. Java has become *the* language that the majority of today's programmers want to use. J2EE provides many of the sophisticated capabilities embodied in the CORBA specifications, yet brings it to the Java programmer as a set of ready-built services that the programmer does not need to worry about. The proliferation of feature-rich and inexpensive Java application servers, along with the visual development tools to support them, has allowed the market to blossom. This does not imply that only J2EE-based application servers are having success. More complicated environments often demand the multi-language support and sophisticated services of a pure CORBA or mixed J2EE/CORBA approach.

In this chapter, the technologies and concepts discussed in previous chapters are illustrated in real-world examples of application servers in actual production environments. The intent is to illustrate that application servers are practical and have provided tangible benefits to a wide range of different enterprises, ranging from relatively young companies to older and established, Global 1000-class enterprise organizations.

Next, a survey of some of the application server products available on the market today is provided. The intent of this section is to provide the reader with a sense of the great variety of different solutions available. While this overview does not (and cannot) detail each and every application server available today, it highlights some of the dominant themes (such as the prevalence of J2EE adoption) and provides a sense of the relative strengths of the solutions from various vendors.

Implementation Examples

Application servers are not a new, untested product category. Application servers have been implemented by a wide variety or organizations. Financial services organizations utilize them to implement home banking, stock brokerage, insurance quotation, and other services. Telecommunication firms implement them to provide Web-based access to account billing information. New E-commerce and E-business firms ("dot-coms") utilize them as the basis for their application infrastructure. State, federal, and local governments utilize them to provide public access to public records. The list goes on. It would be difficult to find a category of organization of any size in any geography that has not implemented application servers in the quest to achieve E-commerce or E-business.

The benefits recognized by the organizations that implement application servers are as varied as the organizations that implement them. Nonetheless, in general, the benefits include:

1. ability to support large numbers of simultaneous users or requests
2. achievement of near-100 percent availability, 24 hours a day and seven days a week
3. ability to quickly implement new business logic that has sophisticated transactional capabilities and state management
4. integration with enterprise standards for security and management
5. ability to leverage off-the-shelf application components for rapid delivery of new applications
6. integration with a wide variety of legacy data sources and applications
7. achievement of E-business goals

National Discount Brokers (NDB), a successful online stock brokerage firm, implemented application servers to support its large and growing trading volumes, which in February of 2000 had reached up to 25,000 trades per day. The system NDB implemented currently handles approximately 5000 simultaneous log-ins while maintaining satisfactory end-user responsiveness. Although impressive, the firm plans to double or even triple that capacity soon. Prior to its application server implementation, the firm's homegrown Web-based systems had hundreds of sub-components with complex back-end connections written in C and C++. What the firm needed was a system that would provide server clustering, load balancing, and fault tolerance so that it could add capacity without changing any code. They were attracted to a J2EE-based implementation because the open standards approach would allow integration of pre-built and custom-built extensions to the firm's back-end and legacy systems. NDB chose to implement the iPlanet Application Server with its built-in Web clustering, load balancing, and fault tolerance capabilities.[1]

Vodafone, a mobile telecommunication giant and the United Kingdom's second-largest company, turned to application servers to consolidate its multiple billing systems to enable the company to keep pace with its rapidly expanding mobile telephone business. The new solution, called Unibill, replaces two legacy billing systems and several other internal applications. By consolidating these systems into a single, comprehensive, application server-based solution, Vodafone was able to vastly simplify and streamline its billing process. In addition, the comprehensive billing system is able to assist in fraud detection and also provides real-time billing data over the Web to Vodafone's partners. While a key goal was to streamline and unify the billing process, the new system also scales beautifully. It was originally designed to support a volume of 12 million calls per peak day, but the system now regularly handles more than twice that volume of calls. Vodafone selected IBM's WebSphere Application Server, Enterprise Edition, as the solution for its Unibill system.[2]

Cable & Wireless HKT is a telecommunication firm in Hong Kong and, until 1995, it had an exclusive franchise to provide local telephone service in Hong Kong. With the expiration of its exclusive franchise, the company quickly faced new competitors. The company needed to protect its market share by offering new and expanded services while reducing customer service-related costs. Like many large enterprises, the company had a number of legacy systems (IBM mainframes and DEC VAXes) that needed to be integrated into any final solution. Cable & Wireless HKT decided that a three-tier architecture based on application servers met its requirements for application partitioning and also would allow the company to build an infrastructure that includes state and session management, transaction management, database access, and result-set caching. The company was able to implement the new solution, based on the iPlanet Application Server, for its most important commercial customers in less than three months. The solution met all of the company's requirements, and provided a quick time to market as well.[3]

Honeywell's Aircraft Landing Systems is an example of a very large, traditional manufacturing organization that has complex systems supported by a variety of legacy systems. The organization previously created custom applications based on procedural programming techniques that were unique to each particular situation. The organization's development costs were high, and the resulting systems were not completely flexible. When the organization decided it needed to move to a new Web-based application model, it decided to put an architecture in place that would allow the organization to make the optimal use of the existing legacy systems while allowing them to migrate into the world of customized off-the-shelf (COTS) software. A distributed object, three-tier architecture backed up with solid visual development tools and message queuing software was the right approach for the Honeywell division. The organization selected a combination of IBM software: WebSphere Application Server, MQSeries, and VisualAge for Java. The new development environment has dramatically reduced the organization's software development costs, improved response times sevenfold, and preserved the investment in the variety of legacy systems.[4]

These examples demonstrate that application servers have been gainfully and profitably implemented by some very diverse enterprises. They also demonstrate that application servers have been utilized in mission-critical environments. The following two sections take a closer look at the environments and the decision processes of two relatively young companies, BuildPoint Corporation and FoliQuest International N.V. These case studies illustrate the types of issues and considerations that are facing large and small enterprises alike.

Case Study: BuildPoint Corporation

BuildPoint Corporation is a premier example of a new type of business that the Internet has spawned — a B2B E-commerce marketplace that electronically brings together buyers and sellers for the purpose of efficiently procuring and selling materials, supplies, equipment, and surplus or used goods. BuildPoint.com[SM] is targeted at the building and construction industry and offers the industry's first Internet-based procurement solution. Its goal is to bring together general contractors, subcontractors, and suppliers to make possible a vastly superior way of managing the construction bidding and procurement processes. BuildPoint's online marketplace delivers fast, reliable, and secure E-commerce applications for the construction industry's largest community focused on contractors and suppliers, and is the leading online destination for increasing efficiency, streamlining business processes, creating new business opportunities and partnerships, and saving time and money.

Founded in May 1999, BuildPoint is a stellar example of a successful Silicon Valley-based B2B start-up and has already won recognition by technology industry watchers for its innovative and comprehensive E-commerce site, BuildPoint.com. More than 15,000 member companies transact business over BuildPoint.com, including 40 of the *Engineering News Record's* Top 400 General Contractors. Since November 1999, more than $20 billion in project volume has been transacted over BuildPoint.com. The company has (as of this writing) grown to more than 160 employees, including a nationwide salesforce made up of more than 60 people with construction industry experience.

BuildPoint.com is an online marketplace that allows buyers and sellers to negotiate for and procure construction products and services online; provides online bid solicitation management and lead generation; and offers financial services including insurance and lending. This is made possible with BuildPoint's Open Trading Platform, an E-commerce platform comprised of Web servers, application servers, and database servers. This platform allows all users to access the various marketplaces and conduct business using a standard Web browser. The platform is built with scalability and fault tolerance in mind. Quite simply, if the system is unavailable, then the company is unable to make any money and its customers may transact their business in other ways.

When the company began its operations, it initially implemented all of its marketplace capabilities using the Microsoft Internet Information Server (IIS) Web server with Active Server Pages (ASP) technology to formulate the dynamic content. However, BuildPoint, with its rapid and dramatic early success, soon outgrew this technology. According to André Taube, BuildPoint's Vice President of Engineering, the original Web server approach was well suited to relatively small environments. "Once there are many engineers involved and a complex set of data to deal with," Taube states, "it is necessary to start separating the data from the business logic and the business logic from the Web page design." Taube came to the conclusion that a three-tier solution, with application servers at the center, was essential to give the appropriate separation of function and also promote a design that is maintainable and fault tolerant. Taube also decided that the new application server design should be implemented on Sun Microsystems hardware running the Solaris operating environment to promote scalability. Exhibit 7.1 illustrates the current Open Trading Platform implemented by Taube and his team.

Once the decision was made to implement a three-tier solution, distributed object approach, Taube evaluated the alternatives. A Microsoft COM+ approach was considered because the current Web server was Microsoft's IIS, but Taube preferred to move to a UNIX-based platform, feeling that the Microsoft technology

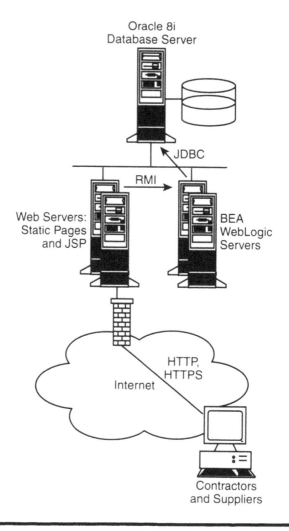

Exhibit 7.1   Architecture of BuildPoint.com

was not as widely accepted by the industry as a whole. Taube also felt that it was extremely important to base the design on a technology that had widespread support from a number of different vendors to avoid being locked in, in the future, to a particular vendor's solution. Taube's opinion was that the right approach would be an application server that implements the Sun Java 2 Enterprise Edition (J2EE) platform, with Enterprise JavaBeans (EJB) and the Java Enterprise APIs.

With the decision to implement a J2EE solution on Sun hardware, Taube evaluated the offerings of different vendors. The WebLogic Server from BEA Systems was selected because it is a market leader and, in Taube's opinion, offers the most complete implementation of J2EE. It was felt that sticking with a market leader was important because it indicated that many other companies had proven the product in a number of different production environments.

All users of the Open Trading Platform are using standard Web browsers communicating with the BuildPoint.com Web servers via HTTP/HTTPS. The Web servers serve static Web pages and also create dynamic pages using Java Server Pages (JSP) technology. Once a user is beyond the first few pages on the BuildPoint.com site, the majority of the remaining pages are dynamically created based on interaction with the user.

The Web servers communicate over the internal BuiltPoint.com network to a pair of Sun Enterprise 420 stackable servers, running the Solaris operating environment and the WebLogic Server. The two servers are configured identically with the same set of enterprise beans. Invocations are load balanced between these two servers; and if one of the servers fails, then the remaining server acts as a failover server. The application server supports all types of enterprise beans — stateless and stateful session beans and entity beans. Taube indicates that his team is not currently using the WebLogic Server's ability to provide failover on stateful session beans, although they plan to do so in the future. BuildPoint has designed the system to scale, and plans to implement two more servers within the next six months.

Because BuildPoint is a relatively new company, it does not have a number of legacy systems that it needs to tie into. Therefore, the back-end tier of this implementation is quite straightforward. It consists of database servers running Oracle8i software. The WebLogic Server communicates with the database engines via the JDBC interface.

A key component of BuildPoint's business model is these Web-based transactions. How mission-critical are the BEA WebLogic Server and the enterprise beans running on the server? It is simple. If they are not available, then BuildPoint is losing money and possibly losing customers. Taube and his team are absolutely aware of this fact, and they have designed and implemented a system that will support BuiltPoint.com today. More importantly, they have designed a system that will be able to continue to seamlessly grow as the needs of the company grow.

By insisting on implementing technology that has widespread support from the vendor community, Taube has the assurance of knowing that BuildPoint.com is not going to be stranded with obsolete technology. By selecting technology of market leaders in each segment — Sun Microsystems, Oracle, BEA Systems — Taube also knows that the products implemented at BuildPoint have been proven in countless other mission-critical environments. Taube and his team have laid a solid foundation upon which BuildPoint can continually build.

Case Study: FoliQuest International N.V.

FoliQuest International N.V. is on the leading edge when it comes to providing unique Internet-based sales services to the financial industry. The company is based in The Netherlands, but also has operations in Australia. Formed in late 1996 and now 40 employees strong, the company enhances the usual

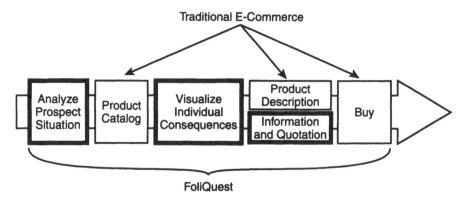

Source: FoliQuest International N.V.

Exhibit 7.2   FoliQuest Augments the Traditional E-Commerce Process

E-commerce experience by providing a unique and useful interface to a prospect for financial and insurance products. Through a Web-based dialog with the prospect, the FoliQuest Sales Support product derives a customized visualization of the products available using the prospect's own unique data. This customized visualization helps guide the prospect to a purchase decision. Exhibit 7.2 presents how the unique FoliQuest technology and processes augment the traditional Web-based E-commerce process.

FoliQuest's direct customer is the financial services or insurance company offering products to consumers over the Internet. The FoliQuest Sales Support product is used within the FoliQuest client's operations to enhance customer relationship management and customer support. For example, a financial services firm may have an in-house staff of financial advisers that access the system to provide complete financial management services to its customers. The in-house users access the system using a Windows client, while prospects access the system using a standard Web browser. Exhibit 7.3 illustrates the model for FoliQuest Sales Support.

FoliQuest provides its customers with the choice of where they would like FoliQuest Sales Support implemented. If a customer chooses to host the application in-house so that it can be responsible for all security related to this sensitive customer financial information, then FoliQuest will provide recommendations about the choice of platforms and assistance in the implementation. If, on the other hand, the customer prefers to outsource the application, then FoliQuest will work on an ASP-based implementation. FoliQuest provides a complete range of services, including situation analysis, project estimation, API development (where necessary), and implementation.

Krishnan Subramanian, lead developer at FoliQuest responsible for the server-side architecture and development, indicates that FoliQuest had several requirements in designing the infrastructure for FoliQuest Sales Support. First and foremost, the technology needed to be based on open, vendor-independent standards and interfaces so that FoliQuest is free to implement products from any vendor. Second, FoliQuest needed a distributed

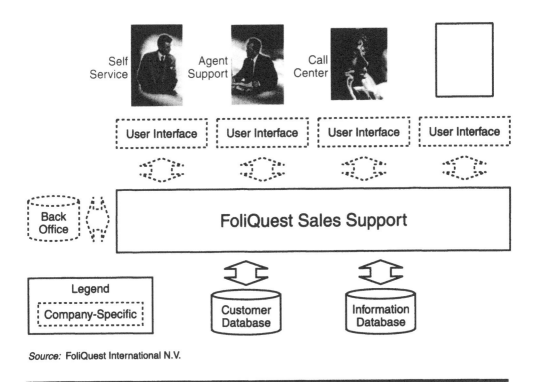

Source: FoliQuest International N.V.

Exhibit 7.3   Model for FoliQuest Sales Support

object-based system that would also seamlessly support Web-based users. In addition, FoliQuest needed a system that would easily attach to a wide variety of back-end data sources and legacy applications, because each of FoliQuest's customers may have a unique set of systems and applications that would need to be integrated with the FoliQuest system. Last but not least, FoliQuest needed a system that would support scalability, load balancing, and fault tolerance because FoliQuest clients demand that Internet services be available 24 hours a day, seven days a week.

The FoliQuest technical team evaluated a number of different solutions. Not satisfied with relying on the vendors' claims, the team carefully evaluated each of the potential solutions in terms of functionality, scalability, manageability, and fault tolerance. The team also checked to make sure that the solutions had been implemented in other production environments and had proven to be reliable and scalable in these real-world situations. Finally, the team evaluated products in terms of the ease of development and the support for development tools. The team selected the Inprise Application Server as the centerpiece of the solution. Exhibit 7.4 illustrates the architecture of the solution.

At the client side, FoliQuest must deal with two different types of users. The prospects for the financial services are consumers on the Internet, and therefore these users access the system via a standard Web browser. FoliQuest does not implement applets, applications, or client-side objects for this user base, in order to keep the system open to the widest possible set of potential users. These users connect to the Web server of the financial services or insurance company.

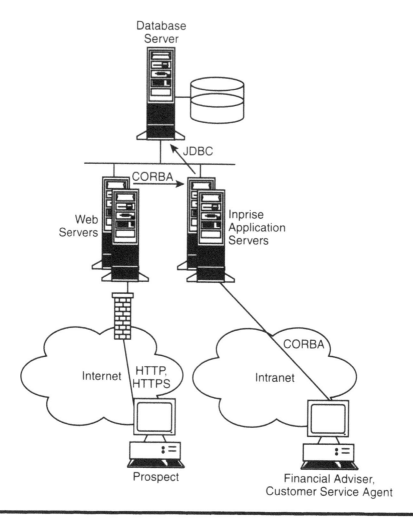

Exhibit 7.4   Architecture of FoliQuest Sales Support

The Web server hosts the company's static pages in addition to Java Server Pages (JSPs) that provide the dynamic content. Therefore, when filling in a form with name and financial information, the prospect is doing so using a JSP. The JSP, in turn, invokes an object on the application server that implements the business logic. This division of function, where the JSP is on the Web server and the business logic is on the application server, is important to promote a fault-tolerant design.

Internal users (e.g., financial advisers and customer service representatives) use Windows clients that run an Inprise Delphi client provided by FoliQuest. The Delphi client code is based on the CORBA 2.2 specification, and these users connect directly to the Inprise Application Server which in turn provides access to back-office systems running Customer Relationship Management (CRM) software or a variety of financial management applications. FoliQuest's implementation of the client-side code allows them to easily switch server-side technology from EJB to Inprise MIDAS, if required in the future, without requiring a change to the client code.

The Inprise Application Server (IAS) 4.0.x runs on one or more NT, UNIX, or Linux servers and supports the Inprise VisiBroker 4.0 ORB. This version of the Inprise ORB supports the CORBA 2.3 specification. To provide a scalable platform, Subramanian recommends a multiprocessor system with sufficient memory and disk. The development platform used in-house by FoliQuest is a Quad Xeon Pentium III with 1 GB RAM and 512 KB internal cache running Windows NT, which provides ample processing power and memory to support the development configuration in addition to a separate configuration to support testing and commercial demonstrations. The development platform was implemented with Windows NT due to its ease of use and the internal expertise of the FoliQuest staff, although the team has also run the system on Linux and AIX with very satisfactory results.

Because the Delphi client and IAS support different levels of CORBA specifications (2.2 and 2.3, respectively), the FoliQuest technical team devised a very clever and efficient wrapper that resides on the IAS server and performs the needed translation or mapping between the client and the server.

The FoliQuest internal test system supported approximately 4000 CORBA object instances that represented about 300 enterprise beans. The enterprise beans are evenly split between stateless session beans, which implement the business logic, and entity beans, which communicate with the back-end databases using JDBC. Each entity bean maps to a particular table in the customer database. The FoliQuest technical team decided to adhere to standard JDBC calls without using any database-specific features such as stored procedures and triggers. This is so that the system can be seamlessly integrated into any database environment a customer happens to support (e.g., IBM DB2, Oracle) without rewriting any code. The architecture, based on EJB and J2EE, is flexible enough to connect to a wide variety of other legacy systems that may exist in a particular customer's environment.

The decision to support stateless session beans rather than stateful session beans was based on two factors. First, the nature of the application is such that each invocation results in a combination of atomic database calls to allow a high degree of flexibility in identifying and setting transaction isolation levels. The second, and perhaps more important, consideration is to provide a fault-tolerant environment. Because the failover of stateful session beans is problematic at best (as discussed in Chapter 6), a stateless session bean architecture provides better protection from failure.

The FoliQuest internal test system mentioned above was a test environment in which 20 simultaneous clients called every method on every bean simultaneously. This environment approximates the load of approximately 200 to 400 simultaneous real-world end users. Based on the test results, the FoliQuest technical team estimated that a production system configured similarly to the development system (the Quad Xeon) should easily be able to handle 80,000 CORBA object instances and thousands of real-world simultaneous users while maintaining acceptable levels of performance.

The FoliQuest technical team recommends that each customer implement at least two IAS servers. Each server is configured to support the same enterprise beans and can work in either a primary-with-hot-standby mode, or can work in tandem with load balancing between the nodes. With an architecture based on stateless session beans, the failure of one server does not impact end users because the next operation they perform will be directed to the surviving server(s). In addition, with the Inprise product, the stateless session bean resources are pooled so that multiple users can share a single bean instance. When the number of users on the server increases, IAS is aware of the fact and will create more instances of the bean to support the increased work. This keeps performance acceptable to all users and supports linear scaling of the server. IAS also pools database connections in a similar manner, automatically increasing and decreasing the number of connections based on user load.

Because the Inprise Application Server is based on the company's full-fledged ORB product (VisiBroker) and IAS supports full CORBA implementations, the team had a choice of either implementing EJB-based CORBA objects or non-EJB-based CORBA objects (which could be written in any CORBA IDL supported language, such as Java, C++, Delphi, etc.). The FoliQuest technical team decided to implement the business logic of the system using EJB rather than Java CORBA for two important reasons. First, an EJB implementation is more portable. Second, and perhaps more important, a CORBA approach would require more development work on the part of the team. With EJB, the entity beans handle all of the transaction management, including commit and rollback, and the session beans incorporate transaction isolation levels as well. With a CORBA approach, the team would have had to write the transaction management into the application (with the help of the CORBA transaction services). Similarly, database access, load balancing, object location, remote object life-cycle management, and other facilities were automatically made available to the team through the EJB container and EJB interface architecture.

The results of the efforts of the FoliQuest technical team are outstanding. The team has a platform that it knows is scalable and fault tolerant, has selected the products and technologies that fit with today's requirements, while also knowing that the CORBA/EJB architecture selected will be flexible enough to support tomorrow's requirements. Because one cannot dictate or control the platforms or applications that potential customers have implemented, the team has designed an approach that will work in almost any environment that might be encountered. The team has created a technology base that FoliQuest can rely on as it continues to grow and dominate the market in providing advanced Internet-based sales services to the financial industry.

A Survey of Application Servers

Thus far, there has been only a brief discussion or mention of actual application server products available on the market. The reasons for this are twofold.

First, the focus of this book has been on concepts, not products. Second, the product-specific information becomes dated very quickly. A detailed feature-by-feature description of a product or a feature-by-feature comparison of products would be out-of-date by the time this book goes to press. Even the list of companies providing application servers changes over time, as new vendors enter the market, existing vendors exit the market, and previous competitors consolidate their operations and product lines.

Nonetheless, it is important in understanding the overall market to get a sense of the diversity of vendors and solutions available. Therefore, this section provides a high-level overview of the offerings of some of the current leading application server vendors; a description of where the application server product(s) fit within that vendor's overall product family; and the vendors' relative competitive strengths in the current market. This information is then summarized in two matrices at the end of the section. The first matrix lists the application server(s) and the related products offered by 17 current vendors. The second matrix focuses on the application server product lines of these companies and summarizes the product line in terms of its support of platforms, Java/CORBA/COM, back ends, development tools, and other differentiating capabilities.

Allaire Corporation

Allaire Corporation, founded in 1995, claims to have introduced the industry's first Web application server, ColdFusion®. The company is headquartered in Newton, Massachusetts, and has offices in Europe and Asia Pacific. Allaire, a publicly traded company, has reached profitability and posted revenues of $59.9 million during the first six months of 2000.

The cornerstone of the company's product line is ColdFusion, a Web application server based on ColdFusion Markup Language (CFML), a proprietary, tag-based server scripting language. Although the server language is proprietary, the communication with users and other servers is via standard HTML/XML. The server supports back-end communication with database servers, e-mail servers, other distributed object systems (CORBA, COM, EJB), LDAP servers, and FTP servers. The product supports server clustering and integrates with Cisco's LocalDirector load balancer. ColdFusion includes its own visual development tool, ColdFusion Studio. ColdFusion was released in 1995, long before the EJB specification was available. Because it was geared to Web developers and authors, and did not have the complexity of a CORBA system, the product gained widespread adoption. Allaire claims that ColdFusion continues to be one of the most widely used application servers and states that tens of thousands of companies have deployed the server.

Allaire Spectra is a set of packaged components and services built on top of ColdFusion that include:

- content management
- workflow and process automation
- roles-based security

- personalization
- business intelligence
- syndication

Despite the historical success of ColdFusion, Allaire has entered the Java application server market with its JRun product. The JRun Server is a J2EE-based application server that is offered in three different editions. The Professional Edition represents the low end of the product line and provides support only for Java Server Pages (JSPs) and Java servlets. The Enterprise Edition adds support for EJB, messaging server (JMS), transaction server (JTS), and server clustering. The Developer Edition is a performance-limited version of the Enterprise Edition (excluding server clustering) and is available for free for development purposes only. Allaire claims that its product focuses on ease of use and implementation. In addition to standard Java JSP and servlet support, JRun supports a customer tag library. The JRun Studio is the companion integrated development environment; it is a separately licensed product.

Art Technology Group (ATG)

ATG, publicly traded and headquartered in Cambridge, Massachusetts, was founded in 1991 as a provider of Internet products and services. The company's revenue was $21.5 million in the first three months of 2000.

The company offers two suites of products under the product line named the Dynamo® E-business Platform. The two suites are built on a common set of server-based products. The ATG Dynamo Customer Management Suite provides capabilities to enable online customer relationship management. This suite is built with four server products: Dynamo Scenario Server, Dynamo Personalization Server, Dynamo Application Server, and Dynamo Control Center. The second suite of products, the ATG Dynamo Commerce Suite, provides online commerce capabilities. It is built on five ATG Dynamo server products — the four that are included in the Customer Management Suite, plus the Dynamo Commerce Server.

The framework for both suites is built with the ATG Dynamo Application Server. This application server now provides full J2EE support. Other capabilities provided with this server include:

- *wireless support:* support for the Wireless Markup Language (WML)
- *messaging support:* a messaging infrastructure based on the JMS API
- *transaction management:* a transaction manager is built in; supports two-phase commit
- *security:* supports a security API
- *session federation:* supports the live exchange of customer information across servers
- *scalable page building design:* pages using the proprietary Dynamo Server Page templates are compiled quickly and efficiently using object and thread re-use

- *server clusters:* sessions are load balanced across multiple servers based on server load; request and session failover is supported

The Dynamo Scenario Server allows an organization to create customized sequences of customer interactions over the life cycle of the relationship with the customer. The Dynamo Personalization Server utilizes user profiling and content targeting to customize the presentation of Web information. The Dynamo Commerce Server supports B2B and B2C features such as product catalog presentation, multiple pricing schemes, multiple payment types, multiple shipping addresses, and recurring purchasing events. The Dynamo Control Center is the management component; it supports a unified user interface to allow all components within the Dynamo E-business Platform to be administered and managed.

BEA Systems

BEA Systems, Inc., formed in 1995 and based in San Jose, California, is a leading provider of middleware software solutions. The company's annual revenue is approximately $464 million (as of January 31, 2000) and it operates in about 26 countries worldwide. The company has formed strategic alliances with a number of heavyweights in the industry, including IBM, Sun, Hewlett-Packard, Compaq, PeopleSoft, and Unisys. It counts some impressive E-business names among its customers: Amazon.com, E*TRADE, and FedEx, to name a few.

BEA Systems was formed with the purpose of supplying middleware software solutions. Its original product, BEA Tuxedo®, is a transaction processing monitor that has been implemented by a number of large enterprise accounts. The company entered the application server marketplace in September 1998 by acquiring WebLogic, and now is considered by some research firms to be the leading application server vendor. BEA also offers a host integration server (BEA eLink™), the BEA WebLogic Commerce Server™, the BEA WebLogic Personalization Server™, and the WebGain Studio.

BEA offers two application servers: BEA WebLogic and BEA WebLogic Enterprise. The BEA WebLogic server is a J2EE-based application server. The company has long been an advocate of Java application servers, and claims that its latest version (5.1.0) has the first implementation of the yet-to-be-finalized EJB 2.0 specification. WebLogic Enterprise extends the product line and includes a native C++ CORBA ORB implementation and a transaction processing (TP) framework that leverages the company's Tuxedo technology and shields the application programmer from some of the complexities of a CORBA implementation. The WebLogic servers provide sophisticated scalability, load balancing, and failover capabilities.

BEA offers two related products that leverage the company's database connectivity capabilities. BEA WebLogic Express™ is a subset of the BEA WebLogic server that combines the WebLogic JDBC interface with Java-based presentation capabilities to allow developers to quickly and easily implement

Web-to-database applications. The BEA WebLogic jDriver family provides a family of two-tier and multitier drivers for accessing different databases using the JDBC standard.

The WebLogic Commerce Server is built on top of the WebLogic Server. It provides many of the capabilities common to E-commerce sites, including catalog, shopping cart, inventory management, order management, shipping components, and a product recommendation engine. All components are written in Java, and the Commerce Server includes the Personalization Server. The Personalization Server allows organizations to easily define rules that associate particular Web site content to individual users or groups of users.

The WebGain Studio supports a variety of different development tasks, including HTML authoring; JSP editing; development of Java applets, servlets, applications, CORBA objects, and EJB components; and mapping of back-end data sources with components. WebGain Studio supports a variety of different application servers, including WebLogic, and is separately licensed.

The BEA eLink product is a platform for connectivity to a variety of different legacy systems. It supports different adapter types, each of which plugs into a particular legacy system or application. BEA supports adapters for ERP, CRM, Telco, and mainframe applications. The company also provides a development kit for those organizations that need to build a specific adapter type.

Bluestone Software

Bluestone Software, a public company headquartered in Philadelphia, Pennsylvania, was formed in 1995 and was one of the first companies to offer a Web application server product. The company booked approximately $16.7 million of revenue in the first half of 2000. The company's flagship product was its Sapphire/Web® application server.

The Sapphire/Web product has been renamed the Total-e-Server in order to align the product within the company's burgeoning product portfolio. The application server is a part of the Total-e-Business platform (TeB platform) that encompasses the complete Bluestone portfolio. The other products within TeB include Total-e-B2B, Total-e-B2C, Total-e-Wireless, and Total-e-Global.

The Total-e-Server application server currently supports the J2EE platform, although the product has been around for number of years and the base architecture predates the availability of J2EE. Therefore, the implementation is a hybrid that is written in Java and can run in any JVM. It supports both EJBs and Java objects. The internal communication between elements in the server, however, leverages XML because the company was an early supporter of XML technology. Therefore, persistence management and state management, among other features, is implemented using XML internally. The architecture of the product has long supported scalability through server clusters and load balancing and failover. The server supports a connector architecture for connectivity to back-end data and application sources, and the company offers a number of prebuilt connectors.

The remaining products in the TeB platform are built on top of the core Total-e-Server. Total-e-B2B allows organizations to exchange real-time information with a variety of constituents, including business partners and suppliers. This facilitates the automation of the supply chain and enhances logistics operations. Total-e-B2B is based on XML technology for cross-platform communication. Total-e-B2C provides the ability to customize the online experience of customers and provides a ready-to-deploy storefront to expedite the E-commerce implementation. Total-e-Wireless extends the legacy systems and corporate databases reached by the new applications to users with cellular phones, personal digital assistance, and other handheld devices. Total-e-Global is a package of all the other elements of the TeB platform: Total-e-Server, Total-e-B2B, Total-e-B2C, and Total-e-Wireless.

GemStone Systems

GemStone Systems is one of the veteran companies offering application servers. Formed in 1982, the company developed applications and application servers for Smalltalk environments. Therefore, the company has a rich history in distributed object technologies. An early devotee of Java, the company offered one of the industry's first Java application servers. Headquartered in Beaverton, Oregon, the company has operations in Germany, the United Kingdom, France, and Switzerland, and has a worldwide network of distributors. GemStone Systems is currently a privately held company, although German E-business software provider Brokat Infosystems AG signed a definitive agreement in June 2000 to acquire GemStone.

The company offers two products, both application servers. GemStone/S is the company's Smalltalk-based application server. It was first made commercially available in 1986 and has been refined over time. Smalltalk is one of the early object-oriented programming languages. The server supports Smalltalk clients and Java clients natively, and can communicate with CORBA-compliant applications using the optional GemORB. GemStone/S has a back-end connector, GemConnect, that integrates with the Oracle database. Developers can construct wrappers to communicate with a variety of other back-end data sources and applications. The GemStone/S architecture can manage state for up to one billion objects and can support transaction-intensive applications involving gigabytes of data and hundreds of concurrent users.

GemStone/J is the company's Java application server, first introduced in 1997. GemStone/J offers a line of four different products, offering a range of capabilities.

1. *Web Edition:* low end of the product line; supports JSP, servlets, JNDI, XML; optional JDBC, JMS, SSL
2. *Component Edition:* adds EJB and JTA to capabilities in Web Edition
3. *Enterprise Edition:* adds JDBC and JMS as core APIs and also adds all four Java security APIs (JSA, JCA, JCE, JAAS) to capabilities in Component

Edition; includes ORB, Persistent Cache Architecture (PCA) for scalability, and Extreme Clustering™ for server clustering

4. *Commerce Automation Edition:* adds process automation engine to capabilities in Enterprise Edition to simplify building of B2B site

HAHT Commerce, Inc.

HAHT Commerce, Inc., is a privately held company headquartered in Raleigh, North Carolina. It was formed in 1995 and operates seven direct sales offices in the United States. The company also maintains international offices and regional headquarters at seven additional locations. The company positions itself as a leading supplier of B2B E-commerce solutions.

The company was an early entrant into the application server market with its HAHTsite Application Server, now renamed the HAHTsite Scenario Server. This product, unlike many of the other application servers on the market, provides full and native support for Microsoft's DNA (COM/DCOM) architecture. The product also supports XML, Java, and CORBA. The server currently provides support for Java servlets and a number of the Java enterprise APIs: JNDI, JTS, JDBS, and others. It does not yet support the full J2EE specification, although the company indicates that it is committed to provide full J2EE support in the future. The product provides support for CORBA by bundling the Inprise VisiBroker for Java with the HAHTsite Scenario Server.

The HAHTsite Scenario Server supports back-end data and application sources in a variety of different ways. The HAHT Java e-Connector (JEC) for SAP R/3 is an HAHT-provided connector that is integrated with the server and also the HAHT Scenario Workbench, the company's IDE. It creates proxies that can be accessed by both Java and HAHTtalk Basic applications. Database access is available to JDBC, ODBC, and OLE DB data sources. Another technology that can be utilized for back-end connectivity is the company's Enterprise Solution Modules (ESM) rapid application development enhancements that allow developers to rather easily integrate ERP, mainframe, security, and other systems with the HAHTsite server. Finally, XML can be used to access XML-enabled Enterprise Application Integration (EAI) environments and third-party middleware components.

The server is augmented with two development tools. The HAHTsite Scenario Workbench is a full IDE tool that supports the creation of HAHTsite applications and links to back-end sources. The HAHTsite Scenario Publisher is a complementary product that offers a subset of functionality. It is intended for Web site authors and designers who do not have to deal with the creation of application code.

The company offers a range of products intended to support the complete B2B E-commerce life cycle, branded the HAHT Commerce e-Scenarios product line. HAHT Market helps attract new customers through personalized B2B interactions and channel campaign management. HAHT Shop supports the selling process by providing knowledge-based product selection and configuration in addition to cross-sell and up-sell capabilities. HAHT Track supports the fulfillment process with real-time order and shipment information. HAHT Support provides an ongoing service relationship with the customer. Additional products include the HAHT Catalog, which can be used stand-alone or with the HAHT Commerce e-Scenarios products, and HAHT Sellside Links, which provides links from the Commerce e-Scenarios platform to multiple E-marketplaces.

IBM

Once the industry's dominant computer company with a majority market share in many different segments (i.e., system hardware, peripherals, software, and networking), IBM has changed considerably over the last couple of decades. The company was unable to hold onto its dominance in the face of rapid changes such as the migration to client/server and distributed computing models and the movement to TCP/IP-based networks. Nonetheless, the company is still the 800-pound gorilla in many of the markets in which it competes, and boasts a 1999 revenue line of $87.5 billion. Mainframe sales continue to be strong, and the company is doing well selling its UNIX-based servers and other servers as well. Its service and consulting product lines are growing rapidly and the company is dominating many of the software markets in which it participates.

The IBM software product lines are diverse and include Lotus groupware, Tivoli management software, DB2 database management, MQSeries message queuing software, and a growing list of software products to facilitate E-business. The WebSphere product line is the called the "software platform for E-business." The WebSphere branding has been applied to a wide variety of software tools and products, from the VisualAge line of development tools, to MQSeries, and even Web site analysis tools. At the center of the branding, however, is the WebSphere Application Server line of products.

There are three different products within the WebSphere Application Server product line. The Standard Edition represents the low end of the product line. It supports key Java server technologies (JSP, servlets, JDBC) but does not support EJBs. The Standard Edition also provides an integrated IBM HTTP server and XML/XSL support. The Advanced Edition, the middle product in the product line, includes everything in the Standard Edition and adds full EJB support; IBM LDAP Directory; DB2 server; deployment support for EJBs, servlets, and JSPs; and support for distributed transactions and transaction processing. The Enterprise Edition represents the high end of the IBM application server product line. It includes all of the features of the Advanced Edition and adds complete CORBA ORB implementation (via IBM Component Broker), support for MQSeries® and TXSeries™, component backup and restore support, XML-based team development functions, and integrated Encina support. The IBM WebSphere product line provides support for a very comprehensive set of operating systems. The list of operating systems supported include Windows NT/2000, Sun Solaris, IBM AIX, IBM OS/400, HP-UX, Red Hat Linux, Caldera Linux, Novell NetWare, and IBM OS/390 (*note:* not all editions and versions support all operating systems).

IBM offers a wide variety of related products, most of which have been branded with the WebSphere brand. Several solutions build on top of the Application Server to accelerate the implementation of E-business solutions: WebSphere Commerce Suite, WebSphere B2B Integrator, and WebSphere Business Components. The WebSphere Host Integration Solution provides integration with a wide variety of legacy back ends and Web-to-host capabilities. A number of the products are geared to Web site design and delivery: WebSphere Site Analyzer, WebSphere Portal Server, and WebSphere Personalization, among others. The WebSphere Studio combines many IBM development tools, such as the VisualAge line, into a comprehensive suite of tools. Finally, there are a variety of different network services and related products (e.g., WebSphere Edge Server) that augment the overall WebSphere Application Server environment.

iE

iE (formerly Intelligent Environments) is a United Kingdom-based company, publicly traded on the London Stock Exchange (AIM). The company was formed in 1985 and operates internationally through offices in London, Boston, and Chicago. The company's mission is to become a leading supplier of E-commerce applications to the finance industry. It sells and distributes product in more than 20 countries and counts many leading banking and insurance companies as clients.

The company provides a comprehensive family of financial applications, iE NetFinance, to support sales and service to banking, insurance, and investment clients. The company also provides three technology products that are sold separately: iE AM, iE ScreenSurfer, and iE Integrator.

iE AM is a client/server development tool for creating graphical user interface (GUI) applications that integrate mainframe data for the traditional "fat client." Originally supported on OS/2, the product now supports the Windows family of operating systems.

iE ScreenSurfer is an HTML conversion gateway product that translates host screens (3270 or 5250) into standard HTML. ScreenSurfer can be deployed stand-alone, or it can be integrated with an Allaire ColdFusion application server or any Web server implementing Microsoft Active Server Pages (ASP) technology. The ScreenSurfer server then becomes a co-processor to these servers, providing host access middleware functionality.

iE Integrator is the company's application server product. It is unique in that the focus of the product is on providing connectivity to a variety of legacy back ends, including many legacy datastream applications, transaction systems, and messaging systems. The product is based on a Microsoft COM/DCOM engine. The development language supported by the platform is Microsoft JScript (Microsoft's implementation of JavaScript). It interoperates with Java-Beans and CORBA objects (based on the CORBA 2.1 specification). iE Integrator can deliver content from a single application to HTML, XML, DCOM, and CORBA clients. The product is optimized to run on Windows NT/2000 and is integrated with many of the Microsoft server-based products and technologies such as SNA Server, Transaction Server, SQL Server, Exchange Server, and NT security.

Inprise Corporation

Today's Inprise Corporation represents a combination of Borland, a maker of development tools and middleware, and Visigenic, a renowned CORBA ORB provider. The company currently is posting revenue of approximately $93 million for a six-month period, or almost $200 million annually. The company has operations around the world and is headquartered in Scotts Valley, California.

Inprise has three different product families: (1) the Developer Tools product family, which maintains the Borland name through branding, provides many rich and leading tools to support Java, C++, and Windows development efforts; (2) the Enterprise product family, which generally leverages the Inprise name for branding, includes the AppCenter management platform, the Inprise Application Server, Entera middleware, and VisiBroker; and (3) the product family comprised of a miscellaneous collection of products, including Pascal tools, C++ compilers, and database products.

The Inprise Application Server is built on the company's VisiBroker ORB. The VisiBroker ORB is the most widely implemented CORBA ORB, and is OEM'd by a number of companies. The ORB also supports the latest OMG specifications, including the Portable Object Adapter (POA) and Objects by Value (OBV). The Inprise Application Server also offers a complete implementation of the J2EE platform. Therefore, the Inprise Application Server is a hybrid CORBA/J2EE platform, with comprehensive support for objects of both types. For example, CORBA objects and enterprise beans can reside in the same container. The product supports RMI-over-IIOP, but also IDL-to-Java mapping and Java-to-IDL reverse mapping to support full interoperability between CORBA objects, CORBA clients, EJBs, and EJB clients. The product supports flexible configurations of containers and objects in a cluster environment. Different containers in a cluster can contain a different set of beans/objects, and beans/objects can reside in different containers on different servers to provide failover for one another. The product supports failover of stateless session beans, stateful session beans, bean-managed persistent entity beans, and container-managed persistent entity beans. The Inprise Application Server implements scalability, load balancing, and fault tolerance by clustering different servers together using the CORBA Naming Service. The product also pools server resources and performs other optimizations to maximize scalability within a single server.

The company offers, as an optional extension to the Inprise Application Server, several separate CORBA services implemented by Prism Technologies. The optional services are available under the product line name OpenFusion and include Trading Service, Notification Service, LifeCycle Service, Property Service, Collection Service, Concurrency Service, Relationship Service, and Time Service. Another option offered is the Secure Gatekeeper, which supports SSL over IIOP for secure CORBA object communication.

The Inprise Application Server supports a visual administrative interface and a variety of capabilities that are included with the server. However, the company also offers a stand-alone management platform, AppCenter, that integrates with the VisiBroker ORB and the Inprise Application Server and augments the native administrative capabilities of those products. AppCenter is a visual tool that allows the administrator to manage to the object or component level. It visually displays all containers and ORB, along with the objects and components associated with them.

Borland built a highly respected name in the software development community by providing advanced tools for a number of different languages and environments. The company's JBuilder is one of the leading Java integrated development environments and supports the visual development of Java applications, applets, servlets, EJBs, JavaBeans, and CORBA objects.

IONA Technologies

IONA Technologies, which dubs itself the "Enterprise Portal Company," was formed in 1991 and posted revenues of $105 million in 1999. Headquartered in Dublin, Ireland, the company maintains its U.S. headquarters in Waltham, Massachusetts, and offices in 25 countries. The company provides E-business infrastructure solutions that allow its customer to build enterprise portals, E-commerce sites, and large-scale distributed applications.

The company made its name in the industry by providing CORBA-based products. The company claims that it is the market leading CORBA supplier and that its Orbix ORB is the "world's most popular" ORB. Orbix 2000 is a CORBA 2.3-compliant ORB that forms the basis of the iPortal family of products. The company also offers a newer version, Orbix 3, that is compliant with the new CORBA 3.0 specification and is also part of a new product family. Besides Orbix 3, this family includes OrbixWeb, a Java ORB implementation; OrbixOTM, an IONA Object Transaction Monitor; Orbix for OS/390, an implementation of Orbix on IBM's mainframe operating system; and messaging products to support asynchronous messaging based on CORBA Events and Notification services.

IONA has augmented its traditional CORBA product line with the addition of the IONA iPortal Suite. This is an integrated product line offering server-based solutions for designing, developing, and deploying robust enterprise portals. The iPortal Suite is a modular offering that includes the following individual products:

1. *Orbix 2000.* Orbix 2000 is compliant with the CORBA 2.3 specification, and supports IONA's patented Adaptive Runtime Technology™ (ART) to allow individual services and code to be added dynamically during runtime. It supports IONA's Portable Object Adapter and the CORBA 3.0-compliant Persistent State Service (PSS) and Asynchronous Messaging Interfaces (AMI).

2. *iPortal Server.* This is the "Web-facing" element that separates the business logic from the content. It supports XML/XSL and communicates with the application server and other elements (EJBs, CORBA objects, etc.).

3. *iPortal Integration Server.* This is the hub-and-spoke messaging platform that supports publish and subscribe and multicast messages. It supports adapters that connect to a wide variety of applications, including SAP R/3, PeopleSoft, CICS, IMS, and custom applications.

4. *iPortal OS/390 Server.* Built on Orbix for OS/390, the iPortal OS/390 Server enables mainframe-based applications written in COBOL, PL/I, Java, or C++ to take advantage of the distributed object environment. It supports connectors for RACF, SNA, DB2, MQSeries, and other mainframe systems.

5. *iPortal Application Server.* This is a J2EE-based application server built on the ART and the IONA Portable Object Adapter for a scalable EJB container that supports hot pluggability and hot reconfiguration. It includes Graphical Application Builder, a drag-and-drop component assembly and deployment environment.

iPlanet

In March 1999, the iPlanet alliance was formed by Sun, Netscape, and AOL. The alliance is headquartered in Mountain View, California, and has presence in the local offices of Sun and AOL around the world. The purpose of the alliance is to build, market, and service E-commerce infrastructure solutions. The alliance offers a broad range of consulting services in addition to its software products.

The alliance offers a broad array of software E-commerce solutions in the following categories:

1. *Web servers:* iPlanet Web Server and Netscape FastTrack Server
2. *application servers:* iPlanet Application Server, iPlanet Application Builder, iPlanet Application Server (Process Automation Edition), Netscape Extension Builder
3. *directory and security services:* iPlanet Directory Server, iPlanet Meta-Directory, Netscape Delegated Administrator, iPlanet Certificate Management System
4. *messaging and collaboration software:* Netscape Messaging Server, Sun Internet Messaging Server, iPlanet Calendar Server
5. *E-commerce software:* iPlanet ECXpert, iPlanet TradingXpert
6. *corporate procurement software:* iPlanet BuyerXpert
7. *online selling applications:* iPlanet SellerXpert, iPlanet MerchantXpert
8. *content information services:* Netscape PublishingXpert
9. *online bill presentment and payment:* iPlanet BillerXpert

It should be no surprise, given Sun's involvement in the alliance, that the iPlanet Application Server is a pure Java, J2EE-based application server. It supports JSPs, Java serlvets, and EJBs. The alliance claims that its latest release, in beta testing as of this writing, is the industry's first application server product to achieve full J2EE certification. The product's primary emphasis is on full support for J2EE, but the product is also known for its ability to scale and to provide load balancing and fault tolerance. The server allows applications to be distributed across multiple CPUs and multiple machines, and supports connection caching, pooling, and results caching for scalability. The server supports failover by distributing transaction state and session information across multiple servers in a cluster. It is one of the handful of application servers that supports failover for stateful session beans. The product includes connectors that integrate the J2EE applications with SAP R/3, PeopleSoft, IBM CICS, and BEA Tuxedo systems.

The iPlanet Application Builder is a companion tool for the application server that allows developers to easily build and deploy applications for the iPlanet Application Server. The tool provides an integrated workspace of graphical tools for a stand-alone development environment, but also interoperates with a number of leading integrated development environments (IDEs).

The iPlanet Application Server integrates with the iPlanet Web Server and the iPlanet Directory Server. With this approach, the Web server and directory server monitor any updates made to the application server clusters or applications so that the administrator does not have to reflect the changes manually. The directory server manages the password policies and user groups for the application server. The load-balancing and clustering capabilities of the application server are performed by the directory server.

Microsoft

Microsoft, the world's largest software company, has long supported both server and client software product lines. Prior to the release of the Windows 2000 operating system, the company's server product line was branded the Microsoft BackOffice family of products and included products such as Microsoft Internet Information Server (IIS), Microsoft SQL Server, and Microsoft SNA Server, among others.

Until recently, Microsoft did not have a stand-alone application server product *per se*. It has offered the Microsoft Transaction Server (MTS) as a part of the BackOffice family since 1996, which provided some of the capability of other application servers. However, with the release of Windows 2000, the company has now released the Microsoft Application Center 2000, a COM/DCOM- and Windows 2000-specific product that is tightly integrated with the Windows 2000 server.

Application Center 2000 is a COM+ platform that provides the transactional support previously found in MTS and the message queuing support found in the previous MSMQ. The server provides many of the capabilities of a CORBA or EJB system, such as the support for persistent and non-persistent objects.

However, it only supports objects based on the COM/DCOM architecture and there is no built-in interoperability with EJB or CORBA systems at this time. Please note that the product was still in beta testing as of this writing and features will change over time.

The big news of the Application Center 2000 is its Web clustering, network load balancing, and component-based dynamic load balancing that the product gains by working with the Windows 2000 operating system. Scalability has been a concern in the past with Microsoft's MTS when compared to other application servers and transaction systems, especially when compared to systems running on high-end UNIX servers or even mainframe systems. The Application Center 2000 components are automatically replicated across multiple servers running in a cluster. Failures are automatically routed around and, in some cases, the transaction will continue without a hitch. Load balancing is based on server response time rather than a simple round-robin approach. Developers can use their familiar development tools, such as Visual Basic and Visual C++, to develop applications for the Application Center 2000.

Oracle Corporation

Oracle Corporation is the industry's leading supplier of software for information management and the world's second-largest independent software company. Formed in 1977 and headquartered in Redwood Shores, California, the company operates in 145 countries and has 43,000 employees worldwide. The company has annual revenues in excess of $10 billion.

Oracle has made a huge investment over the last few years in Internet-enabling its product lines. The company now markets a wide variety of products and applications designed to expedite and enable the process of implementing an E-business strategy. Its E-Business Suite of products provides a set of applications designed to support all of the E-business initiatives of a large, complex, global enterprise. The E-Business Suite provides Web integration of marketing, sales, service, manufacturing, supply chain, financial operations, project management, human resources operations, and business intelligence systems.

At the foundation of the Oracle family of products is the Oracle Internet Platform. The centerpiece of this product line is the company's Internet-enabled database management platform, Oracle8i. Interestingly, Oracle8i is fully equipped with Java technology and can serve as a stand-alone, database-centric Web server. Nonetheless, included in the Oracle Internet Platform product line is the Oracle Internet Application Server (iAS) 8i. The company positions Oracle8i as the product that manages the data, while the Oracle iAS is the product that runs all the applications. The Oracle Internet Platform line also includes development tools, business intelligence tools, connectivity product, an Internet file management products, an integration server, systems management, and data warehousing products.

Oracle iAS, like many application servers, supports the J2EE specification and so therefore supports EJBs and the Java enterprise APIs. What sets it apart from other application servers is the product's very tight integration with Oracle8i and its sophisticated data management and data caching capabilities. For example, it supports data caching to offload processing from the back-end Oracle8i server. It also supports the company's own PL/SQL Server Pages technology that allows SQL statements to be embedded within HTML. The product also supports a PL/SQL engine that executes PL/SQL stored procedures.

Oracle iAS, like many other application servers, includes an HTTP server and will execute servlets, JSPs, and scripts. Although many application servers include this same functionality, most vendors do not position the application server as an all-in-one Web server with application and business logic support. Oracle, on the other hand, positions the combination of Oracle8i and Oracle iAS as a comprehensive, total solution for organizations wishing to deploy Web-based applications such as portals, transactional applications, business intelligence facilities, mobile applications, and enterprise integration.

The Oracle iAS comes in two versions: Standard Edition and Enterprise Edition. The Standard Edition is a comprehensive version that includes HTTP server; JSP and servlet engine; Perl script interpreter; PL/SQL page support; and a full JVM that contains EJB, CORBA, and database stored procedure call support. The Enterprise Edition adds PL/SQL execution, middle-tier caching, forms and reports services, Discoverer Viewer support, and enhanced management server.

Orbware Ltd.

Orbware Ltd. is a United Kingdom-based company that was incorporated on December 17, 1999, the same day that Sun released the EJB 1.1 and J2EE 1.2 specifications. Orbware's primary objective is to provide a high-quality commercial application server that fully implements the J2EE specification.

The company claims to have one of the first application server products that does not predate the EJB specification. The advantage, it claims, is that it does not have a legacy infrastructure or proprietary technology underpinning the application server. The current product available is the OrCAS Enterprise Server v4.0 for EJB, which is a clean-room implementation of the EJB 1.1 specification. The product runs on Windows NT, Sun Solaris, and Linux operating systems. It is very aggressively priced, starting at $795 per server. In addition, developers can use the product without charge for an unlimited amount of time.

The next product that will be released by Orbware is the OrCAS Enterprise Server v5.0 for J2EE. This version will combine the OrCAS EJB server implementation with the Apache Web server and the Tomcat Java servlet and JSP engine.

Orbware also offers a hosting solution for Application Service Providers (ASPs), which the company claims is the first ASP solution offered by a J2EE licensee. The OrCAS Hosting Solution includes the OrCAS Enterprise Server and features that facilitate the provision of hosting services for J2EE applications, including:

- virtual hosting to run multiple applications in a single server instance
- billing and metering capabilities
- a Web interface for uploading and managing applications

Persistence Software

Persistence Software was founded in 1991 and is headquartered in San Mateo, California. The company operates five sales offices in the United States and has offices in ten additional countries. The company is publicly traded and posted revenues of approximately $14.4 million in 1999 and $4.2 million in the first quarter of 2000.

The company has almost a decade of experience in application servers. Its original product, PowerTier for C++, is still being sold, and the company has added to the PowerTier product line with the PowerTier for EJB server. The company also has a new product line, Dynamai, that provides dynamic, application-aware caching of Web content.

PowerTier for C++ is defined as a "transactional application server." Its emphasis is on efficient and fast data access that is based on two technology patents. The first patent provides object-relational mapping that automates persistence of CORBA objects. The second patent is a shared transactional object cache that improves data access performance by providing an in-memory cache of objects and their relationships rather than using disk-based storage. The product is integrated with IONA's Orbix ORB.

The Persistence PowerTier for EJB utilizes the technology in its predecessor to reduce the development time for EJBs. According to the company, the object-relational mapping technology that is a part of the PowerTier Development Kit can reduce the development time by up to 20 times compared to other EJB tools. The technology automatically generates container-managed entity beans directly from a database schema or object model, which eliminates the need to directly code JDBC function calls. PowerTier for EJB supports the JTS specification of J2EE, provides a servlet container system, and supports a variety of different clients, including Java, HTML, XML, C++, COM, and CORBA. The product does not implement the entire J2EE specification.

SilverStream Software

SilverStream Software, based in Billerica, Massachusetts, is publicly traded on the NASDAQ exchange. It began shipping its first product in November 1997. The company posted revenues of over $31 million for the first six months of 2000, compared to only $7.8 million during the same period in 1999.

The company's product line, named the SilverStream eBusiness Platform, is comprised of four products. The centerpiece of the product line is the SilverStream Application Server. Offered as a separate option is the company's jBroker, a complete CORBA ORB written in Java. Two new products, ePortal and xCommerce, are built on top of the company's application server and offer specific solutions for customer relationship management (CRM) and B2B, respectively.

The SilverStream Application Server is a J2EE application server. It supports a number of features to support scalability within a server. It also supports server clustering, server load balancing, and session-level failover. It comes equipped with the company's jBroker ORB and can support CORBA objects; it also supports COM objects. jBroker is compliant with the CORBA 2.3 specification and supports the Portable Object Adapter, Objects by Value, IIOP over SSL, and other key new CORBA capabilities.

The SilverSteam ePortal solution provides a framework and components to facilitate the flexible creation of B2B, B2C, and B2E portals. SilverStream's xCommerce family consists of three products: (1) the xCommerce Server is a Java framework that runs on top of the SilverStream Application Server or other J2EE-compliant Java application server; (2) the xCommerce Enterprise Enablers are adapters that provide XML-enablement to a variety of legacy back ends such as IBM mainframe applications; and (3) the xCommerce Designer is a visual environment that integrates XML-formatted information with XML documents.

Sybase, Inc.

Sybase, Inc., founded in 1984 and headquartered in Emeryville, California, is one of the leading database management software suppliers and one of the ten largest independent software vendors. Sybase posted revenues of $460 in the first six months of 2000. It operates in 60 countries worldwide and focuses on certain vertical markets: financial services, health care, telecommunications and media, the public sector, retail, and wireless. The company has two wholly owned subsidiaries and three product divisions: the Enterprise Solutions Division, the Business Intelligence Division, and the Internet Applications Division.

The Sybase Enterprise Application Server is actually an integrated set of different application servers. It consists of PowerDynamo, Jaguar CTS, Application Integrator (AI) for CICS, Application Integrator (AI) for Stored Procedures, Application Integrator (AI) for CORBA, and Adaptive Server Anywhere.

PowerDynamo is a Web server that serves static and dynamic pages. It supports DynaScript, which is a Sybase, JavaScript-like scripting language that embeds SQL or COMPONENT statements within HTML pages. PowerDynamo can access the Jaguar server components through Java, ActiveX, SQL queries, or PowerDynamo tags.

Jaguar CTS is the distributed component engine for the Sybase Enterprise Application Server. According to the company, it combines the features of a transaction-processing monitor and an ORB. It provides full J2EE support with the exception, at the time of this writing, of JSP support.

AI for CICS and AI for Stored Procedures enable Jaguar to access stored procedure and mainframe COBOL programs. AI for CORBA allows developers to create EJBs for Jaguar that can communicate with existing CORBA objects.

Adaptive Server Anywhere is a full-featured SQL database server that supports the Jaguar server.

The Sybase Enterprise Application Server is sold in three different editions. The Small Business Edition supports a limited number of connections to Jaguar. The Advanced Edition provides unlimited connections and adds server clustering for scalability, load balancing, and fault tolerance. The Enterprise Edition adds a transaction monitor, object persistence, and CICS and stored procedure connectivity.

Summary of Offerings

Exhibit 7.5 summarizes the names of the application server and related products offered by the vendors examined.

Exhibit 7.6 summarizes the capabilities of the application server products. The matrix contains a single entry for each product line. Therefore, the information in that row could apply to any of the individual products within the line. For example, a cell that indicates "J2EE" as the Java support only means that at least one product in the line provides full support for the J2EE platform (i.e., EJB plus enterprise APIs); individual products within the line may only support a subset of the platform. The information for this matrix was drawn from publicly available sources and any errors or omissions are unintentional.

A Look Ahead

To be sure, the field of competitors providing application server solutions is crowded. That is both good news and bad news to the IT manager trying to make a strategic decision. The good news is that there are several competent products from which to choose. The bad news, of course, is that there are just as many options, and vendors make many similar-sounding claims about scalability, fault tolerance, ease of development, etc.

The J2EE platform, while spurring this market to greater growth, has added to the number of vendors providing solutions and also has blurred the distinction (at least on the outside) between the various products. Many vendors claim full J2EE support. However, there is a lot of latitude in how that support is implemented within a particular product. There are many questions to ask about a particular implementation. Some application server offerings today seem more like a bundle of separate products rather than a fully integrated solution that works seamlessly together. And while J2EE support implies that an ORB is the foundation of the product, that does not mean that a J2EE-compliant application server provides the rich and full set of CORBA services specified by the OMG (nor is the full set of services required in many environments). The point is that it is difficult to evaluate a complex and rich product like an application server solely based on the information printed on a glossy data sheet.

Exhibit 7.5   Application Server and Related Products of Some Vendors

Vendor	Application Server(s)	Related Products
Allaire	ColdFusion JRun	ColdFusion Studio JRun Studio Spectra

ATG	ATG Dynamo Application Server	ATG Dynamo products:
		  Scenario Server
		  Personalization Server
		  Commerce Server
		  Control Center

BEA Systems	BEA WebLogic:
	  BEA WebLogic Server
	  BEA WebLogic Enterprise
		BEA WebLogic products:
		  Express
		  jDriver
		  Commerce Server
		  Personalization Server
		  BEA WebGain Studio
		  BEA eLink product line

Bluestone	Total-e-Server	Total-e-Business platform:
		  Total-e-B2B
		  Total-e-B2C
		  Total-e-Wireless
		  Total-e-Global

GemStone Systems	GemStone/J GemStone/S	GemBuilder tools GemORB

HAHT Software	HAHTsite Scenario Server	HAHTsite Scenario Workbench
		HAHTsite Scenario Publisher
		HAHT Commerce e-Scenarios:
		  HAHT Market
		  HAHT Shop
		  HAHT Track
		  HAHT Service
		  HAHT Catalog
		  HAHT Sellside Links

IBM	WebSphere Application Server:
	  Standard Edition
	  Advanced Edition
	  Enterprise Edition
		WebSphere products:
		  Commerce Suite
		  B2B Integrator
		  Business Components
		  Host Integration Solution
		  Site Analyzer
		  Portal Server
		  Personalization
		  Edge Server
		  Studio
		  Transcoding Publisher
		  others…

iE	Integrator	AM ScreenSurfer

Exhibit 7.5   Application Server and Related Products of Some Vendors (Continued)

Vendor	Application Server(s)	Related Products
Inprise	Inprise Application Server	VisiBroker (ORB) AppCenter (management platform) JBuilder (tools) Optional CORBA services Secure Gatekeeper

IONA Technologies	iPortal Application Server	Orbix 2000
		Orbix 3 family:
		  Orbix 3 ORB
		  OrbixWeb
		  OrbixOTM
		  Orbix for OS/390
		  Messaging products
		iPortal Suite:
		  iPortal Server
		  iPortal Integration Server
		  iPortal OS/390 Server

iPlanet	iPlanet Application Server	iPlanet Application Builder iPlanet Directory Server iPlanet Web Server iPlanet ECXpert
Microsoft	Microsoft Application Center 2000	Windows 2000 Server Microsoft SQL Server 2000 Microsoft Host Integration Server 2000

Oracle	Oracle Internet Application Server 8i	Oracle Internet Platform:
		  Oracle8i
		  Development tools
		  Business intelligence tools
		  Connectivity products
		  Internet file management
		  Integration server
		  System management
		  Data warehouse
		  Oracle E-business Suite

Orbware	OrCAS Enterprise Server v4.0 for EJB OrCAS Enterprise Server v5.0 for J2EE	OrCAS Hosting Solution
Persistence Software	PowerTier for C++ PowerTier for EJB	PowerTier Object Builder PowerTier Bean Builder Dynamai Web Caching
SilverStream Software	SilverStream Application Server	jPortal ORB ePortal xCommerce

(continues)

Exhibit 7.5   Application Server and Related Products of Some Vendors (Continued)

Vendor	Application Server(s)	Related Products
Sybase	Sybase Enterprise Application Server	Database Servers Enterprise Portal Business Intelligence iAnywhere Wireless Server Financial Fusion Server

When evaluating different application server solutions today, it is important to keep the future in mind. This market, like many technology product markets, will undergo consolidation. In fact, the early signs are already there because some vendors have already exited the market, and some mergers have taken place. Within the next few years, the leaders will emerge and any other remaining solutions will be targeted to specific niches or verticals. Nobody has a crystal ball to map the future with precision, but the current leaders are likely to continue to gain market share. The second tier of vendors will be comprised of those that have standards-based solutions but also provide good, solid support for the enterprise deployment issues covered in Chapter 6 — namely, security, scalability, load balancing, fault tolerance, and management. Good tools that speed the development process will also be an important differentiating factor.

Another thing to keep in mind about the future is that neither CORBA nor Java specifications are "complete" or "finished." CORBA 3.0 specifications are available and products are already becoming available that support the specifications. With CORBA 3.0, the integration of EJBs and CORBA objects will be more complete; CORBA objects and enterprise beans will be able to co-reside in the same container. The CORBA component container will provide many of the services already provided by EJB containers, and will simplify the development task by automatically taking care of some of the transactional, persistence, and security capabilities. CORBA naming services will support URLs, and Internet firewall support will be built into the specifications. Further enhancements to CORBA will support specific computing environments such as embedded systems.

Just as CORBA is not sitting still, Java and J2EE will continue to evolve as well. The Java Community Process[SM], which is the program utilized by Sun to foster the evolution of Java technologies using an open forum approach, is continuing to solicit and evaluate ideas and requests for enhancements from the community. Some recent requests that have been accepted by the JCP and will eventually result in new platforms or standards include:

- J2EE 1.3 specification
- JDBC 3.0 specification
- Java servlet 2.3 and JSP 1.2 specification
- J2EE Management
- RMI Security
- Generic Security Services API
- Java APIs for XML Messaging
- and many others…

Exhibit 7.6 Summary of Application Server Product Line Functionality

Product Line	OS	Java	CORBA	COM	Back-ends	Dev. Tools	Strengths
Allaire ColdFusion	Win NT, Win 2000, Solaris, HP-UX, Linux	*	*	*	ODBC databases, e-mail, FTP, LDAP	ColdFusion Studio	Huge installed base, quick and easy, Spectra packaged services
Allaire Jrun	Win NT, Win 2000, Solaris, HP-UX, AIX, Red Hat Linux, SGI Irix, Compaq Tru64 UNIX	J2EE	*		RDBMS, OLTP, messaging, naming/ directory	JRun Studio	Free Developer Edition
ATG	Win NT, Solaris, AIX, HP-UX	J2EE	*		OLTP, RDBMS, messaging, Dynamo Repository API	Developer Workbench (included)	Customer management and commerce suites

(continues)

Exhibit 7.6 Summary of Application Server Product Line Functionality (Continued)

Product Line	OS	Java	CORBA	COM	Back-ends	Dev. Tools	Strengths
BEA WebLogic	Win NT, Win 2000, Solaris, HP-UX, AIX, OpenVMS, Sequent Dynix, OS/400, Red Hat Linux, SGI Irix, SNI Reliant, Unisys OS1100, Unisys Burroughs, IBM OS/390	J2EE	Full ORB and services	*	OLTP, RDBMS, messaging, naming/ directory, BEA Tuxedo	WebGain or any compliant tool	Market leader, full J2EE implementation, clustering and failover support, wide system support

Bluestone Total-e-Server	Win NT, Win 2000, SunOS, Solaris, AIX, HP-UX, SGI Irix, Linux, OS/390, OS/400	J2EE	*	Java APIs for OLTP, RDBMS, messaging, naming/directory; Connector architecture for RDBMS, ERP systems, transaction systems, legacy systems	Multiple HTML/JSP authoring tools or Java IDEs	XML integration, JSP TagLibs, load balancing and fault tolerance, portfolio of security services (SSL, X.509, LDAP, EJB security), extensive back ends via connectors
GemStone GemStone/S	Win NT, Win 2000, Solaris, AIX, HP-UX	*	*	Oracle, others built with wrappers	GemBuilder for Smalltalk, GemBuilder for Java, others	Scalable to support up to one billion objects, transaction-intensive applications
GemStone GemStone/J	Win NT, Win 2000, Solaris	J2EE	ORB	Java APIs for OLTP, RDBMS, messaging, naming/directory	Any Java IDE	Extreme clustering technology for scalability and fault tolerance

(continues)

Exhibit 7.6 Summary of Application Server Product Line Functionality (Continued)

Product Line	OS	Java	CORBA	COM	Back-ends	Dev. Tools	Strengths
HAHT HAHTsite Scenario Server	Win NT, Win 2000, Solaris, AIX, HP-UX	Servlets, JDBC, JNDI, JTS	Bundled Inprise ORB	COM/DCOM	SAP R/3, RDBMS (ODBC, JDBC, OLE DB), CICS, DB2, IMS, VTAM, LDAP, Notes, more	HAHTsite Scenario Workbench, HAHTsite Scenario Publisher	Support for COM, CORBA, and Java; rich back-end support; session-level failover, load balancing, clustering
IBM WebSphere	Win NT, Win 2000, Solaris, AIX, HP-UX, NetWare, OS/400, OS/390	J2EE	Full ORB and services	*	MQSeries, TXSeries, RDBMS, IMS/CICS, naming/directory, transaction systems, SNA apps	VisualAge Component Development (included), others	Comprehensive product line and related products, full CORBA services, enterprise functionality, Encina transaction monitor
iE Integrator	Win NT, Win 2000	* (Java Beans)	* (CORBA 2.1)	COM/DCOM	RDBMS, CICS, MTS, Tuxedo, MQ/Series, 3270/5250, VT100/220, Viewdata, ICL, HP3000, others	iE Builders (uses Microsoft JScript)	Rich set of legacy back ends, Microsoft COM/DCOM support

Product	Platforms	Standard	ORB		Services/APIs	Tools	Features
Inprise	Win NT, Win 2000, Solaris, AIX, HP-UX, Linux	J2EE	Full ORB and services	*	OLTP, RDBMS, messaging, naming/directory	JBuilder, others	Scalability, load balancing, fault tolerance through the CORBA Naming Service; distributed transactions with OTS/JTS and two-phase commit
IONA Technologies iPortal Application Server	Win NT, Win 2000, Solaris, HP-UX, OS/390	J2EE	Full ORB and services		Java APIs for OLTP, RDBMS, messaging, naming/directory, others through iPortal Integration Server	Graphical Application Builder	Patented Adaptive Runtime Technology for scalability and fault tolerance
iPlanet Application Server	Win NT, Solaris, AIX, HP-UX	J2EE	*		RDBMS, OLTP, messaging, naming/directory, SAP R/3, PeopleSoft, IBM CICS, BEA Tuxedo	Application Builder, plug-in for VisualAge, VisualCafé, JBuilder, others	J2EE compliance, scalability, load balancing, fault tolerance

(continues)

Exhibit 7.6 Summary of Application Server Product Line Functionality (Continued)

Product Line	OS	Java	CORBA	COM	Back-ends	Dev. Tools	Strengths
Microsoft	Win 2000			COM/DCOM	SQL, ODBC, messaging, legacy host through Host Integration Server	Visual Basic, Visual C++, others	Tight integration with Web clustering of Windows 2000; pure COM/DCOM implementation
Oracle	Win NT, Solaris, HP-UX, AIX, Compaq Tru64 UNIX	J2EE	*		Java APIs for OLTP, RDBMS, messaging, naming/directory, integrated with Oracle 8i	Internet Developer Suite	Tight integration with Oracle8i, strong data management capabilities
Orbware OrCAS Enterprise Server v4.0 for EJB	Win NT, Solaris, Linux	J2EE	*		Java APIs for OLTP, RDBMS, messaging, naming/directory	Any Java IDE	Clean-room implementation of J2EE specs, no legacy technology
Persistence Software PowerTier for EJB	Win NT, Solaris, HP-UX, AIX	EJB, JTS	*	*	Oracle, Sybase, Informix, SQL Server, DB2, other ODBC databases	PowerTier Object Builder, PowerTier Bean Builder	Quick deployment of high-performance database-oriented applications

	OS/Platform	J2EE	Full ORB and services	COM/DCOM	APIs	Development tool	Features
SilverStream Software Application Server	Win NT, Win 2000, Solaris, HP-UX, AIX, Red Hat Linux	J2EE	Full ORB and services	COM/DCOM	Java APIs for OLTP, RDBMS, messaging, naming/directory; Connectors for SAP, PeopleSoft, Lotus Notes, others from third parties	SilverStream Designer, or any Java IDE or EJB builder tool	Comprehensive IDE support, scalability with fault tolerance
Sybase Enterprise Application Server	Win NT, Solaris, AIX, HP-UX, Linux	J2EE (except JSP)	*	COM/DCOM	ODBC and JDBC RDBMSs; CICS, Java APIs for OLTP, messaging, naming/directory	PowerBuilder or other (PowerJ, Visual C++, Visual Basic)	Integrated Encina transaction monitor, Java and CORBA transactional interfaces, good load balancing options

* Supports interoperability with systems supporting objects of this type.

Of course, J2EE 1.3 is the biggest Java news on the horizon for application server customers and vendors. Without this specification, which formalizes many new enhancements such as a standard connector framework for integration with back-end systems, the vendor community will fragment and begin to offer proprietary extensions to J2EE 1.2 to solve certain needs. The good news is that most of the application vendors mentioned in this chapter are members of the group finalizing the definition of J2EE 1.3, so it is a good bet that most of them will implement it fairly quickly once it is finalized.

Although the focus of much of the industry is on J2EE and CORBA, it is important to also recognize the potential importance of COM/DCOM in the future. Microsoft, with its release of Windows 2000 and the Application Center 2000, has built in key capabilities such as clustering, load balancing, and fault tolerance that will be important for many customers. Of course, the Microsoft approach is based on Intel hardware and Microsoft operating systems only. This will limit its role in many large enterprises to departmental environments. Nonetheless, many enterprises will need to accommodate interoperability with COM/DCOM platforms.

The application server is not a fad. It is a platform and a framework that can facilitate the single challenge facing many large enterprises — the achievement of E-business. IT organizations that have not already done so should immediately put in place plans to evaluate a three-tier architecture centered around application servers. They should begin with a pilot project to become familiar with the technology and the options. Once they are familiar with the technology and can visualize the place it has within the enterprise, the staff should begin to define an architecture and a set of requirements that are specific to the environment. When they get to the point of evaluating alternative products, special attention should be given to adherence to standards, scalability and fault tolerance, and support for the back-end systems within the enterprise's infrastructure.

As shown with the National Discount Brokers and Vodafone examples, organizations should plan for success when they are architecting the three-tier environment. It is not uncommon that, once rolled out into production, the demand for E-business and E-commerce systems doubles or triples in a very short timeframe. This increased demand can be easily accommodated if the staff architects a system, up front, that can scale smoothly and in a linear fashion. Another key to being able to adapt and grow a system is to implement standards wherever possible so that new services and new components can be easily implemented as required. This includes knowing a vendor's commitment to the continued support for new standards. As CORBA and J2EE evolve, it is important to select a vendor that has a firm commitment to the continued implementation of standards, as opposed to vendor-specific and proprietary extensions.

Once the architecture is in place, IT organizations will find that they now have an environment that is incredibly flexible and powerful. As demonstrated in the Honeywell Aircraft Landing Systems example, organizations can dramatically cut their application development costs and lead-times by using a distributed object approach leveraging the rich services of application servers. They will also have a system, as demonstrated by FoliQuest, that can be seamlessly integrated into a wide variety of different environments due to the widespread support for standards and interoperability. Finally, and perhaps most importantly, organizations of all sizes, in all industries, and in any locale can realize the goal of achieving E-business. New organizations such as BuildPoint Corporation can be created to accomplish E-business; and established enterprises such as Cable & Wireless HKT can transform their existing customer service processes while simultaneously slashing costs and increasing customer satisfaction. By setting in place a three-tier, distributed architecture based on application servers, IT organizations can literally transform all of the key business processes of the enterprise and, at the same time, leverage the pervasiveness and the power of the Internet.

Notes

1. http://www.iplanet.com/solutions/customer_profiles/ndb/index.html.
2. http://www2.software.ibm.com/casestudies/swcsweb.nsf/customername/ F542555943BCCF070025683A0005F827.
3. http://www.iplanet.com/solutions/customer_profiles/hktelecom/index.html.
4. http://www2.software.ibm.com/casestudies/swcsweb.nsf/customername/ C1116B143828BED500256943001C49B7.

About the Author

Lisa M. Lindgren is an independent consultant, freelance high-tech marketing specialist, and co-editor of Auerbach's *Communications System Management Handbook 2000* and *Web-to-Host Connectivity*. She has more than 16 years of experience working for leading enterprise-networking vendors, most recently Cisco Systems. She is a lecturer at Plymouth State College in Plymouth, New Hampshire, teaching E-Commerce and other marketing courses. She has an M.B.A. from the University of St. Thomas and a B.A. in computer science from the University of Minnesota.

References

Clark, Tim, 2000. Proactive Performance Management, *Communications Systems Management Handbook*, 6th ed., Auerbach Publications, New York.

Cobb, Edward, Dave Frankel, Dave Curtis, Martin Chapman, and Patrick Thompson, 1999. *CORBA Components* (Microsoft Powerpoint presentation), Object Management Group, URL http://www.corba.com/library/csmar99.ppt.

Comer, Douglas, 1988. *Internetworking with TCP/IP: Principles, Protocols, and Architecture*, Prentice-Hall, Englewood Cliffs, N.J.

Curtis, David, Christopher Stone, and Mike Bradley, 1997. *IIOP: OMG's Internet Inter-ORB Protocol, A Brief Description*, Object Management Group, URL http://www.corba.com/library/iiop4.html.

Deshpande, Salil, 2000. *Clustering: Transparent Replication, Load Balancing, and Failover — Building Scalable and Highly Available E-commerce Applications with the Inprise Application Server*, CustomWare, San Carlos, CA.

Edwards, Michael, 1997. *Let's Talk about Java Portability*, URL http://msdn.microsoft.com/library/backgrnd/html/msdn_javaport.html.

Gurugé, Anura, 2000. Why Parallel Sysplex is a Must for Today's IBM Data Centers, *Web-to-Host Connectivity*, Auerbach Publications, New York.

Lai, Charlie, Li Gong, Larry Koved, Anthony Nadalin, and Roland Schemers, 1999. User Authentication and Authorization in the Java Platform, *Proceedings of the 15th Annual Computer Security Applications Conference*, Phoenix, AZ.

Lindholm, Tim and Frank Yellin, 2000. *The Java™ Virtual Machine Specification*, 2nd ed., URL http://java.sun.com/docs/books/vmspec/2nd-edition/html/VMSpecTOC.doc.html.

Linthicum, David S, 2000. Microsoft May Have App Server Winner, *Enterprise Development*, DevX.com, Inc., Palo Alto, CA.

McClain, Gary R, 1992. *The Handbook of International Connectivity Standards*, Van Nostrand Reinhold, New York.

Musciano, Chuck and Bill Kennedy, 1997. *HTML: The Definitive Guide*, 2nd ed., O'Reilly & Associates, Inc., Cambridge, MA.

Object Management Group, 1999. *CORBA/IIOP 2.3.1 Specification*, URL http://www.omg.org/technology/documents/formal/corba2chps.htm#ia.

Object Management Group, 2000. *Security Service V1.5*, URL http://cgi.omg.org/cgi-bin/doclist.pl.

Orfali, Robert and Dan Harkey, 1998. *Client/Server Programming with Java and CORBA*, 2nd ed., John Wiley & Sons, New York.

Radding, Alan, May 22, 2000. Java Emerges as Server-Side Standard, *InformationWeek.com*, CMP Media, Inc., Manhasset, New York.

Rosenberg, Jothy, 1997. *Javax: An Approachable Examination of Java, JavaBeans, JavaScript and All the Related Java Technologies*, URL http://developer.iplanet.com/docs/wpapers/java/javax.html.

Scallan, Todd, 1999. *A CORBA Primer*, Segue Software, Inc., URL http://www.corba.com/library/whitepapers.html.

Sun Microsystems, 1995. *The Java Language: An Overview*, URL http://java.sun.com/docs/overviews/java/java-overview-1.html.

Sun Microsystems, 1999. *Java 2 Platform, Enterprise Edition Frequently Asked Questions*, URL http://java.sun.com/j2ee.faq.html.

Sun Microsystems, 1999. *Simplified Guide to the Java 2 Platform, Enterprise Edition*, URL http://www.javasoft.com/j2ee/white.html.

Sun Microsystems, 2000. *Enterprise JavaBeans Technology*, URL http://www.javasoft.com/products/ejb/index.html.

Sun Microsystems, 2000. *The Java Platform: Five Years in Review*, URL http://java.sun.com/features/2000/06/time-line.html.

Sun Microsystems, 2000. *The Java Tutorial*, URL http://www.javasoft.com/docs/books/tutorial.

Thomas, Anne, 1998. *Enterprise JavaBeans Technology: Server Component Model for the Java Platform*, Patricia Seybold Group, Boston, MA.

Thomas, Anne, 1999. *Java 2 Platform, Enterprise Edition: Ensuring Consistency, Portability, and Interoperability*, Patricia Seybold Group, Boston, MA.

Týma, Paul M., Gabriel Torok, and Troy Downing, 1996. *Java Primer Plus*, Waite Group Press, Corte Madera, CA.

Vogel, Andreas and Keith Duddy, 1998. *Java Programming with CORBA*, 2nd ed., John Wiley & Sons, New York.

Walsh, Aaron E., 1997. *Java for Dummies*, 2nd ed., IDG Books Worldwide, Foster City, CA.

Yeager, Nancy J. and R. E. McGrath, 1996. *Web Server Technology: The Advanced Guide for World Wide Web Information Providers*, Morgan Kaufmann, CA.

For More Information

The author found many useful Web sites in the process of researching this book. The sites listed below offer a great deal of useful and in-depth information for readers who want to examine a particular subject in more detail.

Site Name or Title	URL	Description
Worldwide Web Consortium	www.w3c.org	Provides detailed and current specifications on evolving Web standards; also provides good Web history information
Internet Engineering Task Force	www.ietf.org	Information about the IETF, its working groups, and all RFCs
Sun's Java site	www.javasoft.com	Contains complete information about Java and its technologies; source of downloadable products and documentation
Object Management Group (OMG)	www.omg.org	Contains complete information about the OMG; includes technical specifications free for download
CORBA site	www.corba.org	Contains success stories, information on CORBA implementations, beginners' introduction to CORBA
OneLook® Dictionaries	http://www.onelook.com/	Searches a variety of dictionaries for words; includes technical dictionaries specific to computing — a great research tool!
ServerWatch™	http://serverwatch.internet.com/appservers.html	Site about application servers
DevX App Server Zone	http://www.appserver-zone.com/	Site about application servers
TechMetrix Research	http://www.techmetrix.com/lab/benchcenter/asdirindex.shtml	Application server directory

The Web sites of application server vendors provided invaluable product information:

Vendor Name	Web Site
Allaire Corporation	www.allaire.com
Art Technology Group (ATG)	www.atg.com
BEA Systems	www.bea.com
Bluestone Software	www.bluestone.com
GemStone Systems	www.gemstone.com
HAHT Commerce	www.haht.com
IBM	www.ibm.com
iE	www.ie.com
Inprise	www.inprise.com
IONA Technologies	www.iona.com
iPlanet	www.iplanet.com
Microsoft	www.microsoft.com
Oracle	www.oracle.com
Orbware	www.orbware.com
Persistence Software	www.persistence.com
SilverStream Software	www.silverstream.com
Sybase	www.sybase.com

Index